Ahead of the Curve

Ahead
of the
Curve

A Commonsense Guide to

Forecasting Business

and Market Cycles

Joseph H. Ellis

Harvard Business School Press
Boston, Massachusetts

978-1-59139-691-8 (ISBN 13)

Library of Congress Cataloging-in-Publication Data
Ellis, Joseph (Joseph H.)
    Ahead of the curve: a commonsense guide to forecasting business and stock
    market cycles / Joseph Ellis.
        p. cm.
    Includes bibliographical references and index.
    ISBN 1-59139-691-3
    1. Economic forecasting. I. Title.
    HB3730.E55 2005
    330'.01'12—dc22

                                                                    2005012862

To my mother, Aline Taylor, whose unwavering
confidence in me has been a constant in my life
and to my wife, Barbara, whose love, patience,
and understanding have been the bedrock
of a rewarding life and career

Contents

Preface and Acknowledgments   ix

Part I: "Seeing" The Economy
Creating Order from Chaos

1. Seeing Around Economic Corners   3
2. Making Sense of the Economy   11
3. Redefining Economic Downturns   25
4. An Antidote for the Recession Obsession   33
5. Smart Economic Tracking   49
   Getting the Noise Out
6. The Nature of Leading Indicators   61

Part II: Consumer Spending
The Cornerstone of the Economy and the Stock Market

7. Consumer Spending Drives the Demand Chain
   in the Economy   73
8. Consumer Spending, Corporate Profits, and
   the Stock Market   91

Part III: Forecasting Consumer Spending
Understanding the Key Indicator Relationships

9. Forecasting Consumer Spending   107
   Numbers, Not Psychology

Contents

10. Real Earnings   117
    The Powerhouse of the Economy

11. Employment and *Unemployment*   137
    The Economy's Deceptive Laggard

12. Interest Rates, Inflation, and the Economic Cycle   153

13. Interest Rates and the Stock Market   163
    A Concerned Look Forward

14. The Link Between Federal Deficits and Interest Rates   171

Part IV: From Theory to Practice

Applying the Charting Discipline to Your Own Forecasting

15. Forecasting for Your Own Industry or Company   181

16. Making Economics Happen   203

    Appendix A: Credit: Consumer Spending's
    Swing Factor   209

    Appendix B: Does Charting Economic Cause
    and Effect Work Outside the United States?   217

    Appendix C: Major Industry Data Series   237

    Appendix D: www.AheadoftheCurve-theBook.com   255

Notes   257
Bibliography   265
Index   267
About the Author   275

Preface and Acknowledgments

Almost everyone interested in the economy, from lay businesspeople and investors to the most sophisticated CEOs and investment managers, feels lost in the morass of anecdotal and often conflicting economic reports that fill daily newspapers and TV news broadcasts. While the accumulated flow of reports usually provides an underlying tone—"the economy is strong" or "the economy is getting weaker"— little of it is accessibly analytical, and the audience is generally left confused. The resulting sense of uncertainty in dealing with the economic and investment outlook is a universal problem for business managers, investment professionals, and individual investors.

This book presents a methodology I developed over a twenty-five-year career as a Wall Street investment analyst for simplifying and clarifying the use of economic data in forecasting the basic direction of the economy and, with it, the likely direction of the stock market. From 1970 to 1994, I specialized in the analysis of the retail industry—its economic trends and the performance of individual companies within it. The ultimate purpose of my work was to advise clients of Goldman Sachs about the investment outlook for the retailing industry as a whole and the shares of individual retailers such as Wal-Mart, Federated Department Stores, and Gap.

Early in my career, I came to realize that I simply could not wait for economic trends to manifest themselves in the stock market and in the sales and profits of the companies I was charged with covering. I had to see whether it was possible to get ahead of the curve in forecasting consumer spending and general economic trends. I couldn't excuse myself from this task simply by noting that few economists themselves had been successful at this. As much for self-preservation, I suppose, as from curiosity, I began to investigate how I might develop an improved method for forecasting consumer spending and, with it, the rest of the economy. Furthermore, I wanted to document the basis for my forecasts with such clarity that my clients would understand not only the forecast but also the rationale supporting it.

I recognized that it would be essential to study the relationships among various economic indicators over many decades and economic cycles. The primary question in this endeavor would be: Were there consistent and repetitive cause-and-effect (i.e., predictive) relationships among these series in the past that might be used to forecast future developments?

I soon discovered—with considerable excitement—that economic events are not as random and unpredictable as I had previously thought. There were numerous cause-and-effect relationships in the economy that had practical value in forecasting, but many of the most effective ones had gone largely underappreciated and underused, even in the world of professional economists. Some of these relationships were well known and others less so, but most had simply not been placed into an analytical framework or working discipline that allowed their effective use.

Thus my task was to develop (1) a simplified, user-friendly method for monitoring and analyzing the various economic data series that describe economic advances and declines and equally, (2) a framework for understanding the *sequence* of events that manifests itself in a typical cycle. Intuitively, I recognized that it would not be possible to gain mental control of long columns of figures covering forty years or more of economic history. I found that only charts provided the means of visualizing whatever long-term relationships existed among key economic data series. I learned that, far from having to rely on anecdotal reportage about consumer confidence, durable-goods orders, interest rates, and "what Alan Greenspan is going to do," I could actually *view* valuable cause-and-effect relationships among economic series that have repeated themselves cycle after cycle over many decades and remain highly relevant today. Essentially, via effective charting I could "see the economy."

The four most dangerous words in assessing economic and stock market cycles are, "It's different this time!" In fact, you will see in this book that almost every cycle over the past four decades has followed the same chronology of cause and effect, and often with a similar dimension of advance or decline in the various sectors of the economy. Far from finding more differences among cycles, I found greater similarities.

This comforting discovery suggested that I could apply these findings to forecasting economic direction in future cycles. By tracking not the absolute numbers themselves, but the *rates of change* in the most effective leading indicators, I was usually (though not always) able to catch key inflection points—upturns and downturns in trend—ahead of the prevailing economic forecasts. In short, I became much more adept than I had been in predicting the next change of direction in the economy and positioning myself to take advantage of it.

By the mid-1970s, I began using my charts of economic cause and effect in timing my forecasts of consumer spending, the outlook for retail stocks, and the stock market in general. Happily, my new method worked effectively and provided me with considerable competitive advantage in my work. I didn't always catch the economic turning point far in advance, but my new discipline more often than not allowed me to position myself ahead of other investment professionals, and I always had a strong understanding of where we were in the cycle of the economy and the stock market. I have now successfully used the approach set forth here for enough years that I believe it has real value to the lay businessperson and investor. That is why I have written this book.

What This Book Is About

I would like you to think of this book as having two broad purposes:

- *To help us understand and then overcome major flaws in the way most economic information is reported and digested by the business, investment, and economist communities.* A new framework for analyzing economic data is essential if we are to foresee turning points in the economic cycle before most of the damage (or benefit) has already occurred. I have attempted to provide that perspective in part I.

- *To put this new framework to work in forecasting.* In parts II and III, we will identify and track the key drivers of economic cycles and the sequence of indicators as they unfold in economic advances and declines. In part IV, we will drill down a little deeper into the economy and apply the same approach to individual industries and even companies.

The methodology detailed in this book results from empirical observations I developed and carefully recorded over my three decades as a working investment analyst on Wall Street. Using this approach, I was able to put the economy and the stock market into a context that made sense: where the economic cycle had been, where it was at the time, and where it was headed. When my leading indicators were equivocal, I was equivocal; however, when the leading indicators pointed unequivocally upward or downward, I was unequivocal in my forecasts. Throughout this book, I also relate the stock market to the chronology of events that occurs in every economic cycle, because the stock market itself is a key economic indicator and obviously of great importance.

Key Findings

Let me simplify here the key premises of this book so that, having a preliminary grasp of its findings from the outset, you can make the best use of it as we travel through it together.

1. Cause-and-effect relationships among key economic indicators, and the sequences in which they occur, repeat themselves in cycle after cycle. These relationships can thus be used to forecast future economic cycles.

2. To put these relationships to work, we must first correct several key flaws in the way economic data are typically reported and analyzed. These flaws include the following:

   - The overreliance by most observers on "recession"—(two successive quarters of *absolute decline* in the economy)—as the key measure of economic harm. Recession is, in fact, such a lagging indicator of a slowing economy that it is largely useless to business managers and investors. Most damage to the economy and the stock market is done when *rates of growth* in consumer spending and other economic drivers *peak* and begin to slow. This decline in growth rates typically precedes recession (again, an *absolute decline* in economic activity) by as much as a year. Thus if we are to get ahead of the curve, we must train ourselves to spot the early stages of declining rates of growth, rather than recession, as the key measure of economic downturns.

- The widespread practice of measuring economic data on a quarter-versus-previous-quarter or even month-to-month basis. This attempt to provide short-term sensitivity to economic trends, although a laudable goal, in fact creates such noise and confusion that it obfuscates valid and underlying relationships among economic data series.

3. Chapter 5 shows that tracking and analyzing economic data series, based on *year-over-year rates of change,* provides a clarity that enhances our ability to use these series to predict future events. I employ the acronym ROCET (rate of change in economic tracking) to describe a preferred new approach to monitoring economic data. Once we master these technicalities, we will see that charting is the analytical method by which we can best track one economic data series versus another to reveal their predictive capabilities.

4. Consumer spending is by far the largest part of the U.S. economy, and drives the rate of economic change in most other economic sectors. Other sectors of the economy simply don't have the size or causal characteristics to be more than secondary drivers of the business cycle. As obvious as this fact is, it is not heeded by economic forecasters to the extent it should be. If we can predict turning points in consumer spending, we can also successfully predict inflection points in the economy at large and, often, the stock market. This book follows the sequence of events that begins with consumers' real (unit) hourly earnings— my favorite leading indicator of consumer spending—and

proceeds through the demand chain to consumer spending, industrial production, capital spending, and corporate profits.

5. *Lagging* economic indicators, such as employment and capital (business) spending, are often mistakenly viewed as primary economic drivers. These lagging indicators therefore can actually deceive the unwary into remaining positive well past the peak in the economy and stock market and remaining pessimistic well beyond the trough. Identifying these laggards helps us sit above the fray as others become lost in it.

6. To forecast uptrends and downtrends in a number of individual industry sectors, we can drill down beneath the macro economy. You may well find smaller components that will help you forecast the demand cycle for your own industry or company.[1]

The Two Poles of Economic Discourse

Books and other publications on the economy have tended to move toward two poles, each of which has left us, as lay readers, with few tools to employ and little to pursue in forecasting the economy as we seek to maximize our business and investments.

The first is purely verbal, often devoid of any seeming dependence on, or relationship to, real numbers. Many of these deal with consumer and business psychology—for example, how consumers and businesses make investment and purchase decisions, rationally or irrationally. These verbal discourses may offer valuable and even entertaining insights and are more easily read, but invariably lack a pragmatic *working discipline* for forecasting. This leaves us with no process or prospects for looking forward at the economy— which can only be measured and predicted in terms of *numbers*.

The second direction—the polar opposite of the first—belongs to the mathematicians and theoreticians, whose complex formulae and hypotheses represent the highest level of statistical thinking in academia, but are accessible only to those few scholars who have reached this level of study. More importantly, few theories emanating from this realm have actually proved readily usable in the real worlds of business and investment, and have been totally inaccessible to lay audiences. Bottom line: if these abstruse approaches had resulted in more accurate forecasting of economic and stock-market directions and turning points, we might accept their value and simply use them, despite our personal inabilities to comprehend the processes themselves. However, this has not been the case.

In both cases, our inability as lay users (and I include in this group professional businesspeople and investors) to perceive the *working discipline* in the forecasting process results in the high level of uncertainty we all feel. Ironically, this makes our lives easier: we simply throw our hands into the air, conclude that there is little to be done, and relieve ourselves of any analytical effort beyond listening to the evening news! We thus settle into a state of conveniently lazy resignation.

I have written this book in the belief that there is an accessible and pragmatic middle ground between these poles of economic discourse. We must begin with the recognition that developing a forecasting discipline for the economy and stock market warrants a somewhat higher level of ongoing effort. Adopting *Ahead of the Curve*'s methodology will ask more of you—a bit of time and intellectual engagement in mastering a simplified, working-discipline approach to understanding the economy and its elusive companion, the stock market. However, the main tools you will need are free. It's really not very hard, and this book will show you how.

What This Book Is Not

Ahead of the Curve is not an economics textbook, nor is it meant to be a complete survey of all key subjects relating to the economy. Its purpose is, quite simply, to help place into context the confusing array of economic data series we receive daily. Occasionally I have been asked why I do not spend more time referencing the considerable body of scholarly work relating to many of the economic indicators discussed herein. The answer itself is a sort of statement of purpose for the book: as described earlier, although a good deal of worthy theoretical and diagnostic work has been done at both the macro- and the microeconomic level, much of it has been conducted at abstruse levels not accessible to most readers. In many instances, the practical benefit of such work is not apparent to businesspeople, investors, and policy makers who need to forecast the economy. This book is about empirical, statistical observation of how key economic indicators have played out in past cycles, and it is geared to pragmatic forecasting of the macro economy and the stock market in a framework that is comprehensible and usable to those who lack advanced degrees in economics, mathematics, or psychology. Unless a hypothesis can be shown to have *clear practical value in forecasting*—in terms that are understandable to lay businesspeople and investors—it does not fall within the mission of this book.

For example, *Ahead of the Curve* does not delve into the increasingly popular field of behavioral economics. There is no denying that psychology and behavior play a role in the economy, particularly when major political and international events (wars, terrorism, etc.) are involved; however, these effects are primarily event-driven and therefore highly unpredictable. Furthermore, the charts in this book suggest few instances in which psychology trumped statistical economic indicators in forecasting. Anecdotal and difficult-to-measure political and psychological factors often make interesting reading, but in my opinion they remain part of the nebulous minefield that we must skirt as we establish a *working discipline* for tracking the primary drivers that make more successful forecasting possible.

In addition, I have not dealt with some undeniably important economic subjects that now and then play a significant role in the economic cycle but more often are secondary in their effects. For example, major imbalances in foreign trade and significant related surpluses or deficits in the balance of payments can be major factors at any given time. Indeed, as I write, the United States has a major trade deficit that is resulting in (1) an uncomfortably high share of U.S. national debt being held by other countries, (2) a dollar that remains weak against other currencies, and (3) the possibility of sharply rising interest rates to keep foreign and domestic investors buying U.S. debt. Although this situation may have a material effect on the U.S. economy over the next several years, it is not a factor that regularly plays a principal role—as opposed to a secondary (one of many) role—in determining the course of our economic cycle. As an economic subject, it certainly deserves major investigation in economic textbooks, but it does not lend itself to this book's analytical discipline based on the repeating primary drivers that require our closest focus in forecasting of the economy year after year and cycle after cycle.

We might view the economic cycle as being a bit like the four seasons of the year, always occurring in the same sequence. Affected by extraneous forces, some summers will be warmer than others, and some winters colder. But summer will always come and will be warm, and winter will always come and be cold. We will see that, in the same way, economic cycles by their nature are reflected in uptrends and downtrends, some of which are longer, others shorter, some reaching higher-than-normal rates of growth, and still others sagging to greater declines. But my charts reveal that the *sequence* of leading and lagging economic indicators rarely changes, just as leaves will always fall from the trees before the snows arrive. This book is designed to do two things: highlight those indicators and sequences that have proven to have predictive value, and render them accessible for the purpose of predicting business and stock market cycles.

Many if not most of the indicators and relationships I emphasize are well known to academic economists, but the framework and methodology are, I believe, novel. In emphasizing the importance of accessibility to non-academics interested in the economy and the stock market, I do not mean to suggest that this book would not prove useful in the realm of academic economics as well. Indeed it is my hope that it will.

About the Charts

This book includes numerous charts. Many—occupying a full page to accommodate more than forty years of data—demonstrate that the cause-and-effect relationships explained in the text really do occur as described. Most juxtapose, over four or more decades, as many as four variables:

- One line representing an economic data series that is a leading— or causal—indicator.

- A second line that is the lagging indicator—that is, one whose direction is likely driven by the first line.

- Vertical shaded bars representing stock market declines. These allow us to assess where, in the cycles defined by the two economic data series, stock prices were in a state of decline.

- Black bars (at the bottoms of the charts) denoting a recession. As I have noted, a recession typically is identified too late to be of use to either businesses or investors.

As you read the charts you will have to come to grips with all four variables if you are to place these economic indictors into context with the stock market and recession. These large-scale historical charts are crucial, for they provide the needed proof that these cause-and-effect relationships have played themselves out in the economy in much the same way cycle after cycle. You can judge for yourself whether the case for each one is compelling. Without these charts and that proof, the forecasting discipline established in this book would mean little. Forecasting economic and stock-market cycles and turning points is more science than art and depends, I believe, on sound statistical/empirical disciplines. Theory alone, without documentation that is accessible to the lay reader, has little value.

---

www.AheadoftheCurve-theBook.com

I am confident that you will find many of the charted cause-and-effect relationships in this book persuasive in providing a new understanding of sequential developments in the economy and as the basis for greatly improving your forecasting. Obviously the charts in this book are static, with most of the data ending as of 2004. As time goes on, you will need additional data if you are to put these charts to use. To make this process easier, we have created a companion Web site for this book: www.AheadoftheCurve-theBook.com. This site contains URLs for the economic data series for nineteen of the most important charts in the book (listed in Appendix D), which will allow you easily to access the data series at government Web sites and other bureaus that report this data, so that you may create and update your own charts. As a further service to readers of this book, www.AheadoftheCurve-the-Book.com will maintain monthly updated versions of these nineteen charts, so that in the future you may easily refer to them for an updated perspective on the current economic and stock market outlook. The material on the Web site is free regardless of whether you purchase the book. I hope that this will allow *Ahead of the Curve*'s precepts to be of the greatest value to you over an extended period of time.

How to Use This Book

If you are company CEO or business unit head, I urge you to do the following:

1. Identify a computer-literate and clear-thinking associate in your corporate planning department to read this book and master the methodology for creating cause-and-effect charts.

2. Work with this associate and your corporate planning department to identify leading indicators at both the macro- and the microeconomic levels that might pertain to your company, your division, or the category of your product or service.

3. Create charts that provide the best perspective on economic developments that will affect your business and give you the best chance for forecasting the business cycle in your sector.

4. Arrange for monthly distribution and review of the charts, accompanied by simple and comprehensible observations.

This process is potentially important not only for company and divisional CEOs and business managers but also for all professional and private investors, most of whom currently rely strictly on conventional economic forecasts. Investors would do well to establish their own empirical economic tracking and analytical disciplines based on the cause-and-effect charting methods offered in this book, at both the macro and the industry level.

If you are a professional investment manager or an individual investor, you will benefit from the charting method, established in chapter 7, of marking bear markets with vertical gray bars as a means of comparing stock market declines against key economic indicators over forty or more years of charted history.[2] The results show, in many cases, remarkable consistency in the timing of bull and bear markets versus key economic indicators. And the disciplined application of the consistent sequence among consumer spending, industrial production, and capital spending will certainly help analysts and investors in these sectors to understand the order in which companies in these sectors participate in economic uptrends and downtrends, with commensurate effects on the performance of their stocks.

To lay readers, I urge you to put this method to work in your own business or portfolio. If you find several of the cause-and-effect relationships in this book persuasive, go to the Web sites provided in appendix D and download the two series—a leading series and a lagging one—beginning with 1960. Thereafter, simply update and observe the progress of the series each month, using the leading series to forecast the lagging one. Or you may take a far easier course and simply go to www.AheadoftheCurve-theBook.com and view the nineteen charts that will be maintained on an updated basis there.

In this way, you will gain economic perspective and begin to reduce your dependence on economic blurbs in newspapers and fifteen-second economic reports on the evening news. These are economically volatile times, at home and abroad, and we are flooded with information. It is hard to know how to interpret most of the data and analysis that flow our way. *Ahead of the Curve* is intended to bring analytical discipline and context to your evaluation of economic reporting and to empower you in enhancing your understanding of the outlook for the business cycle and the stock market.

Acknowledgments

This book, from its concepts to its individual charts and exhibits, is the result of more than three decades of work with my talented associates at Goldman, Sachs & Company. It began with my colleagues Ellen R. Harris and Marcia Krieger in the 1970s, long before personal computers facilitated the easy retrieval, manipulation, and charting of economic data. In those days, data were obtained from government journals; rates of change were tabulated on a mechanical calculator or even a slide rule; and charts were drawn by laboriously pasting taped lines on large white posterboards, which were then photographed for publication. The work continued during the 1980s and early 1990s with the help of my able statistical assistant, Felicia Sotillo, to whom the original production of many of the charts in this book can be attributed. We made great strides in recent years with the skill and hard work of my associates Karim Mirshak, Sophia Savul, Stephanie Froes, and Prashant Bothra, each of whom contributed fresh ideas as plans for this book took shape. I am particularly indebted to Prashant for his hard work and commitment to detail as work with my editors at Harvard Business School Press intensified.

I was fortunate over many years to work with retail-analyst colleagues Stephen Mandel, David Bolotsky, George Strachan, and Matthew Fassler, who not only used this forecasting method but also added to its efficacy. And I can never sufficiently thank my administrative assistant for more than eighteen years, Julie Loprete, whose exceptional capabilities and friendship supported all my efforts at Goldman Sachs.

Many learned colleagues, friends, and advisers have read drafts of the book at various stages and have contributed to its content. These include the following:

William Dudley, chief U.S. economist, and Jan Hatzius, senior economist, of Goldman Sachs, who offered important guidance on economic issues during the early writing.

Barrie Wigmore, retired partner of Goldman Sachs and author of *The Crash and Its Aftermath: A History of the Securities Markets in the United States, 1929–1933* and *Securities Markets in the 1980s: The New Regime, 1979–1984.*

John Sweeney, president and CEO of Swiss RE Company and an accomplished economist and investment thinker.

Morris Williams, partner of Miller Anderson & Sherrard, for his wise guidance in clarifying the structure of this book.

Gary Loveman, CEO of Harrah's and former associate professor of business administration at the Harvard University Graduate School of Business Administration, an accomplished economist in his own right.

John Gilbertson of Goldman Sachs, whose incisive observations regarding the chronology of the economic cycle and charting methods helped significantly at the early stages in the writing of this book.

Bernie Sosnick of Oppenheimer & Co., who provided wise advice at the very earliest stages of this project.

Brian Thomas of Swiss RE Company, good friend and most astute reader, whose thoughtful commentary on the book helped me improve its readability.

David Larr, a longtime family friend and expert in the organization, possibilities, and vagaries of historic economic data.

I have indeed been fortunate to gain the good counsel of my son, Jonathan Ellis, and my daughter, Claire Ellis. Jon, a professor of philosophy, thoroughly reviewed key parts of the draft, provided important observations with a nuance worthy of his field, and helped develop the concept of asymmetrical circular causality. Claire, who spent a number of years in book marketing and publicity, has been of great value in thinking through the marketing aspects of the book.

Finally, I have been extraordinarily fortunate in the editorial assistance I have received in the later stage of the writing and final preparation of the book. Victoria Larson, formerly of Texere, a business publishing firm, expertly guided me through a first reorganization of the draft before its submission to Harvard Business School Press.

I am deeply indebted to Jacque Murphy, my principal editor at Harvard Business School Press, who quickly identified important issues of organization and readability in earlier drafts. She and her associates skillfully guided me through the entire process of preparation and publication.

I was fortunate to work with Jane Isay in reorganizing and bringing greater narrative life to this book. The subject matter is, of course, often technical and intense, and Jane showed the way to increase the book's readability and accessibility. I am also most grateful to Jane for leading me to Julia Kagan, who took full charge of the many figures and tables in this book and with unflagging dedication saw to their accuracy, consistency, and placement. She also identified and worked with Bruce Campbell of Bruce Campbell Design, who with equal ardor adapted the data and charts I used at Goldman Sachs over the years into a format appropriate for this book. Without Jane, Julia, and Bruce, I would not have been able to complete this project.

Finally, I am deeply grateful to my wife, Barbara, for her patience and understanding over the several years during which this book absorbed much of my spare time that otherwise might have gone to being with her and our family. I am truly blessed to have had this support.

I

"Seeing" The Economy

Creating Order from Chaos

CHAPTER ONE

Seeing Around Economic Corners

Businesspeople, policy makers, and investors—indeed, most people in the United States—have a significant stake in understanding the outlook for the economy. Are we at the beginning or middle of an economic advance—or a downturn, with more to go? Or are we at the end of the current trend? Are we about to encounter a significant change in direction for the economy and, if so, for the better or for the worse? Is it even possible for economic forecasters to determine, most of the time, what the next six to twelve months hold, particularly in predicting major turning points? And what are the implications for the stock market?

Any corporate CEO or investment manager will confirm that even though economists have made outstanding contributions in many areas of theory, data gathering, and specialized analysis (labor, health care, etc.), the profession as a whole has had difficulty in forecasting key economic turning points with sufficient timeliness to prove useful. Quarterly and annual forecasts are published by virtually every government and financial institution; theories are espoused; and Nobel Prizes are awarded. However, few, if any, individual forecasters or groups of economists have track records sufficiently accurate to warrant their being relied on by the business or investment community.

It's true that government, businesses, and investors all subscribe to or monitor certain economic publications and forecasters, but they rarely do it with confidence in the outcome. They use economic projections the same way the host of a gala July Fourth picnic uses weather forecasts: even if, based on experience, he completely distrusts five-day weather forecasts, on June 29 he feels compelled to tune to the Weather Channel to survey the chances of a sunny afternoon for the picnic five

3

days from then. Given the paucity of successful predictions of major turning points in economic activity in the past, the audience is highly skeptical, but most people nevertheless feel compelled to pay continuous attention to the flow of economic forecasts.

Yet in spite of our skepticism, it is essential for analysts and investors, not to mention executives in every industry tied to economic cycles, to forecast major trends—as the title of this chapter has it, to see around economic corners—if they are to position themselves in advance for economic and stock market uptrends and slowdowns. The stock market as a whole, and the industry sectors within it, is a sensitive *discounting mechanism*—that is, stocks rise or decline in advance of their companies' and industries' actual operating results.

Overcoming Anecdotal Economics

Given the daily avalanche of economic reports, it is not surprising that the business and investment communities—and sometimes even economists themselves—lapse into what might be called an anecdotal approach to forecasting the economic and business outlook. By "anecdotal," I mean responding ad hoc to the deluge of data released by the government and trade groups as well as newspaper and magazine headlines and television broadcasts—not to mention personal experiences. Each piece of the picture may be an individual stimulus, but in the absence of a disciplined context relating it to other inputs, the result is confusion on the part of the entire economic audience.

A headline in the February 28, 2003, *New York Times* business section said it all: "Economic Data Point in Both Directions." This was not a generic statement. In fact, the article reported that separate sets of data posted the day before had pointed in opposite directions: sale of new homes had fallen while orders of durable goods rose, the latter exceeding expectations. The headline simply manifested what readers of economic reports experience virtually every day—a confusing crosscurrent of conflicting indicators that for all intents and purposes renders it impossible to foresee where the economy is headed, or even *is*.[1]

On any given day, a quick scan of the *Wall Street Journal*, the *Financial Times*, *The Economist*, *Fortune*, and other business publications

"The rise in unemployment, however, which was somewhat offset by an expanding job market, was countered by an upturn in part-time dropouts, which, in turn, was diminished by seasonal factors, the anticipated summer slump, and, over-all, a small but perceptible rise in actual employment."

yields brief reports on the latest of a great variety of economic data series. In each, an advance or decline per se is seen to be "positive" or "negative." However, few of these reports contain any longer-term history of the series and its relationship to another economic data series. For example, if we see a report on the rise or fall in a consumer confidence index, rarely is it accompanied by a chart tracing that index's historic relationship with, and implied causality of, uptrends or downtrends in consumer spending. How can readers be informed by economic reports if the latest reading on the economic series in question is presented in a vacuum?

The *New York Times* reported on Saturday, August 2, 2003, "Stocks dropped on reports of lost jobs and a lower than expected reading for a manufacturing index." A few days later (August 6), the *Wall Street Journal* reported, "Consumer confidence is down, but gross domestic product is up. Unemployment is relatively high, as are sales of new homes, but producer prices are down. The budget deficit is up, which is bad, but interest rates are down, which is good. With so much data giving such mixed signals, it's not surprising that many economists are waffling about the state of the U.S. economy."

Month by month, businesspeople absorb these reports with varying levels of credulity. Although we usually receive the disclosed economic data at face value, we lack a framework or context provided by the government bureaus that release the data and the journalists who report it.

This lack of context usually results in a profound latent sense of unease and frustration, or at the very least, a deep-seated lack of confidence in the data's forecasting value.

Need: A Discipline and a Context

One of the primary dilemmas faced by business managers, investors, and policy makers—key users of economic data—is that of placing current monthly and quarterly data in historical context. Why should we care about today's unemployment report unless we can see its relationship in past years—leading or lagging—to economic advances and slowdowns? But discovering this relationship means surveying data for many decades, enough to cover multiple economic cycles. The answer, as you will see throughout this book, is the careful construction of charts that allow us to determine whether one economic series has consistently led another over many years and is likely to do so in the future.

Ironically, the form in which most economic information is presented is perhaps the biggest culprit in preventing our understanding it. When the information is presented in words only, as on television and radio (as well as in many publications), historical context is totally lacking. Even when we receive the information in a newspaper or magazine, if a chart of the data is included, it typically is allotted inadequate space for presenting the relationship of one series to another over the long period needed to assess its consistency.

To assess the latest economic developments in their proper context, we must pull current data into charts large enough to encompass several decades of data in a highly readable fashion. There is no excuse for not doing so. It requires only an ordinary personal computer, Excel or some other widely available data management software, and access to the many free Web sites where the data is available.

Some people will argue that we can get better results using *econometric* analyses: complex computerized statistical analyses that economists have to come rely on to track and relate the greatest possible number of variables driving the outcome of a series being forecast. However, after years of observing forecasting results based on computerized models, I believe that the rigidity of data models and their remoteness as "numbers in a machine" reduce their usefulness in forecasting, neutralizing the presumed benefits of computerized intelligence. They actually *remove* key cause-and-effect relationships in the economy from economists' continuous consciousness. Unless we actively "see" the relationships in action on a week-to-week and month-to-month basis, much of the value of the data is lost.

One conclusion is unavoidable: if the results of econometric modeling had advanced materially in recent years—if businesses and investors in recent cycles had found econometric modeling actually capable of forecasting economic trends and turning points to a greater extent than in the past—then they would now rely on econometrics for this purpose. However, this has not been the case. I am reminded of the comments of economist Paul Samuelson, winner of the Nobel Prize in economics:

> *Back when I was 20, I could perceive the great progress that was being made in econometric methods. Even without foreseeing the onset of the computer age, with its cheapening of calculations, I expected that the new econometrics would enable us to narrow down the uncertainties of our economic theories . . . My confession is that this expectation has not worked out. From several thousands of monthly and quarterly time series, which cover the last few decades or even centuries, it has turned out not to be possible to arrive at a close approximation to indisputable truth. I never ignore econometric studies, but I have learned from sad experience to take them with large grains of salt. It takes one econometric study to calibrate another . . . But it seems objectively to be the case that there does not accumulate a convergent body of econometric findings, convergent on a testable truth.[2]*

In short, frustration with economic forecasts, including the dramatically increased contribution from econometrics, has increased, rather than declined, in recent decades. Just as computers have not yet composed more beautiful music, have not designed more pleasing cars, and have not proven capable of more adept investing, they also have not yet proven capable of forecasting economic trends.

For these reasons, I embarked upon the task of simply constructing charts to track what I hoped would be clear cause-and-effect relationships between key economic data series. My aim was to see whether I might determine that A leads B and B leads C—and, if so, whether I might monitor A as the basis for forecasting C—i.e., "what leads what" in the economy. I was elated to find that this is indeed possible.

A Working Methodology Ready for Widespread Use

By charting and graphing key relationships between economic data series, we see that these relationships have not only been the primary drivers of the U.S. economic cycle over the past fifty years but also continue to dominate today's economic cycles. Charting economic relationships is a simple, articulate, and self-sufficient way to understand economic and stockmarket cycles for the purpose of forecasting economic developments six to eighteen months in advance.

You may well ask, "Don't economists and other interested parties already chart many of these relationships? If so, why aren't we already getting the right answers?" Excellent question! The answer is, yes, for years economists, analysts, and others have used charts to evaluate predictive relationships in the economy. However, this work often contains key flaws in how data are measured and the charts are constructed, and these flaws have prevented their fully yielding important basic truths that exist in the data being tracked. Chapters 4 and 5 investigate and explain how to correct these dysfunctions, including the need to replace the current focus on absolute increases versus absolute declines in economic data with a new ROCET (rate of change in economic tracking) approach. Changing how we organize and track economic data is essential as a prelude to analyzing the relationships themselves in the chapters that follow.

Many of the cause-and-effect relationships demonstrated in this book will be useful not only to business and investment readers but also in some cases to economists. The simplified methodology should help to uncover useful and predictive relationships in the economy with sufficiently improved clarity that even those who have advanced educations in economics will benefit from their enhanced presentation. Thus, the audience for this book extends (in descending order of economic education) from those who deal every day in the forecasting of economic cycles to lay business and investment readers who have only a modicum of economic training.

My goal is to describe a fundamental working discipline that will allow you to make sense of, or contextualize, the daily barrage of economic information.

This means identifying and separating in your mind the role of leading versus lagging indicators—mastering the leading indicators for forecasting purposes and ignoring the lagging ones. When you read that unemployment has increased sharply, it is often reported as a sign that the economy is headed for worse times. This assumption is erroneous and potentially harmful to the observer's understanding. In fact, employment is a lagging indicator; the economy may have started a recovery even though employment has not yet caught up. If you possess a chart showing (as one of many economic cause-and-effect relationships) that consumer spending and the economy drive and *lead* employment rather than vice versa, you will be able to place the news of rising unemployment in its necessary and correct context.

It is vital to put both positive and negative reports of economic data into a long-term, sequential context, because any single piece of information may be misleading if it is taken out of its past, consistent sequencing in the economic cycle. It is not the responsibility of the press to give us this framework. Rarely do reporters have the time, space, or inclination to do so. Therefore, it is paramount that investors and business leaders themselves develop and maintain this context so that information is comprehensible to them and that they can apply it to their companies and portfolios. Providing this discipline is the core mission of this book.

CHAPTER TWO

Making Sense of the Economy

As I set about the initial detective work in my attempt to clarify the economic cycle and its key cause-and-effect relationships, I knew that common sense had to be my guide. I also knew that a good deal of my focus would be on consumer spending, better known in economists' parlance as *personal consumption expenditures* (PCE). There were two reasons for this focus:

- The first was specific to my job responsibility. As an analyst of retailing companies, I needed particularly to understand the ebb and flow of consumer spending as a whole, including the considerable portion (spending such as that on education, medical care, and housing) that does not occur in retail stores but competes with stores for consumers' dollars.

- With consumer spending representing roughly two-thirds of all economic output (*gross domestic product*, or GDP), it was clear that understanding what drives consumer spending was likely to be key to understanding the economy as a whole, even in the simple terms I hoped I could preserve in my analysis.

The fact that consumer spending is a large portion of the economy is also helpful in psyching out how the economy works. We are all consumers, and, if consumer spending is the primary force in the economy, we can relate personally to many of the factors that drive it. Perhaps the biggest obstacle non-economists have in understanding and gaining a forward-looking sense of the economy is the difficulty of demystifying it. We are subject to all sorts of arcane economic reports and developments, such as the balance of payments, the money supply, and "what the Fed is going to do." However, when assessing consumer spending, we may feel safe in the assumption that most of the forces driving it are understandable to us as consumers. This accessibility may enable us to fiercely defend ourselves, from a commonsense point of view, against any notion that the spending of tens of millions of households is driven by esoteric or cosmic forces known only to PhD economists. It should be possible to determine and monitor the key forces that drive consumer spending and therefore those other parts of the economy that depend on it.

From this platform, I began to see my way clear to designing the architecture of an analytical model focused on the sequence of events that drives a typical economic cycle, including, most importantly, its upturns and downturns. And if I could design a working discipline for tracking those economic indicators that lie at the front end of the economic sequence, or chronology, I might get a leg up on the rest of the world in forecasting key economic trends that would affect sales and profits of my retailing industry and companies—and perhaps, in the process, in better understanding other sectors as well.

The Chronology of the Economic Cycle

Basically, *economic growth* is the rate of change in the nation's total demand for and output of goods and services. So it seemed logical, in seeking a chronology of "what leads what" in the economic cycle, to do the following:

- Begin by tracking consumers' spending on goods and services.

- See how consumer spending drives the production of goods and services.

- Determine how production, in turn, drives the demand for the machinery and equipment, office buildings, and factories— broadly known as *capital spending*—that supports the production of goods and services in the first place.

I hoped that, during this voyage of economic discovery, I would also find out where—or more importantly, *when*—rising and falling stock markets reflected the uptrends and downtrends in the significant areas of economic activity.

What I found was clear: a chain of cause and effect does, indeed, extend from consumer spending at the front end of the cycle, through industrial production, and on into companies' spending on plant and equipment. This chain revealed itself with remarkable clarity when each link of cause and effect was charted over four decades and eight economic cycles.

This chain of cause and effect—essentially a chronology of the economic cycle—is presented in figure 2-1, in which primary cause-and-effect relationships are designated by the large arrows and secondary cause-and-effect relationships by the smaller, dotted arrows. Please have patience in studying this sequence. It is not as complex as it seems. It is based in common economic sense, and later chapters in this book demonstrate the validity of each link.

- Personal income—largely wages and salaries—is the primary driver of consumer spending, by far the largest sector in the economy. Credit and borrowing play a role, but if we can identify the most important indicators of spending power through wages, we have a shot at forecasting consumer spending.

- Uptrends and downtrends in consumer spending drive advances and declines in manufacturing and services.

- In turn, the capital spending sector of the economy, which includes companies' spending on plants and equipment, follows, like clockwork, the trend set by production and services, and consumer spending before them.

- These three sectors of economic activity—consumer spending, industrial production and services, and capital spending—represent the core of corporate profits produced in the United States, so the dependence of corporate profits on consumer spending is also clear.

- The stock market, which advances and declines as a sensitive predictive mechanism reflecting corporate profits, is therefore also tied closely to consumer spending at the front end of the cycle. This makes it easier to understand the sequencing of the

FIGURE 2-1

The chronology of the economic cycle

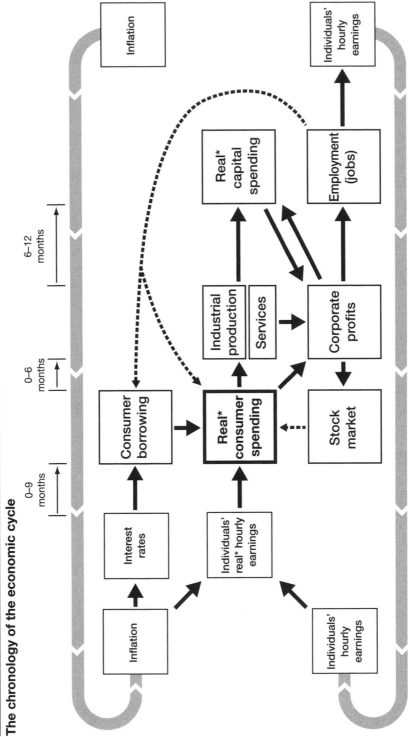

stock market in this chain of cyclical events, with major stock market advances and declines tending to occur at similar points in successive cycles.

- Because businesses hire or fire workers based on the respective rise or fall of sales and profits, employment—jobs—follows rather than leads the economy. Mastering this fact is one of the core hurdles in overcoming emotional but erroneous reactions to economic news.

Each of these indicators has a sequential position in the cycle that is remarkably similar in cycle after cycle. Forthcoming chapters explore the sequential causal relationships between these indicators. We will also see—in charts covering more than four decades—that the sequencing of these relationships over many cycles has been sufficiently consistent that we can use these relationships to understand where we are in the current cycle and, likely, where we are headed.

Everything Starts with the Consumer

Let's define some of the key sectors of the economy. Most of us intuitively grasp the meanings of the terms *consumer spending, industrial production,* and *capital spending,* but certain nuances in the definitions, labeling, and construction of these economic data series will prove useful for all but highly trained economists who work daily with these terms and concepts.

The central figure of the U.S. economy is, without question, the consumer. Consumer spending—or personal consumption expenditures (PCE), as it is labeled by the government bureaus that report it—is comprised broadly of consumer expenditures on durable goods, nondurable goods, and services. It accounts for more than two-thirds of total gross domestic product (GDP), the nation's total output of goods and services. Throughout this book, I refer to real consumer spending (equivalent to real personal consumption expenditures). The term *real* here refers, in economic parlance, to consumer spending measured in units and not dollars—in other words, adjusted to remove the effect of inflation. Real consumer spending is calculated by dividing consumer spending by the *personal consumption expenditures deflator*, an index that measures price inflation across the entire spectrum of consumer spending.

Logically, consumer spending on goods and services is, through the retail and distribution pipeline, the key determinant of cyclical swings in industrial production (the manufacture of goods purchased). And accelerations and decelerations in industrial production (manufacturing) are, in turn, the key drivers of capital spending (manufacturers' outlays on plant and equipment for productive capacity to produce those goods).

In 2004, total GDP in the United States totaled $11.7 trillion, as shown in figure 2-2, comprised of consumer spending, capital spending, and government spending. Each of GDP's major categories can, in turn, be broken down further into numerous categories, classifications, and subclassifications. For example, consumer spending can be segmented broadly, as in figure 2-3.

FIGURE 2-2

Composition of gross domestic product (GDP), 2004

$11.7 trillion

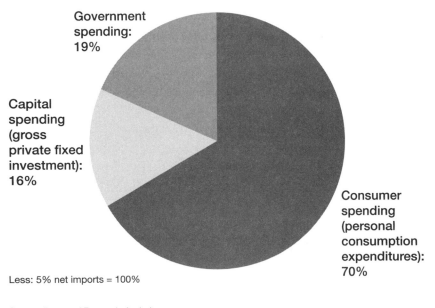

Government spending: 19%

Capital spending (gross private fixed investment): 16%

Consumer spending (personal consumption expenditures): 70%

Less: 5% net imports = 100%

Source: Bureau of Economic Analysis

16

FIGURE 2-3

Composition of consumer spending (PCE),* 2004

$8.2 trillion

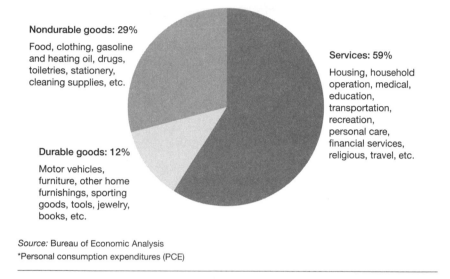

Nondurable goods: 29%

Food, clothing, gasoline and heating oil, drugs, toiletries, stationery, cleaning supplies, etc.

Services: 59%

Housing, household operation, medical, education, transportation, recreation, personal care, financial services, religious, travel, etc.

Durable goods: 12%

Motor vehicles, furniture, other home furnishings, sporting goods, tools, jewelry, books, etc.

Source: Bureau of Economic Analysis
*Personal consumption expenditures (PCE)

Within these categories of PCE are innumerable classifications. Appendix C contains a detailed list, down to levels as fine as small electric appliances (in durable goods), beef and veal (nondurable goods), and cellular phones (services).

It is vital to realize that each of the major sectors of GDP—consumer spending, plant and equipment spending, and government spending—represents *final sales*: the ultimate value of a product or service when it is purchased by the final user. In other words, each final sale is the culmination of a long series of embedded transactions consisting of the production and sales of materials, parts, and labor that went into the final product. Consequently, consumer spending of $8.2 trillion in the United States in 2003 represented final sales that included multiple layers of hidden transactions and processes whose combined value exceeded that of the final sales.

Industrial production is the largest sector of economic activity that lies embedded within the final sales number. For example, personal consumption expenditures (consumer spending) might include a Whirlpool refrigerator purchased by a family in Peoria for $500 from a local appliance dealer. This sale to the consumer is defined as the refrigerator's final sale value. However, Whirlpool produced the refrigerator and may have sold it to the dealer in Peoria for $370. Whirlpool's manufacture of the refrigerator and its sale to the dealer are considered part of industrial production and are not counted in the $500 final sale that showed up in the PCE and GDP numbers. To include the $370 as part of GDP would be to double-count its impact in total economic output. After all, it is only one refrigerator!

Similarly, other manufacturers' sales to Whirlpool of the refrigerator's compressor, ice maker, shelving, and steel are also embedded in the $500 final sale recorded as part of consumer spending; but these sales are compiled separately as industrial production by the Federal Reserve Board. Just as PCE is reported down to very fine classifications, annual data on industrial production is provided for such specific products as industrial gas sales, creamery butter, tires, and glass and glass products. And yes, major appliances. Appendix C provides a listing of industrial production categories and classifications.

Another significant example of an economic data series tallied separately by the government but embedded in total consumer spending and GDP is retail sales. About half of all personal consumption expenditures are consumer purchases of goods and services from retail businesses (primarily stores, but also catalog and online retailers) that sell products and services directly to the consumer. These comprise *retail sales* data, which are gathered from all types of retail stores by the Department of Commerce in a large number of individual classifications. The data are aggregated in the monthly "Retail Sales" report, which is widely commented on in the business press as an important measure of the health of consumer spending. The retail sales series is not overtly reported as part of GDP but rather is used as source data by the Bureau of Economic Analysis in its calculation of consumer spending, which *is* part of the GDP tabulation. Appendix C presents the composition of the retail sales series, ranging from categories as broad as department stores and discount department stores to retail niches as specific as luggage and leather goods stores and heating oil dealers, each selling directly to consumers.

Similarly, personal consumption expenditures on services—such as medical care, insurance and banking, education, car washing, dry cleaning, and the like—are composed of layers of product and labor transactions that represent costs and transactions embedded in the final sale. For example, within the room charges of a hotel lie the labor of the housekeepers and door attendants, the production and commercial purchase of carpeting in the halls, the natural gas that heats the hotel, and so on.

In this manner, major economic series such as industrial production, retail sales, personal income (including wages and salaries), durable goods orders, and the like, although not recorded directly in GDP, can be thought of as layers of economic activity that contribute added value to the final sales represented by consumer spending. The various categories can be calculated separately so that we can analyze their various parts, but they are considered under the umbrella of personal consumption, which, again, represents more than two-thirds of GDP.

Beyond Consumer Spending

Capital spending is another major sector of GDP that, like consumer spending, is subject to cyclical influences. Its official name in the Department of Commerce's Bureau of Economic Analysis reports is *gross private domestic investment*, but this book refers to it by its more popular name, *capital spending*. In most instances, I will refer to real capital spending, which, as with real consumer spending, denotes units and not dollars—adjusted to remove the effect of inflation. Capital spending consists of spending by businesses on factories and offices and their equipment, as well as housing. (Note: references to real capital spending later in this book will exclude the "residential structures" portion of gross private domestic investment in order to focus on business capital spending.) Figure 2-4 shows its three major categories, and Appendix C shows its individual subcategories, down to such specific products as mining and oilfield machinery and engines and turbines.

In addition to capital spending, there are two major economic sectors other than consumer spending that influence economic growth:

FIGURE 2-4

Composition of capital spending,* 2004

$1.9 trillion

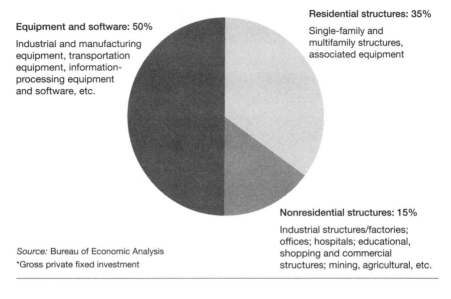

Residential structures: 35%

Equipment and software: 50%

Single-family and
multifamily structures,
associated equipment

Industrial and manufacturing
equipment, transportation
equipment, information-
processing equipment
and software, etc.

Nonresidential structures: 15%

Industrial structures/factories;
offices; hospitals; educational,
shopping and commercial
structures; mining, agricultural, etc.

Source: Bureau of Economic Analysis
*Gross private fixed investment

- *Government spending.* It has represented 15 to 20 percent of total GDP in recent years, but in most years (except during wartime or with major spending initiatives during peacetime) it is unlikely to prove sufficiently volatile to provide sufficient stimulus to alter the economic cycle as a whole.

- *Net exports and imports.* These are goods produced for non-domestic consumption and goods manufactured abroad and brought into the United States. U.S. imports exceed exports, with the *balance-of-trade deficit* (exports minus imports) accounting for only 5 percent of GDP (2004).

Just as consumer spending includes embedded industrial production and other activities that support the final sale, similar production and transactions lie embedded in the final sales represented by capital spending and government spending. For example, capital spending includes the production (including materials and labor) of, say, bricks or steel used to build a factory, and government spending would include products used to build interstate highways or jet fighter planes.

Consumer spending represents a dominant portion of GDP and, from a cyclical standpoint, is the key determinant of the short- to intermediate-term direction of industrial production and, in turn, capital spending (an assertion documented in chart form in chapter 7). As a result, consumer spending is also, not surprisingly, the key driving force in the direction of corporate profits. This insight is important for investors, because advancing or slowing growth in corporate profits is one of two key factors in the direction of the stock market (the other is interest rates). Indeed, although the arrow in figure 2-1 points causally from right (corporate profits) to left (stock market), the stock market serves as a sensitive anticipating mechanism for corporate profits, with the chronology, although not necessarily the causation, therefore moving from left to right.

Advancing or slowing corporate profits are also, in turn, the key determinant of intermediate-term uptrends and downtrends in employment. Clearly, strong or weak business activity and corporate profits lead to, respectively, the hiring or the laying off of workers, and employment thus lags most other indicators in the economy. To reiterate an earlier point, we will see later that, from the viewpoint of timing, it is vital for businesspeople and investors to firmly grasp employment's lagging characteristic and thereby avoid the frequent and highly deceptive assumption that, cyclically, jobs drive the economy to a greater extent than vice versa.

Consumer Spending and the Stock Market

Given the causal relationship of consumer spending to corporate profits, we should not be surprised that the stock market, too, behaves in a surprisingly consistent manner in relationship to rates of change in consumer spending at the front end of the cycle. The stock market, as a sensitive predictive indicator, moves up and down with the rate of growth in consumer spending at the front end of the economic cycle. Consequently, forecasting uptrends and downtrends in consumer spending is often another useful key to forecasting the stock market. If consumer spending (A) drives the economic and corporate-profit cycle (B) and if the stock market (C) is a sensitive predictor of (B), *then (A) and (C) are causally linked.*

This is not to suggest that uptrends and downtrends in the stock market are not also driven by myriad other psychological and valuation factors. Nevertheless, we will see that most major stock market advances and declines have a surprisingly consistent relationship to increasing and decreasing rates of change in consumer spending. This relationship is not well recognized by most investors and economists.

In other words, consumer spending is dominant in the economy as a whole to such an extent that it is, by itself, the sector that cyclically determines the direction of the overall economy. This being the case, carefully monitoring overall consumer spending—or, even more significantly, forecasting the direction of consumer demand—is the key that unlocks effective forecasting for most other developments and sectors in the economy.

Forecasting Consumer Spending

If consumer spending is the key driver of the rest of the economy, then we must forecast consumer spending itself to get ahead of the curve on uptrends, downtrends, and turning points in the chain of economic demand.

Chapters 9 through 13 investigate the key forces driving consumer spending. By far, the two most important of these are as follows:

- *Individuals' real average hourly earnings.* This number reflects the unit purchasing power of the majority of the population that is employed at any given time. Real average hourly earnings has proven to be an excellent leading indicator of consumer spending over many cycles.

- *Employment.* Although it is more driven by consumer spending than vice versa and therefore lags, employment is still a key factor in the wages and salaries that contribute a significant portion of consumer spending power.

For the neophyte, indeed even for the professional forecaster, the starting point for predicting uptrends, downtrends, and turning points in major economic series is to begin by intuitively positing the key cause-and-effect relationships that might exist between major economic series. One need not have an advanced degree in economics to hypothesize that there would be, for example, a strong cause-and-effect relationship between the sales in retail stores of durable and non-durable goods and the production or manufacture of such goods. Borrowing from the sportscaster cliché, "Let's go to the videotape," throughout this book we will exclaim, "Let's go to the chart!" as we seek to verify whether or not the commonsense cause-and-effect relationships we postulate actually exist when we examine, via charts, the historical data.

But before we embark on the process of proving how consistent most of the cause-and-effect relationships in the economy really are, chapters 3, 4, and 5 tackle—and correct—several major structural flaws in how most economic data series are tracked and analyzed. These flaws have long prevented those wishing to forecast (from the most sophisticated economists to lay businesspeople and investors) from commanding a clear view of the economic cycle. I will offer a new framework for analyzing economic data that I believe will greatly enhance our ability to master the consistent sequence of events in economic cycles by understanding where the economy is today and forecasting where it is headed.

CHAPTER THREE

Redefining Economic Downturns

Early in my career as an investment analyst on Wall Street, I discovered an important truth in providing sound advice to my clients: although my first job was to determine *which* companies and stocks (my specialty was the retailing industry) would provide the best investment returns over an intermediate-term (say, one to three years) or longer-term time frame, my second one was to determine *when* stocks of retailing companies, or the stock market as a whole, might be most favorably owned. Without question, there were long periods during which retail stocks and stocks in general were unrewarding. During such times, a buy-and-hold posture would prove to be destructive. These periods usually coincided with slowdowns in the economy lasting for two or more years. Economic cycles—periods of advancing and then slowing economic growth—were the rule and not the exception. These cycles appeared to occur every three to six years and carried with them corresponding bull and bear markets.

Furthermore, on the downside, there seemed to be a repeating pattern in which businesses and investors were invariably caught, without warning, in economic downturns and the accompanying bear markets. In cycle after cycle, the abilities of the business and investment communities to perceive the downturn as it occurred were typically so belated that there was little capacity for avoiding its damaging effects.

Much of the problem seemed to revolve around businesses' and investors' focus on *recession*—typically defined as two successive quarters of absolute decline in total economic output (real GDP) on a quarter-versus-prior-quarter basis—as the key economic event to be feared, the big bad wolf of the economy, so to speak. Businesses and investors seemed to feel that, if there were no recession, then everything was basically OK. But, repeatedly, business conditions, corporate profits, and the stock market appeared to suffer badly before recessions ever came into view.

The Four Stages of Economic Downturns

I observed four stages of perception associated with these downturns:

- *Stage 1: The peak.* The economic environment would be uniformly favorable. Real GDP and its key component, consumer spending, were increasing at a strong pace, corporate profits were showing superb gains, and the employment picture was clearly favorable. The stock market would be reaching new peaks, with investors enthusiastically embracing a bright business outlook.

- *Stage 2: A modest slowing.* The uniformly bright outlook of stage 1 would give way to a period of moderate slowdown in the *rate of growth* of the economy, particularly in consumer spending at the front end of the cycle. Retail sales growth would slow a bit. Interest rates would be rising gradually in response to the strong economy, and some vague concerns about interest rate and inflation would be raised, but not sufficiently to quell business and investor optimism. Capital spending and employment would still be growing at a strong pace (accompanied by much happy talk about a "full-employment economy"). And corporate profits would still be on the rise, but with percentage increases at a somewhat slower pace than the robust pace of the prior period. Few forecasters would yet fear that a recession—an actual decline in total economic output—was in the cards. And the stock market might well be sideways or, more likely, even down 5 to 10 percent, but believed to be only taking a "breather" after the strong market gains of the prior period.

- *Stage 3: Intensifying worry.* The economy would now enter a period of more intense worry, in which interest rates and inflation were higher, the rate of growth in real consumer spending and real GDP had slowed from a peak of 5 to 6 percent to "moderate growth" of perhaps 2 to 3 percent, and economists and others would begin to contemplate the possibility that the economy could enter a recession. Conjecture would now begin to center on how long and deep such a recession (if it occurred) might be. The stock market by now might have declined an additional 10 percent or more from stage 2; a bear market was now under way. However, some comfort would still be taken from the fact that capital spending was still relatively strong and the unemployment rate remained low.

- *Stage 4: The advent of recession.* Now the economy would actually enter the recession, a period of absolute decline in real GDP, with corporate profits falling significantly, capital spending beginning to weaken, and—perhaps most alarmingly—the first major increases in the unemployment rate. And if an accelerating number of workers were losing their jobs, where would the impetus for an upturn come from? Fears of a protracted decline would now become more widespread, with a great deal of economic discourse devoted to determining when the recession began: when quarter-to-quarter real GDP comparisons fell below zero—that is, began to decline (as if the zero demarcation level were any more important than any other number). During the early phases of stage 4, stocks would continue to decline as investors confronted these fears. As a period of unusually widespread pessimism, stage 4 appeared very much like a mirror image of the unquestioned optimism of stage 1. And, most perplexingly, at some point during the recession, when economic conditions were at their worst, stock prices would stop declining and—mysteriously—would begin to advance.

As an analyst responsible to my clients for providing guidance on the performance of my (retail-industry) stocks, I began to recognize patterns of economic and investment damage. Not only my retail stocks, but also the stock market as a whole, had peaked during stage 1 when economic growth was still at its best and optimism was rampant. Stock prices were already in decline as sales-growth rates for business throughout

"It's true, Caesar. Rome is declining, but I expect it to pick up in the next quarter."

the economy began to slow in stage 2, and this decline intensified in stage 3 as sales increases slowed even further, but *before* an actual recession was even considered likely. By stage 3, it was already too late for most companies to react to slowing business conditions. Investors, too, were faced with a dilemma by the time stage 3 ran its course: the difficult choice of either waiting things out in the hopes that a recession could be avoided, or selling—to avoid further losses—at what could be the bottom.

I now began to understand that the central role given to recession—the advent of stage 4—as the accepted definition of economic harm was itself most damaging to businesses and investors. The emphasis that economists, businesspeople, and investors placed on recession as the key negative economic event actually led them to miss the fundamental fact that the greatest economic damage was done when *rates of economic growth* began to slow, and this period began at the end of stage

1 and continued through the beginning of stage 4, long before stage 4's absolute decline in economic activity. It was in stages 2 and 3 that an unexpected slowdown in sales growth would begin to cause rising inventories, pricing weakness for businesses, falling profits, and declining stock prices. In fact, in a number of downturns (for example, 1966–1967 and 1984–1985) the economy never even reached stage 4; that is, a recession, or actual decline in economic activity, never even occurred. Yet there was clear damage to corporate profits and the stock market.

As I write, I have been tempted to draw a weather analogy with this economic pattern. Stage 1 is the bright, unclouded sunny day, stage 2 is sunny but with a growing haze, stage 3 is cloudy with the threat of thunderstorms developing, and stage 4 is the violent thunderstorm itself. But I then realized how inaccurate this analogy is, and yet helpfully descriptive in its very inaccuracy. With weather, we can wait through hazy and then cloudy and worsening skies (stages 2 and 3) and board up the windows shortly before the onset of the storm (stage 4). But in the economy and the stock market, much of the damage is already done between the end of stage 1 and the end of stage 3, *before* stage 4. In the economy and the stock market, stages 2 and 3 represent, in reality, the first half to two-thirds of the damage, and stage 4—the recession—is the *beginning of the end* of the harm.

Two Great Flaws in Conventional Economic Analysis

It now became clear to me that to get ahead of the curve in predicting the economy, it would be necessary to alter the most widely used methods of tracking economic data. The goal was to correct the two major dysfunctions in the conventional means by which most businesses, investors—and yes, even economists—measure economic cycles.

- *Economic flaw 1: recession as the primary measure of economic slowdown.* To use the concept and definition of recession—a period of absolute economic decline in real GDP—as the most widespread measure of economic harm is fundamentally tardy and, therefore, useless as a pragmatic economic measure for businesses, investors, and policy makers. In every economic cycle—those I experienced in my first decade as an analyst, and those since— by the time a decline in real GDP *occurs*, or is even close at hand, the general economy, businesses, and stock market have already suffered considerable damage. Most damage to the economy, businesses, and the stock market happens much earlier, when the rate of growth in the economy begins to slow from peak levels. By the time the economy is actually declining in absolute terms, most of the damage is already done. Recession needs to be replaced by a more sensitive and agile concept of economic slowdown.

- *Economic flaw 2: tracking economic data on a quarter-to-quarter and month-to-month basis.* The method that is used to track rates of change in most economic series and indicators creates unneeded confusion and often obscures viable economic cause-and-effect relationships that might have been used more effectively to forecast future events. Government data bureaus and other sources of economic data, and most economists, track the rate of change in most major economic indicators on a quarter-versus-prior-quarter basis (headline: "Real GDP rose 3.5% in the second quarter"). This method requires (1) seasonal adjustment of the data for the quarter and then the one that preceded it, (2) multiplication by 4 (or 12, if the data is monthly) to determine a *seasonally adjusted rate of change*, and (3) frequent revision. There are some pragmatic short-term reasons for reporting economic statistics in this manner. But looking at economic data on a quarter-to-quarter basis over longer periods results in so much volatility, or *noise*, that causality between economic series is often obfuscated, when a cause-and-effect relationship in fact exists. I found that, as we seek to find longer-term predictive relationships between economic indicators, the way data is charted is fundamental to achieving clarity.

When we combine recession, as the wrong definition of economic harm, with quarter-to-quarter rates of change as the wrong method for measuring it, the result is confusion that obscures the real inflection points in the business cycle—when rates of change begin to turn.

By correcting these two overarching problems associated with most economic analysis, we can learn to look at the same data everyone else has, but from a different perspective that enables us to see patterns others may miss. Like the pilot of an airplane at thirty thousand feet, we can look down and see patterns that the driver of a car—lost in the maze of "recession," "growth," and confusing quarter-to-quarter data comparisons—will not recognize. Eliminating these two errors will make us better able to evaluate the public conversation from a detached and illuminated point of view and help us wean ourselves from the confusion of much of current economic discourse.

Each of these two major dysfunctions merits its own chapter. Chapter 4 examines the frequency and timing of past recessions and describes how they relate to rates of growth in economic activity, corporate profits, and the stock market. It also provides our first glimpse of the economic-indicator sequence in which a cyclical downturn unfolds. Chapter 5 analyzes how economic growth rates are tracked and explains the overarching need for those who seek to forecast future cycles to abandon quarter-to-quarter measurement and focus instead on year-over-year rates of change. Later, in parts II and III of this book, we will see the consistency of cause and effect in past cycles, a consistency that serves as a guide to the future.

CHAPTER FOUR

An Antidote for the Recession Obsession

I remember my first recession. It occurred during 1969 and 1970, when I was a budding analyst at the Bank of New York. Despite the Vietnam War and growing social unrest, the late 1960s had been a period of considerable growth and prosperity. The stock market had performed strongly in 1968 (the S&P 500 index rose 8%). The rate of economic growth had slowed but remained positive through the second half of 1968 and the first half of 1969 and actually accelerated late in the year. Corporate profits had increased steadily over the preceding year, and the unemployment rate was actually continuing to decline. It was only in the very late months of 1969 that the likelihood of a recession became apparent, and yet the stock market had declined in each quarter of that year, losing 11% for the year as a whole.

In the hindsight of conventional economic measurement, the 1969–1970 recession began in December 1969 and ended in November 1970; but the fact of a recession wasn't verified by the National Bureau of Economic Research until June 1970, *after* the 1969–1970 bear market—which saw the S&P 500 index decline a whopping 36%—had ended.

It was then, and in repeated similar circumstances in later economic slowdowns, that I learned that the damaging effects of economic slowdowns—softening demand, accumulating inventories, slowing growth in corporate profits, and falling stock prices—far precede even the conjecture of recession by professional economists and other forecasters. It became clear that businesses needed to pull in their horns and investors had to sell at a far earlier stage in the slowdown, when the slowing of momentum from peak rates of economic growth was beginning and long before recession—an actual decline in real GDP—was considered a possibility. Indeed, I came to see that a slowdown in year-over-year real GDP growth from +5% to +2% was enough to wreak havoc on corporate profits and produce a bear market. A recession wasn't even necessary for material economic and stock market damage to occur.

How the Recession Obsession Clouds Economic Thinking

Recession is typically defined by the financial press and most casual economic observers as two consecutive quarters of absolute decline in real GDP. (The National Bureau of Economic Research, which is charged with both defining and measuring recessions, uses a somewhat broader and more complex definition, but the operative definition is nevertheless close to the popular usage.[1]) This definition leads to a tendency by many economists and the business press to regard the economy as being in one of two simplistic states: growth (increases of *any* degree in gross domestic product, or overall economic activity) or recession (declines). When real GDP growth is positive—that is, more than zero—most economists consider the economy to be growing or at least not in trouble. In contrast, the existence or even the likelihood of a recession is typically greeted with a great waving of hands and a sense of defeat for government and foreboding for business and consumers alike.

A slowdown in economic growth that fails to reach recessionary proportions is often termed a *soft landing* or *growth recession* and is often viewed as an event not worthy of particular concern. However, having observed economic cycles and stock prices for almost four decades, I believe that "growth recessions" typically do almost as much economic and stock market damage as "official" recessions. Economic slowdowns that failed to reach recessionary proportions nevertheless produced stock market declines of 15% or more in 1953, 1956–1957, 1962, 1966, and 1984. As I asked earlier, why should we regard the "zero" demarcation between growth and recession as any more important than, say, +1.5% or +0.3%?

Recessions: Far Less Relevant Than Economic Slowdowns

One of the central dysfunctions of the conventional view of recession as the key definition of economic distress is that recessions are quite infrequent, occurring less often than economic slowdowns. Table 4-1 summarizes relevant data regarding recessions during the fifty-four years from 1950 through 2004. This period included nine recessions, averaging one every six years. They averaged 10 to 11 months in length, varying from only 6 months in the 1980 recession to 16 months in the 1973–1975 and 1981–1982 downturns. During that time, the United States was in recession for a total of 93 months (7.75 years) out of a total of 660 months (55 years). This represents only 14% of the time: no wonder that the condition of recession, being a relatively rare one, is greeted with excessive concern.

TABLE 4-1

Recessions 1950–2004*

Recession				Number of months
Began		**Ended**		
July	1953	May	1954	10
August	1957	April	1958	8
April	1960	February	1961	10
December	1969	November	1970	11
November	1973	March	1975	16
January	1980	July	1980	6
July	1981	November	1982	16
July	1990	March	1991	8
March	2001	November	2001	8
Total				93

*As defined by the National Bureau of Economic Research

Figure 4-1 provides a sense of the frequency and duration of recessions. Year-over-year changes in real GDP from 1950 through 2003 are represented by the solid line, and recessions are denoted by black bars at the bottom of the chart.

As figure 4-1 shows, the *rate of change* in real GDP (measured year-over-year) from 1950 to 2004 was divided rather evenly between periods of increasing rates of growth and periods of declining rates of growth. And in thirteen instances (numbered in the chart), the year-over-year rate of growth in real GDP fell 4 or more percentage points. However, recessions (again, black bars at the bottom of the chart) occurred only nine times and appeared almost as punctuation marks at the end of periods of declining rates of growth in real GDP.

Clearly, there is a fundamental mismatch between (1) the roughly 50/50 balance of periods in which real GDP growth is accelerating (economic advances) or decelerating (economic slowdowns) and (2) the 86%/14% balance of time between real GDP *absolute* "growth" and "recession" (absolute declines). The more relevant need for businesses and investors, therefore, is to be prepared for periods of declining rates of growth, which are far more frequent than recessions.

A Belated and Generally Useless Measure of Downturns

Figure 4-1 includes an additional visual aid—one used throughout the book—that will help put into perspective the relatively meaningless nature of America's "recession obsession." The vertical gray bars represent *bear markets*, by my definition periods during which the stock market, represented by the S&P 500 index, declined 12% or more. (There is no universally accepted definition of a bear market.)

So the vertical gray bars help us determine when, relative to a myriad of economic indicators, stock prices were in significant decline. Although it is intuitive, it will be useful to remember that the beginning of the vertical gray bars marks when stock prices peaked (the bear market began), and the end of the gray bars marks when stock prices bottomed

FIGURE 4-1

Recessions versus slowdowns in real* GDP: A mismatch

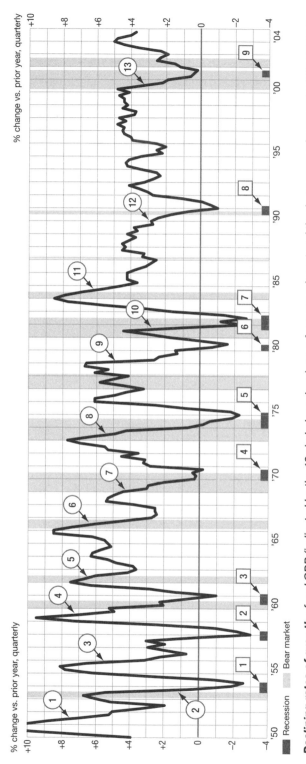

■ Recession   ▒ Bear market

Declining rates of growth *of real GDP (indicated by the 13 circled numbers) are a far more relevant and timely measure of economic difficulty than the less-frequent recessions (denoted by vertical gray bars) usually begin when the year-over-year rates of growth of real GDP are at peak and begin to decline.*

1. Bear markets (designated by vertical gray bars) usually begin when the year-over-year rates of growth of real GDP are at peak and begin to decline.

2. By the time recessions (periods of absolute decline in real GDP) begin, the decline in the rate of economic growth and the bear market are largely over, and most economic damage has already been done.

This makes it essential for investors and businesspeople to learn to forecast the peak of economic growth (discussed in part III of this book) to avoid the economic and stock market harm that occurs as the rates of growth decline.

Source: Bureau of Economic Analysis   *Adjusted for inflation (a new bull market began). Chapter 8 takes a detailed look at some of these bear markets from 1960 through 2004.

But a quick scan reveals that most bear markets *began* when the year-over-year real GDP growth was at or near peak levels of 4% to 8% and occurred primarily as year-over-year real GDP increases fell *toward* the zero level. In other words, most bear markets began when the rate of growth in real GDP was *strong* and occurred as that rate of growth slowed from peak levels. Why? It's because this was also when the rate of growth in corporate profits—driven by consumer spending at the front end of the cycle—began to wane from their peak rates of gain. Most recessions—shown in the charts as black bars—occurred only after the year-over-year rate of change in real GDP *had been declining from peak levels for at least several quarters*, and often more than a year.

It is also clear in figure 4-1 that in most instances, by the time recession was reached, the bear market was largely over. In other words, by the time a recession had occurred and had been validated by economists, most of the economic harm had been done.

Given all this, we can reasonably conclude that the concept of "recession" has little or no analytical value beyond telling us, usually late or after the fact, that a significant slowdown in the overall economic growth rate—to actual declines—has occurred. Although recession is often highlighted in the press with a sense of forward-looking gloom, it is, in fact, the end of the event. Thus, entirely too many words are wasted on the concept of recession in economic and business publications and the media in general. By the time recession is upon us, attention might better be given to leading indicators that would help determine in advance the beginning of the next upturn. So it is crucial for business managers and investors to distinguish between a decline in the growth rate of the economy, when most actual business and stock market harm is done, and an actual decline (recession) in the economy, which, by the time it is recognized, is little more than an afterthought.

A Closer Look at Two Cycles

Charts throughout this book demonstrate how similar most economic cycles from 1960 to 2004 were in their sequence of economic indicators,

FIGURE 4-2

Chronology: Key economic indicators

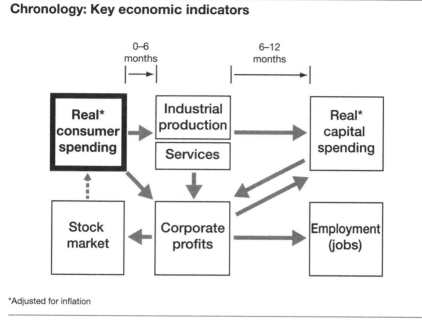

*Adjusted for inflation

which in turn advance and decline. We are going to closely examine two specific economic downturns (1969–1970 and 2000–2002) and show these sequences at work in a shorter time frame. Figure 4-2, excerpted from figure 2-1, is a reminder of the chronology of economic indicators whose uptrends and downtrends follow each other in a typical cycle.

For each of these economic slowdowns, I have pulled together a visual analysis of quarterly changes for six relevant economic data series: real GDP, real consumer spending, industrial production, real capital spending, S&P 500 earnings per share (representing corporate profits), and the unemployment rate. Take some time reviewing these charts. They will reveal our core insight: that damage to business and the stock market occurs as the year-over-year rate of growth slows, well before the economy is in absolute decline (i.e., a recession).

The 1969–1970 Downturn

I discussed earlier my experience in the economic downturn that began in early 1969 and ended with the 1969–1970 recession. As figure 4-3

FIGURE 4-3

Key economic data in the 1969–1970 downturn

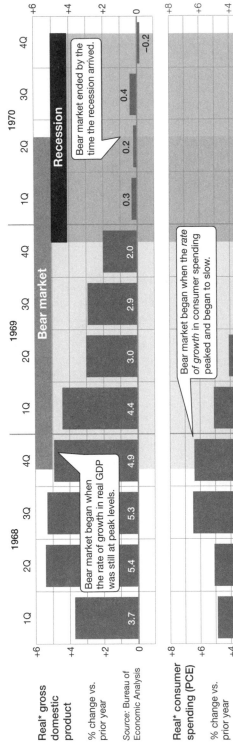

Real* gross domestic product

% change vs. prior year

Source: Bureau of Economic Analysis

Bear market began when the rate of growth in real GDP was still at peak levels.

Bear market

Recession

Bear market ended by the time the recession arrived.

1968				1969				1970			
1Q	2Q	3Q	4Q	1Q	2Q	3Q	4Q	1Q	2Q	3Q	4Q
3.7	5.4	5.3	4.9	4.4	3.0	2.9	2.0	0.3	0.2	0.4	-0.2

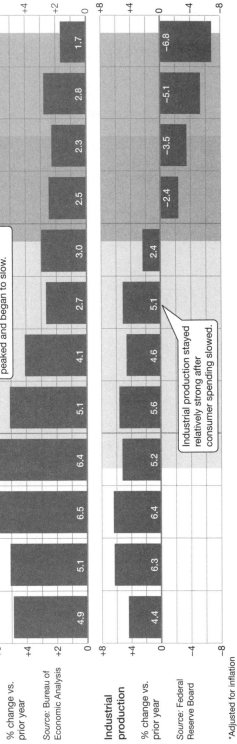

Real* consumer spending (PCE)

% change vs. prior year

Source: Bureau of Economic Analysis

Bear market began when the *rate of growth* in consumer spending peaked and began to slow.

| 4.9 | 5.1 | 6.5 | 6.4 | 5.1 | 4.1 | 2.7 | 3.0 | 2.5 | 2.3 | 2.8 | 1.7 |

Industrial production

% change vs. prior year

Source: Federal Reserve Board

Industrial production stayed relatively strong after consumer spending slowed.

| 4.4 | 6.3 | 6.4 | 5.2 | 5.6 | 4.6 | 5.1 | 2.4 | -2.4 | -3.5 | -5.1 | -6.8 |

*Adjusted for inflation

FIGURE 4-3 (continued)

Key economic data in the 1969–1970 downturn

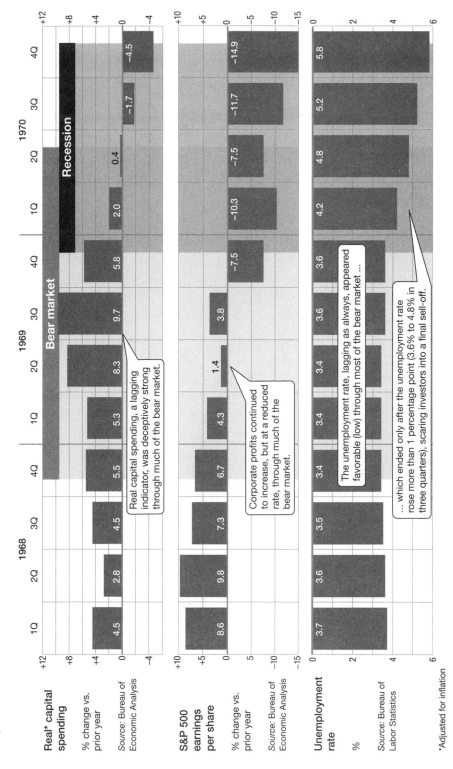

*Adjusted for inflation

shows, year-over-year growth in overall real GDP peaked at 5.4% in the second and third quarters of 1968 and slowed to a rate of –0.2% by the fourth quarter of 1970. Real consumer spending peaked at a year-over-year rate of 6.5% in the third quarter of 1968 and slowed steadily through 1970, but it never reached a year-over-year decline. Industrial production remained solid through much of 1969 but then fell from year-over-year growth of well over 5% throughout 1968 to year-over-year declines throughout 1970.

However, the two notable lagging indicators in the economy—capital spending and employment—stayed deceptively strong right through 1969 and the bear market. Capital spending reached a year-over-year peak of 9.7% growth in the third quarter of 1969 before turning down, and the unemployment rate was still holding at an optimistic cyclical low of 3.4% in the second quarter of 1969. Later in this book we examine how lagging indicators, if they are not correctly perceived as lagging, fool even seasoned observers into remaining positive long after economic peaks, and negative well beyond economic troughs.

As figure 4-3 shows, by the official beginning of the recession in the fourth quarter of 1969, real PCE, industrial production, and S&P 500 profits had all slowed sharply from their peak levels of the prior year. However, as noted earlier, a bear market had been already well under way for almost a year. Indeed, the beginning of the 1969–1970 recession in December 1969 was verified by the National Bureau of Economic Research only in June 1970 (in measuring recession, it is possible to do so only after consecutive declines have actually occurred). However, most of the damage to business (slowing sales comparisons and drastic inventory liquidation) and to investors (the bear market) had already occurred while year-over-year rate of growth in real GDP was slowing from peak levels of 5%-plus in late 1968. Stock prices, as measured by the S&P 500, had already declined 13% from their peak in late November 1968 through the end of November 1969 by the time the recession officially began. Stock prices fell another 26% between the end of November 1969 and the market's (S&P 500) final bottom in late May 1970.

In short, the recession of 1969–1970, like all recessions, was a lagging event, occurring after the rate of change in the economy had been declining for well over a year.

The 2000–2002 Downturn

The economic slowdown of 2000–2002 is the most recent example of this phenomenon. As figure 4-4 shows, real consumer spending growth peaked at 5.5% year-over-year in the first quarter of 2000 and slowed moderately throughout the year, before falling to a nadir of 2.0% in the third quarter of 2001. However, through the entire slowdown, real consumer spending never declined in absolute terms. Industrial production and capital spending both peaked in year-over-year terms in the second quarter of 2000—one quarter later than consumer spending—but both fell sharply to year-over-year declines by mid-2001. S&P 500 profit growth, which had remained strong in early 2000, fell sharply to significant declines throughout 2001. By early to mid-2001, it was clear that the economy was beginning to sag badly. However, a good deal of stock market damage had already been done. The bull market of the late 1990s had already ended in late March 2000, with the market alternately rising and falling through much of 2000 but then suffering a 27% decline between late 2000 and April 2001. It then vacillated throughout mid- to late 2001 (including a sharp decline in reaction to the World Trade Center tragedy, followed by a surprising rally), and in 2002 it declined another 23%.

Although questions of impending recession began to be raised only in mid-2001 and later, a great deal of the setback to businesses and the stock market had already occurred in early and mid-2001. Again, the debate among economists and in the press regarding whether the economy was heading into recession, or would have a soft landing, came far too late to be of use to those who were caught in the maelstrom. Retail stores, manufacturing concerns, capital spending businesses, and, of course, the world of the Internet were already reeling from the drastic downturn in business activity. Economists had issued no advance warning of a dramatic setback in the economy, and belated efforts to define the dimension of the downtrend were already a hollow exercise.

In the end, even in the face of the debilitating effect of the terrorist attacks, 2001 real GDP recovered slightly in the fourth quarter. In fact, it was not until November 2002 that, evaluating newly restated

FIGURE 4-4

Key economic data in the 2000–2002 downturn

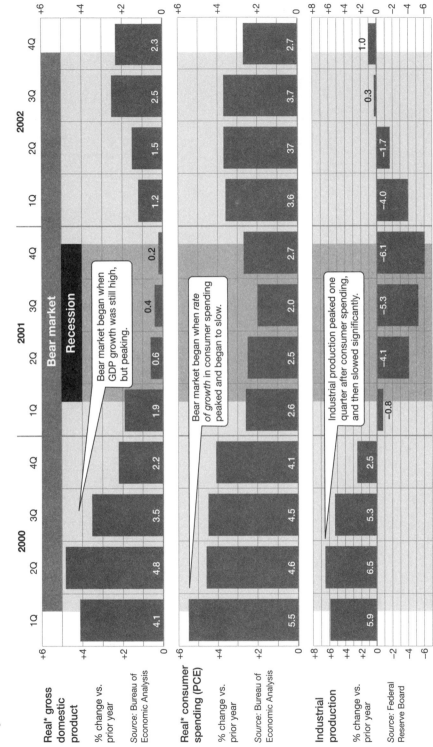

*Adjusted for inflation

FIGURE 4-4 (continued)

Key economic data in the 2000–2002 downturn

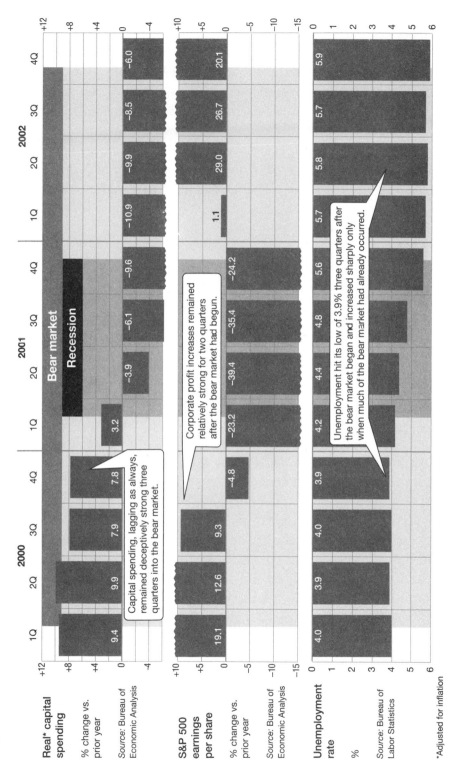

Real* capital spending

% change vs. prior year

Source: Bureau of Economic Analysis

Capital spending, lagging as always, remained deceptively strong three quarters into the bear market.

	2000			2001				2002			
	1Q	2Q	3Q	4Q	1Q	2Q	3Q	4Q	1Q	2Q	3Q	4Q
	9.4	9.9	7.9	7.8	3.2	−3.9	−6.1	−9.6	−10.9	−9.9	−8.5	−6.0

Bear market / Recession

S&P 500 earnings per share

% change vs. prior year

Source: Bureau of Economic Analysis

Corporate profit increases remained relatively strong for two quarters after the bear market had begun.

| | 19.1 | 12.6 | 9.3 | −4.8 | −23.2 | −39.4 | −35.4 | −24.2 | 1.1 | 29.0 | 26.7 | 20.1 |

Unemployment rate

%

Source: Bureau of Labor Statistics

Unemployment hit its low of 3.9% three quarters after the bear market began and increased sharply only when much of the bear market had already occurred.

| | 4.0 | 3.9 | 4.0 | 3.9 | 4.2 | 4.4 | 4.8 | 5.6 | 5.7 | 5.8 | 5.7 | 5.9 |

*Adjusted for inflation

economic data, the National Bureau of economic Research determined that a recession of three quarters had, indeed, occurred during 2001.

Again, the whole recession exercise was a hollow one, at least as a pragmatic tool for businesses and investors. The declaring of recession had value only as a post facto measurement of an absolute decline in the economy—the rather arbitrary "zero" dividing line between up and down. Only an early read on the slowing rate of growth in economic activity in the first half of 2000 would have provided possible protection for businesses and investors astute enough to have seen it.[2]

Needed: A New ROCET Method
for Defining Business Cycles

In short, a recession—and all the hand-wringing over whether or not one has begun—is often meaningless (except as a possible sign of the beginning of a *new* cycle!) by the time it is evident. To give so much analytical and emotional attention to the concept and fact of "recession" is analogous to a municipal department of water resources remaining unconcerned as the reservoir slowly dries up, issuing water restrictions only when the reservoir is nearly empty. Much of the harm in fact occurs as the water level falls from full to one-third full. The fear and alarm caused by the definition of recession as an absolute economic decline are belated and unnecessary, and the definition does not realistically portray the economy's actual movements, which consist of rising rates of growth half of the time and declining rates of growth half of the time.

Many portfolio strategists recognize that stock market declines precede recession, usually by six to twelve months. Therefore, even forecasting a recession by six months represents scant relief—it is the wrong event to forecast. And for the businessperson, by the time the economy approaches recession, it is too late to gear down—and, indeed, it may even be time to gear *up* for the recovery. Basically, too much time is spent by economists and others attempting to forecast the wrong event.

Therefore, although the term *recession* may continue to be useful to economists and newscasters as a means of defining and dramatizing a poor economy—that is, usually incorporating an actual decline in total economic output—the business and investment worlds must develop an alternative approach to measuring economic advances and declines.

It is time for businesses, investors, and even economists to move to a new *rate of change economic tracking* method, or ROCET, in which turning points in the rate of change in economic growth, and not absolute levels, are viewed as the economy's key inflection points. You will find the ROCET approach invaluable in mastering the economy's most important indicators and their relationships to each other and the stock market.

But first, in chapter 5, we must deal with the second major dysfunction of economic analysis: how rates of change can be more advantageously tracked and charted to improve understanding of the economy's most important cause-and-effect relationships and to enhance economic perspective and forecasting.

CHAPTER FIVE

Smart Economic Tracking

Getting the Noise Out

We have identified a fundamental flaw in most economic analysis—the excessive reliance on recession, or absolute decline in the economy (as opposed to slowing rates of change), as a measure of economic distress—and we have seen that this flaw has almost guaranteed that businesses, investors, and economists alike are late in reacting to economic downturns. However, even if we switch to the more facile ROCET approach, we must still correct the second major flaw in much economic discourse and analysis: the standard practice of measuring change over periods of time—quarter to quarter or month to month—so short that a great deal of fluctuation is created and the underlying real trends are missed.

An Example: Acme Shirts

It is easier to understand the problem of quarter-to-quarter or month-to-month reporting when we look at it from the standpoint of a typical business and then expand to a view of how it affects the analysis of most economic data. Suppose we are the owners of Acme Shirt Stores, a retailer of men's shirts. We track our company's unit sales of shirts on a weekly, monthly, and quarterly basis. Columns 1 through 4 in the top panel of table 5-1 show our Acme quarterly sales for 2000, 2001, 2002, and 2003. In addition to the effects of periods of strengthening and weakening consumer spending, our quarterly sales are influenced by changes in weather, fashion trends, special promotions, and competitive

TABLE 5-1

Acme Shirt Stores, quarterly sales tables

	Unit sales (thousands)				% increase, quarterly vs. prior year			% increase, quarterly vs. prior quarter, annualized		
	2000 (1)	2001 (2)	2002 (3)	2003 (4)	2001 (5)	2002 (6)	2003 (7)	2001 (8)	2002 (9)	2003 (10)
Sales, actual										
1st Qtr.	3,951	4,156	4,355	4,499	5.2	4.8	3.3	—	—	—
2nd Qtr.	5,064	5,378	5,642	5,788	6.2	4.9	2.6	—	—	—
3rd Qtr.	4,650	4,904	5,088	5,233	5.5	4.8	2.8	—	—	—
4th Qtr.	6,074	6,396	6,617	6,731	5.3	3.5	1.7	—	—	—
Year	19,739	20,834	21,702	22,251						
Sales, seasonally adjusted										
1st Qtr.	4,854	5,111	5,344	5,536	5.3	4.6	3.6	6.0	2.3	3.9
2nd Qtr.	4,888	5,176	5,411	5,542	5.9	4.5	2.4	5.1	5.0	0.4
3rd Qtr.	4,961	5,234	5,464	5,590	5.5	4.4	2.3	4.5	3.9	3.5
4th Qtr.	5,036	5,313	5,483	5,583	5.5	3.2	1.8	6.0	1.4	(0.5)
Year	19,739	20,834	21,702	22,251						

factors. And every year, sales are particularly strong in the second quarter because of the new spring season and purchases for Father's Day, and in the fourth quarter because of Christmas gift-giving.

As most businesses do, every month and every quarter we look at our percentage sales increases over the same periods in the prior year (top panel, columns 5 through 7). But in a quest for shorter-term *trend* information, we are also interested in how sales are proceeding on a month-to-month or quarter-to-quarter basis. How was our sales rate during the third quarter as a whole compared with the second quarter? And the fourth quarter versus the third quarter? And so we compare our sales for one month with those of the month preceding it, or our sales for one quarter with the one before it.

Now we encounter two significant problems:

1. Because sales in the second and fourth quarter are always stronger than those of other quarters, we must *seasonally adjust* each quarter by applying a multiplier or divisor that reflects over many years the normal seasonal sales divergence of that quarter

vis-à-vis other quarters. This procedure is not totally accurate, but it's doable. And so we seasonally adjust our quarterly sales, as shown in columns 1 through 4 in the bottom panel of table 5-1.

2. But now, to evaluate our quarter-versus-prior-quarter sales increases or decreases in *annualized* terms, we must multiply the quarter-to-quarter rate of change by 4, resulting in the annualized quarter-to-quarter percentage changes shown in the bottom panel in columns 8 through 10.

Here's the problem: each of these steps takes us farther away from the "real" numbers, data we can really analyze statistically with some degree of confidence in their accuracy.

Because of the monthly and quarterly weather changes, sales promotions, and changes in competitive conditions—as well as the inherent errors in the seasonal adjustment process—our quarter-to-quarter annualized sales changes fluctuate a great deal more than the year-over-year percentage changes. In fact, the rates of change move up and down with such frequency that, in our quest for shorter-term sensitivity in analyzing sales, it has actually become more difficult for us to see the underlying trend.

It's easier to see this problem when we chart table 5-1's year-over-year and quarter-to-quarter sales changes, as shown in figure 5-1. You can see in the top panel of figure 5-1 that Acme Shirt sales slowed quite steadily, from a year-over-year increase of 6% in the second quarter of 2001 to less than 2% growth by the fourth quarter of 2003; but the pattern is much harder to read in the annualized quarter-to-quarter changes charted in the bottom panel. With increasing and decreasing rates of change alternating almost quarterly—reflecting the normal vacillations of weather, fashion, and competition, not to mention possible errors in our seasonal adjustment process (which we multiply by 4 to calculate annualized)—at any given time in the downtrend we might erroneously read one of those quarterly upticks as a sign that business is picking up.

Because of these vagaries associated with tracking demand on a quarter-to-quarter annualized basis, most businesses stay with the more reliable approach of evaluating their demand trends by looking at advancing or declining rates of sales growth on a year-over-year basis.

FIGURE 5-1

Unit sales of Acme Shirt Stores

Percent sales increases, quarterly versus prior year

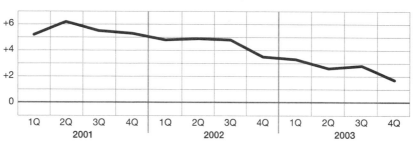

Percent sales increases, quarterly versus prior quarter*

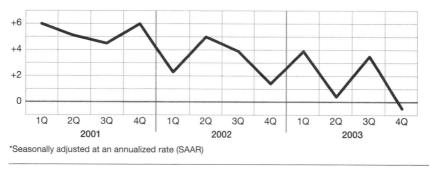

*Seasonally adjusted at an annualized rate (SAAR)

However, in the realm of macroeconomic reporting and analysis, it is another matter altogether.

How Quarter-to-Quarter Charting Obfuscates Economic Clarity

How often have you been confronted with a chart of an economic data series such as gross domestic product, covering many years and perhaps even decades, that looks like the one shown in figure 5-2?

Like the Acme Shirt data in the bottom panel of figure 5-1, the quarter-to-quarter percentage changes in real GDP in figure 5-2 change direction so frequently that it is virtually impossible to determine the trend, much less draw a conclusion about the future. How are we expected, analytically, to make sense of the volatile ups and downs of such a

FIGURE 5-2

A typical "noisy" chart

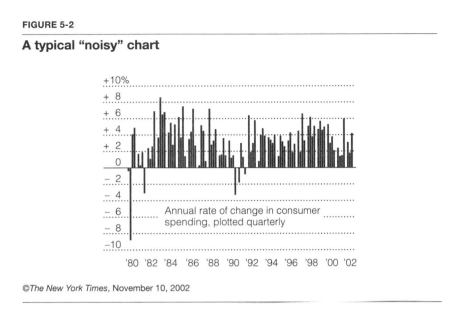

Annual rate of change in consumer spending, plotted quarterly

chart? A similar typical chart showing month-to-month changes in retail sales from the *Wall Street Journal* of November 15, 2002, is also representative; who could possibly determine a business trend in the chart shown in figure 5-3?

Charts with wildly vacillating swings of quarter-to quarter or month-to-month data, without any other context, serve only to confuse, creating in readers a sense of futility with regard to economic analysis: "If the chart can't clarify the meaning of this economic report, how could I ever possibly make intelligent use of this economic data?" The logical next step for the businessperson or investor is to just resign himself, lie back, and let the economy "happen."

Learning to "See" the Economy

As we saw in chapter 1, charts are the most effective means of documenting and understanding past cyclical economic patterns. Seeing an economic series' latest data as part of a continuum in a chart that spans several decades allows the observer to visualize the series' long-term behavior and put today in context. It simply is not possible to do the

FIGURE 5-3

How can we discern a trend in this chart?

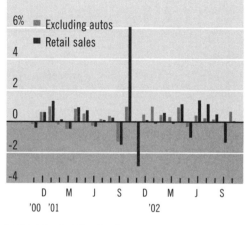

Glimmer of Hope

Month-to-month percentage change in
retail sales and sales excluding autos

Source: Commerce Department

same thing using long columns of figures in tables. And when a data series is charted with another related series that it leads or follows, clear historical patterns of cause and effect may emerge that will prove useful in describing the relative future behavior of the two series.

Charts have long been a widely used means of synthesizing and evaluating data in economics and other analytical disciplines. However, many are so flawed that readers cannot extract from them the necessary information. Readers thus become confused more than enlightened, and we often hear someone say, "I hate charts." This problem has become more acute, if anything, with the ease of using computers to create charts in standardized formats. If the charting of historical economic relationships is to be useful in the application of these relationships to future cycles, it is essential first to follow a few basic principles of execution.

"I've learnt not to worry."

Even casual readers of business and economic news will recognize that much economic data, beginning with gross domestic product, is reported on the basis of quarter-to-quarter rates of change. As in our Acme Shirt example, this means that real GDP for the fourth quarter of 2002 is compared with that of the third quarter, rather than GDP of the same quarter a year earlier. This practice reflects a perfectly reasonable attempt on the part of economic data gatherers to achieve greater sensitivity in recording shorter-term changes in trend. Nevertheless, this shorter-term, trend-driven approach creates the same analytical problems we encountered with Acme Shirt, particularly in tracking and perceiving economic cause-and-effect relationships over long periods.

First, just as Acme Shirt had clear seasonal patterns, the economy as a whole exhibits its own seasonal characteristics. For example, consumer spending, which is more than two-thirds of total GDP, swells in the fourth quarter because of Christmas spending. To achieve a meaningful comparison between the third and fourth quarters, economic data must be seasonally adjusted by a statistical factor, or SAAR (seasonally adjusted at an annual rate of change). Still, such seasonal adjustment factors are bound to have errors.

Second, for analytical purposes, our minds often do not prepare us to measure change on a quarter-to-quarter or month-to-month basis.

Corporate financial statements are presented, and therefore businesses and investors typically reason analytically, in year-over-year terms. Charting longer periods on a month-to-month or quarter-to-quarter basis violates the orderly year-over-year thought processes in which most businesspeople and investors have been (correctly) trained.

Third, and most importantly, as with Acme Shirt, the constant up-and-down changes associated with quarter-to-quarter measurement create such frequent zigs and zags in total economic activity that basic trends can barely be discerned. Comparison with other economic indicators is rendered virtually impossible.

Nevertheless, quarter-versus-prior-quarter charting of economic data is the method most often presented in general-interest, business, and economic publications. It does not have to be this way.

A Simple Solution: The Benefits of Year-Over-Year Charting

Figure 5-4, which charts real personal consumption expenditures in two ways, demonstrates the significant advantages of charting longer-term economic trends on a year-over-year basis. In the top panel, when shown on a year-over-year basis over the forty-five years surveyed, real consumer spending typically ranged between peak growth rates of +6% to +8% and troughs of –2% to +2%. When the data are presented this way, on a year-over-year basis, it is possible to see the underlying cyclical pattern of consumer spending, and the ROCET approach takes on new value. In contrast, the quarter-versus-quarter method (shown in the bottom panel) displays such volatility, or noise, that the chart itself has little analytical value.

The problem of noise is compounded when we attempt to chart causes and effects in the economic cycle by comparing two economic data series. The top panel of figure 5-5, for example, compares the year-over-year rate of consumer spending with the year-over-year rate of change in industrial production (i.e., all manufacturing in the economy) over repeated cycles from 1960 to 2005. It is clear that small changes in real PCE beget wide swings in industrial production (factory production of those goods, a subject explored in chapter 7) when the

FIGURE 5-4

Real* personal consumption expenditures (PCE), charted two ways

Percent change, quarterly versus prior year

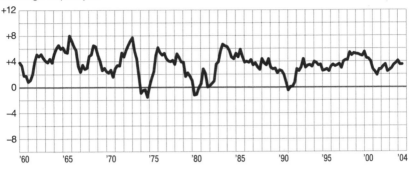

Cyclical patterns in consumer spending—and other economic data—are clearest when charted year-over-year (top panel).

Percent change, quarterly versus prior quarter**

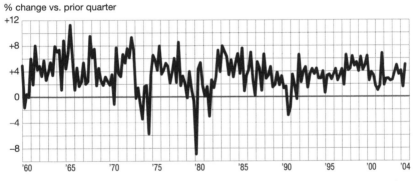

Quarter-vs.-prior-quarter charting of data (bottom panel) often results in excessive volatility and noise, obscuring underlying trends.

Source: Bureau of Economic Analysis
*Adjusted for inflation
**Seasonally adjusted at an annualized rate (SAAR)

data is presented year-over-year, as in the top panel. The bottom panel compares consumer spending with industrial production using the same data, but charted on a quarter-versus-previous-quarter basis, adjusted at an annualized rate. Using this method, the volatility of *both* series creates such a tangle that the reader cannot effectively use what is (presented differently in the top panel) an excellent cause-and-effect

FIGURE 5-5

Real* personal consumption expenditures (PCE) and industrial production, charted two ways

Percent change, quarterly versus prior year

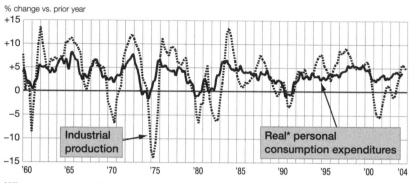

When two economic data series are compared, the clarity of year-to-year charting is particularly important.

Percent change, quarterly versus prior quarter**

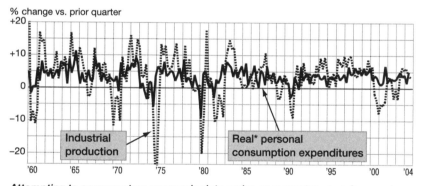

Attempting to compare two economic data series on a quarter-vs.-prior-quarter basis (bottom panel) results in a useless, incomprehensible tangle.

Sources: PCE—Bureau of Economic Analysis; Industrial production—Federal Reserve Board
*Adjusted for inflation
**Seasonally adjusted at an annualized rate (SAAR)

relationship. Figure 5-5 eloquently demonstrates why the quarter-to-quarter methodology popular in reporting key economic numbers is dysfunctional when it comes to visually correlating economic data series on a longer-term historic basis.

Cause and Effect: It Takes Two to Tango

Another major dysfunction in reported data is the common practice in publications of presenting charts with only a single indicator, or line. For example, suppose that an article in the business press commenting on yesterday's release of The Conference Board's Consumer Confidence Index contains a chart tracking the index on a monthly basis for the past ten years. Nothing wrong with that, as long as we do not wish to be *analytical*—to know what consumer confidence results from or what it may lead to. However, the very existence of the Consumer Confidence Index—and, indeed, its very name—implies that a predictive relationship exists between consumer confidence and consumer spending and that the series is supposed to be useful to us in forecasting it. It is incumbent on the writer of any article discussing the latest consumer confidence report, then, to provide a chart tracking both series—consumer confidence and consumer spending—to show that the implied relationship exists and has analytical value. Why should we care about the latest consumer confidence report unless we have clear evidence that it has worth in understanding consumer spending?

Does the Consumer Confidence Index lead consumer spending, or is it coincident, or does it lag? (Chapter 9 deals with this question.) A one-line chart can show cause or effect, but not both. From an analytical standpoint, a one-line chart is a bit like saying either "Gas prices have increased 80% over the past year . . ." or " . . . therefore, I am driving my car 20% less than in the past," without showing causality by linking the two thoughts.

We now have two basic rules of charting that will take us farthest in charting economic cause and effect, thereby improving our understanding of the economic cycle and its sequences and letting us forecast economic trends:

1. Chart year-over-year rates of change, avoiding the volatile and confusing quarter-to-quarter methodology.

2. Whenever possible, include in each chart two lines: a cause and an effect.

Following are a few additional housekeeping rules that will render our charts more readable:

- When necessary, present year-over-year monthly data on a rolling "trailing-three-months" basis (for each month calculating the percentage increase in total data for the latest three months versus that of a year earlier) rather than individual-month basis. This practice reduces excess noise and enhances a chart's clarity.

- If the two series being charted have widely different *amplitudes* (degrees of change), use two scales; denote one series using the right-hand scale, and the other one using the left-hand scale. In this way, you can better compare the two lines.

- Provide horizontal grid lines to facilitate the perception of rates of change, and vertical grid lines to clarify time periods. A tip for the compulsive (from one who is): execute the grid lines in light gray so that they don't visually overwhelm the data series being charted.

- Provide sufficient horizontal space to accommodate visually the several decades of data encompassing a sufficient number of cycles. Ironically, one of the issues that may have prevented economists from realizing the full benefit of cyclical chart analysis covering multiple decades is the tendency to constrain charts to half-pages or even, in most publications, to three-inch columns. These formats prevent the author (not to mention the reader) from effectively and analytically viewing the charted relationships over the periods of forty or more years that encompass seven or eight cycles. (I thank Harvard Business School Press for its wisdom in providing the charts in this book with the full pages they require for easy comprehension.)

Before we look in Part II at how specific economic cause-and-effect relationships play out in the real world of the U. S. economy, let's take one final step: understanding how leading and lagging indicators relate to each other in a typical economic cycle.

CHAPTER SIX

The Nature of
Leading Indicators

Now that we have a simplified method for recording and monitoring key economic data series, let's look at some of the fundamental characteristics of leading and lagging indicators and their relationships to each other. Much of this thought process will be intuitive, but it's important not to overlook the nuances.

If the year-over-year rate of change of one economic series (let's call it series A) consistently leads the year-over-year rate of change in another (series B) in both upward and downward directions over repeated cycles in decade after decade, then we can usually conclude that series A has a causal relationship to series B.[1] This means that we might successfully use advances or slowdowns in series A to forecast advances or slowdowns in series B.

If series A leads series B by six months, then after a long downtrend series A may reverse direction and turn upward, but series B will continue to decline for an additional six months. In other words, it is axiomatic that the leading indicator, series A will, *at turning points*, be headed in a different direction from that of series B, the economic data series predicted by series A. That is not intuitive for most of us. Emotionally, most of us want to extrapolate today's trend for series B in the direction it is heading. However, if we can master the patterns inherent in leading and lagging relationships, we can learn to be more dispassionate in successfully using series A (correctly charted) to overcome our emotional hunches and foresee turning points for series B.

The Cycles of Leading Indicators

We can more easily understand these patterns by viewing our two hypothetical economic data series, series A (the *leading indicator*) and series B (the *lagging indicator*) as they pass through four phases in a typical cycle, as shown in figure 6-1.

- *Period 4 of the previous cycle: positive divergence.* As the rate of growth in series B, our target series, is still approaching its nadir, the rate of change in series A has already begun to turn upward, signaling that growth in series B will also change direction and follow A upward the following year. We might call period 4 in this example a period of *positive divergence*—that is, a phase in which the downward direction of series B, the series being forecast, is counterindicated by the uptrend in series A. Those who have studied the cause-and-effect relationship between the two series will (correctly) be optimistic regarding the outlook for series B despite the latter's current declining state of affairs. Those who have not studied cause and effect, however, may mistakenly regard the current difficulties of series B as a reason, ipso facto, for remaining negative on its future.

- *Period 1 of the new cycle: positive concurrence.* However, in period 1 of the new cycle, the growth rate of series B does, indeed, begin to ascend, following series A, which is now in its second year of uptrend. We might call this a period of *positive concurrence* for series A and series B because the rates of growth in both series are now rising.

- *Period 2: negative divergence.* Now, as the new economic cycle is well under way, the rate of change in our leading indicator, series A, has begun to turn downward, even as the rate of growth in series B continues to accelerate to new heights. This period of *negative divergence* will be a signal for those who grasp the series A and B leading and lagging relationship to become cautious about the future of series B, even as the uninitiated remain optimistic because of its current strength.

FIGURE 6-1

The nature of a leading indicator

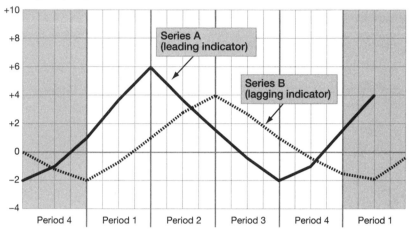

% change vs. prior year

Series A (leading indicator)

Series B (lagging indicator)

Period 4 | Period 1 | Period 2 | Period 3 | Period 4 | Period 1

Characteristics

Positive divergence	Positive convergence	Negative divergence	Negative convergence	Positive divergence	Positive convergence
Leading indicator turns upward, as lagging series approaches a trough	Lagging series turns upward, following (but now also reinforcing) leading indicator	Leading indicator turns downward, as lagging series approaches a peak	Lagging series turns downward, following (but now also reinforcing) leading indicator	Leading indicator turns upward, as lagging series approaches a trough	Lagging series turns upward, following (but now also reinforcing) leading indicator

Forecast for lagging indicator

	Continued uptrend	Reversal in direction to downward	Continued downtrend	Reversal in direction to upward	

- *Period 3: negative concurrence.* Series B's growth rate has now, inevitably, turned downward, following series A's lead of the prior period. For businesspeople and investors, often it is now too late to take corrective measures: series B—whether it be the economy at large (real GDP), a specific sector (e.g., capital spending), or the stock market—will already be suffering the consequences of a business slowdown.

- *Period 4: positive divergence.* We have now come full circle, with the rate of growth in series A turning upward even as the rate of change in series B continues toward its worst. Those who use the charted historic relationship between series A and series B may well begin to turn more positive on the outlook for series B even as those around them despair.

The difficult reality, of course, is that relationships between most leading and lagging economic data series are not nearly so smooth nor as crystal clear as shown in the idealized example in figure 6-1. Over time, I have observed two particularly tricky phenomena that test even astute observers.

The Problem of Variance in Peaks and Troughs

The first pitfall is that the time between peaks or troughs in series A and series B may vary considerably from cycle to cycle. The same is true for the rates of change at these peaks and troughs.

Let's look at a hypothetical example in figure 6-2. In the first cycle, the rate of growth in series A peaks in year 2 and turns down three quarters before series B does. In the second cycle, the time lag (at the end of year 5) between peaks in the two series is much shorter: only one quarter. Similarly, in the first cycle, the rate of growth in series A reaches a peak at 5%, whereas series B peaks at a much higher growth rate of more than 8%. In the second cycle, series A reaches a higher 7.6%, but series B peaks at a barely higher 8.0%. Based on the disparities of timing and dimension between these two series in the two cycles, a computerized analysis might dismiss a predictive relationship between the two series.

However, our eyes tell us a different and more valuable story, *based solely on sequence.* In both cycles, at the peaks as well as the troughs, the rate of growth in series A turns before that of series B, and then series B follows. Therefore, if history is any guide, we can use future turning points in series A as a predictor of turning points in series B. The gap in time or dimension between these peaks and troughs may vary from cycle to cycle, but that is far less important than the advanced notice to users of a forthcoming change in economic direction. One series con-

FIGURE 6-2

Variable time and dimension gaps between leading and lagging indicators

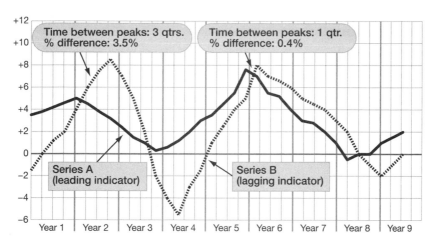

*This chart, showing a hypothetical Series A and Series B, indicates potential variances (1) in time elapsed between A and B at economic peaks and troughs, as well as (2) in the dimension of change at both peaks and troughs. Despite these variances, turning points in Series A lead turning points in Series B **each time**, making Series A an effective leading indicator of Series B. In identifying a leading indicator, the numbers (size or timing of changes) are less important than a consistent sequence.*

sistently leads the other and therefore can reliably be used to forecast it. This is a great lesson in the importance of seeing the economy.

Think of it in the same way that the falling pressure measured by a barometer almost always correctly predicts deteriorating weather. The speed and the depth of the decline in barometric pressure may not always tell us exactly when the rain will arrive or the amount of precipitation. However, it is far more important that the falling barometer warns us of a turn for the worse in the weather. For the observer, it is most important, after the barometer falls, to prepare for that weather and less so to know the exact hour the storm will arrive. Similarly, observers of economic data are best served, after series A peaks and turns down, if they become pessimistic about the prospects for series B and, whether it takes three months or a year, remain pessimistic until series B itself begins its decline.

In part III of this book we'll see how certain leading indicators clearly signaled throughout 1999 a forthcoming downturn in consumer spending, providing a longer-than-normal warning of the devastating economic downturn of 2000–2002. Even though that warning came further in advance than usual, businesses and investors who heeded it (there were few) were well served by reducing their exposure even as the economy and stock market continued to advance throughout that year and into early 2000. Particularly in the investment realm, those who obey early signals of a forthcoming downturn are well rewarded even if it means sacrificing that final period of marginal gains in the stock market as the peak approaches.

The Problem of the Chicken and the Egg

A second and equally tricky aspect of economic cause-and-effect analysis is the fact that many economic cause-and-effect relationships are circular. By "circular" I mean that while, in primary terms, series A drives series B, series B may also influence series A. The effect is somewhat like the proverbial chicken and egg.

A perfect example is the relationship between consumer spending and employment (shown earlier in our chronology of the economic cycle in figure 2-1). We all know that jobs (employment) and the income created by them are key elements in consumer spending power. Yet consumer spending, representing approximately two-thirds of GDP, in turn drives the demand cycle for industrial production, services, and capital spending, which are cornerstones of employment.

The question is, which leads which? The answer is that consumer spending, cyclically speaking, is more powerful in driving employment than vice versa. Chapter 11 shows this: every uptrend, downtrend, and turning point in the year-over-year growth of consumer spending leads to (is followed within six to twelve months by) a similar trend in employment.

I described this circular yet lopsided relationship to my son, Jonathan, a professor of philosophy. Calling upon his philosophy professor skills, Jonathan labeled the phenomenon *asymmetrical circular causality*. Figure 6-3 shows, schematically, what the causal relationships look like (with the size of the arrows representing the degree of cause and effect).

FIGURE 6-3

Asymmetrical circular causality

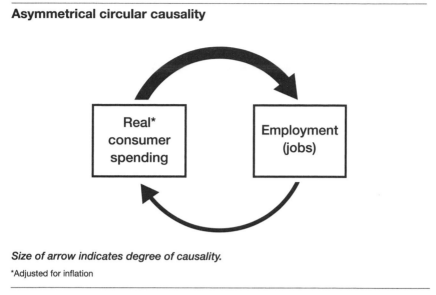

Size of arrow indicates degree of causality.

*Adjusted for inflation

Why is it important to grasp both the primary and the secondary aspects in this circular cause-and-effect relationship? First, perceiving the *primary* causality (that consumer spending drives employment) allows the forecaster to focus on the chronologically correct, and therefore predictive, relationship in rendering an economic forecast. Second, but equally important, the forecaster will not fall prey to the dangerous tendency to use the lagging series (employment in this example) to forecast economic direction when, in fact, it will be among the *last* economic indicators to turn and follow the economy in its new direction.

Asymmetrical circular causality describes many of the economic-indicator relationships set forth in this book. For example, capital spending (outlays for construction and new plant and equipment) virtually always *follows* consumer spending in the economic cycle; this is the case even though a surprising number of forecasters use capital spending, and the job creation it represents, as a basis for forecasting consumer spending. Those who erroneously rely on capital spending as a signal of a strong future economy will always be late in perceiving economic downturns.

Another interesting example is the confusion that often reigns in analyzing the relationship between consumer spending and the stock market. Often, a strong or weak stock market (and its widely heralded "wealth effect") is used as the basis for forecasting continuing strength in consumer spending and the economy overall. This view almost always misleads. Quite the opposite, the primary causality is that rising or falling rates of growth in consumer spending drive a strong or a weak economy and therefore the stock market. If we correctly forecast consumer spending, we enhance our chances of predicting the stock market, but it's never true that correctly forecasting the stock market improves our chances of forecasting consumer spending.

The only means of escaping the mistakes that can come from misapprehending the circular relationships among economic indicators is to master "what leads what," and the best way to do that is through empirical observation via charts of historic cause and effect such as those provided throughout this book. Only by this route can we escape the potential inaccuracies of anecdotal economic commentary as it appears in the business and investment media, by providing ourselves with the necessary context through the use of repeated historical cause and effect.

Much of this book is devoted to documenting that the cause-and-effect relationships can indeed be proven to recur consistently when the two series in question are tracked together on a year-over-year basis on charts spanning four decades or more. As it becomes clear that this is the case, we can place increased confidence in the notion that these relationships may be used to understand the current state of the economic cycle and, with it, enhance our prospects of predicting the future.

Correlation Versus Causality: Let Common Sense Rule

Clearly, as we seek to forecast based on charting economic cause-and-effect relationships, we must have a strong rational basis for expecting changes in one economic data series to cause predictable movements in another. For example, do sales of durable and nondurable goods in the nation's retail stores lead to uptrends and downtrends in manufacturing in the nation's factories? Do increases in national debt actually lead to increases in interest rates?

Ultimately, our charts of cause and effect (and therefore predictability) must meet two important tests:

- That the cause-and-effect relationship being tested is based on compelling common sense

- That when both series are charted, a clear, lead/lag relationship exists

Here, we will run into a perennial question among scholars: the extent to which correlation suggests causality. The mere fact that one series of data leads or has a close correlation to another does not necessarily mean that one *causes* the other. A nonsensical (but surprisingly popular) thesis is that, in years when the National Football Conference champion wins the Super Bowl, the stock market advances. Even if there were perfect synchrony between these two events, reason should tell us there is no way that which conference wins the Super Bowl determines stock market direction; this assertion violates our first rule.[2] Accomplished thinkers ranging from scientists to philosophers often use examples like this to debunk the thesis that correlation implies causality, and to establish higher thresholds of proof. To be sure, this is essential, particularly in precise disciplines within the sciences. However, in economic forecasting, we must also take care that the search for proof does not become a diversion of such intellectual dimension that it eclipses the facile use of logical cause-and-effect relationships that meet the above tests. If we have a compelling reason to believe, for example, that moderate uptrends and downtrends in consumer spending trigger wide swings in industrial production, and subsequently find that the charts corroborate this (as in figure 5-5), then by all means let's move ahead and use it.

The Proof Is in the Charts

As we now move into part II, we will begin to explore the actual cause-and-effect relationships in the economy whose consistency over many cycles makes them the foundation of good forecasting using the methodology we have seen here. In most cases, I will describe why, in commonsense terms, the cause-and-effect relationship in question works and provide a small chart illustrating an idealized example of how the relationship behaves in a typical cycle. This will be followed by a full-page chart containing the actual data from 1960 (or later, when data back to 1960 is not available) through 2004.

The full-page charts in this book, covering more than four decades from 1960 through 2004, represent the empirical proof that the relationship has been sufficiently and consistently valid in the past so that you can trust it to guide you in the future. Lacking this, this book would be no different from many others that offer various and wonderful theories about how the economy and its participants work, but without empirical observation of past data that can give you confidence that the theory can be trusted—in practice—in the future. The charts allow you to decide, based on your own visual assessment, whether the case is effectively made.

So I hope that you will stay with me as we move forward from concept and method to the more demanding process of analyzing the evidence provided in the full-page charts. I am confident that you will find the verification provided in the charts, and the resulting empowerment in looking forward, to be rewarding and worth the effort it takes to assess them.

II

Consumer Spending

The Cornerstone of the Economy and the Stock Market

CHAPTER SEVEN

Consumer Spending Drives the Demand Chain in the Economy

Chapters 4 and 5 explored the two major flaws associated with most conventional economic data tracking and charting.

- The recession obsession has prevented many forecasters from focusing on *rates* of growth instead of absolute growth and declines, and this misdirected approach to measuring economic harm has led to perennial tardiness among businesses and investors in identifying economic turning points.

- Poor charting and tracking methods—particularly a widespread reliance on quarter-to-quarter comparisons—have obfuscated economic cause-and-effect relationships that exist and that with improved charting might have been effectively used to aid us in more deftly forecasting future cycles.

We have seen that, by charting data on a year-over-year basis, we can more clearly see the economy and harness these cause-and-effect relationships, which have repeated themselves over many past decades. Now it is time to demonstrate the repeated and reliable cause-and-effect relationships that exist between key economic data series cycle after cycle. I have found these relationships useful in observing multiple cycles over several decades.

In Chapter 2 I described how, having come to the unremarkable conclusion that consumer spending was the cornerstone of the economy and the key driver of most other economic sectors, I determined to see whether uptrends and downtrends in consumer spending were, in fact, clearly followed by the rest of the economy. As shown in figure 7-1, the commonsense demand chain in the economy begins with consumer spending, proceeds into the production of goods and services that are consumed, and leads to the building of the offices, factories, and equipment used to produce them.

Industrial Production and the Inventory Effect

It is intuitively clear even to the most casual business observer that uptrends and downtrends in consumer spending on goods and services drive more volatile cycles in the production of those goods and services. During an uptrend in consumer spending (i.e., after a period of flat demand)—when consumers are buying, say, 5% more shirts at our Acme Shirts stores than a year earlier—we at Acme must for a while buy 8% or 10% more than we did a year ago to increase our inventories enough to support the new, higher level of demand.[1]

Quite simply, in a consumer spending upturn, retailers, distributors, and manufacturers themselves must build inventories to support the growth in demand. This inevitably results in increases of 10% or more in shirt factory production to support not only the consumer demand in retail stores, but also the building of inventories in distribution pipelines between the factories and the stores. Conversely, when our

FIGURE 7-1

Chronology: The economy's demand chain

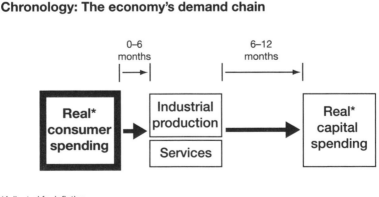

*Adjusted for inflation

Acme business flattens out or even declines, we will stop buying in order to bring our inventories back into line. In the same manner, in a slowdown all retailers and distributors liquidate inventories by reducing purchases from their suppliers, and manufacturers in turn drastically slow their production, resulting in year-over-year declines in shirt production.

The key point here is that because inventories in the retail, distributor, and factory pipelines grow during periods of strengthening consumer spending and shrink when consumer spending slows, the changes in the industrial production that supplies this system are far more volatile than the changes in consumer spending at the front end of the system.[2]

Let's take a look at how this works in the real world of the U.S. economy. We saw in chapter 5 that consumer spending cycles have typically lasted from four to six years (the extended growth of the 1990s was a notable exception). In a typical consumer spending cycle, real personal consumption expenditures (PCE)—measured in year-over-year growth terms—has normally peaked at increases of 5% to 7% and then slowed to around "zero" growth before heading back toward 5% to 7% at the peak of the next cycle.[3]

Figure 7-2 shows a hypothetical cycle, lasting four years, in which year-over-year growth in real PCE (represented by the dotted line), peaked at 5% to 6% in the first quarter of year 1, fell to approximately zero by the fourth quarter of year 2, and recovered to a new-cycle peak of slightly more than 6% at the end of year 4. But because of the inventory accumulation and liquidation cycle that accompanies the uptrends and downtrends in consumer spending, industrial production experienced far greater swings, ranging from year-over-year increases of 8% to 10% or more at economic peaks to quite normal declines of 4% or more at cyclical troughs.

Figure 7-2 is great as an example, but how does it work in the real world of the U.S. economy? Figure 7-3 tracks year-over-year increases in real consumer spending versus those of industrial production for more than four decades, from 1960 through 2004. The chart makes it clear that almost every upturn in real consumer spending over the past four decades spurred a far greater uptrend in industrial production: when year-over-year increases in real PCE (solid line) rose to +5% to

FIGURE 7-2

Typical cycle: Consumer spending, industrial production, and the volatile effect of inventories

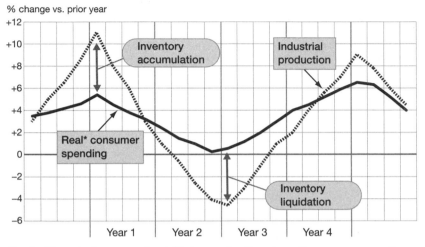

Product inventories respond quickly to accelerations in real* consumer spending (solid line). Result: almost coincident—but much greater—increases in industrial production (dotted line).

Conversely, when consumer spending slows even moderately, inventory liquidation almost always results in precipitously declining industrial production. The depth of this decline usually catches forecasters by surprise.

*Adjusted for inflation

+8%, industrial production (dotted line) accelerated to year-over-year gains of 8% to 10% or more. Conversely, industrial production, in response to downtrends in real PCE of only 3 to 4 percentage points year-over-year, often declined 5% or more at troughs in most of the economic cycles from 1960 to 2005.

Figure 7-3 is the first of our economic cause-and-effect charts. Hopefully you are seeing the consistency of this important economic relationship over a long period and are feeling empowered by understanding this piece of the economy. Why is this important? If you are a manufacturer, or an investor owning the shares of a manufacturer, you need this chart or a similar one to recognize that, if real consumer spending growth slows by 2 to 4 percentage points or more, sales of your company are likely to drop 8 to 10 percentage points or more.

FIGURE 7-3

Real* consumer spending (PCE) and industrial production: The volatile effects of the inventory cycle

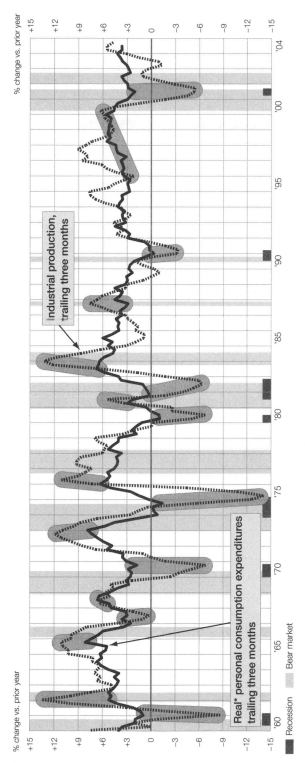

Modest cyclical swings in consumer spending result—due to the buildup and ebbing of inventories in distribution and factory pipelines—in far greater volatility in industrial production (see shaded ovals). Industrial production typically reacts quickly to changes in consumer demand through retail stores, so its cycle is usually coincident with, to slightly lagging, that of consumer spending.

Note how, despite claims in most cycles that "it's different this time," there is considerable similarity in the timing and dimension of the consumer-spending industrial-production relationship among most cycles since 1960, including the 2000–2002 downturn.

Sources: PCE—Bureau of Economic Analysis; industrial production—Federal Reserve Board

*Adjusted for inflation

Many economic commentators saw the 2000–2002 downturn as yet another example of the cliché, "It's different this time"—a downturn driven by unique circumstances, in this case the collapse of interest in the Internet and technology's fall from grace. Yet figure 7-3 makes it clear that it was consumer spending (real PCE) that fell from peak year-over-year increases of more than 5% in 1999 and the first quarter of 2000 to less than 3% by the first quarter of 2001, *leading* industrial production to plummet from a peak year-over-year increase of 6.5% in the second quarter of 2000 to declines of 4% or more throughout most of 2001.[4] The precipitous slowdown of industrial production in late 2000 and 2001, seen as unusually sharp by many observers, was in fact entirely consistent with many past cycles in steepness and degree—a useful perspective offered by the chart.

The cyclical effect of inventory building and reduction accelerates even more for manufacturers that produce basic materials for inclusion in finished products, because they have an extra layer of inventory to rise and ebb between themselves and the final product in the demand cycle. Thus, using the shirt example, the volatility of year-over-year sales comparisons for the producer of the fabric used to make the shirts would be even greater than for the shirt manufacturer. This greater cyclical volatility for manufacturing companies in basic industries such as chemicals, paper, and steel is the reason economists and investors call these industries the "cyclicals."

Despite repeated history, economists, industry analysts, and managers of manufacturing companies almost never foresee increases or declines of such great magnitude in the production cycle, or at least not until such swings are already evident. Why? The answer, quite simply, is that, absent the visual clarity provided by a chart such as figure 7-3, economic forecasters lack the enforced visual discipline that might otherwise result from continuous observation of, and reliance on, the sheer consistency of its graphed relationship. There is no substitute for this visual manifestation of the historical relationship between these two series, which, for the very reason that it is visual, is heightened at all times in readers' consciousness.

The government forces cigarette makers to include on cigarette packs the sentence, "Warning: The Surgeon General has determined that smoking is hazardous to your health." It does so because even though most people already know and accept this fact, if smokers read it each time they see a cigarette pack, it reinforces the fact that smoking causes cancer, a reality that might otherwise recede in their awareness. Similarly, a chart highlighting the consistent cause-and-effect relationship between two economic data series, reviewed monthly by the economic forecaster, has the benefit of continuously and overtly reinforcing that relationship as a tool the forecaster can employ in predicting the economic future with increased confidence.

Just as figure 7-3 documents the clear and consistent cause-and effect relationship between moderate three- to five-year cycles in consumer spending (real PCE) and the far more volatile cycles in industrial production, it is also possible to document similar relationships between cycles in consumer spending (and its segments) and specific sectors of manufacturing. Chapter 15 explores ways that managers in specific sectors of manufacturing and other industries can use these relationships as the basis for forecasting future business trends for their industry sector or company. In this way, they can avoid simply awaiting upturns and downtrends in new orders as signals of improving or deteriorating industry conditions.

Capital Spending: Driven by Consumer Spending and Not Vice Versa

Capital spending largely comprises manufacturers' outlays on plant and equipment, as well as spending on distribution and other processing facilities used by retailers, distributors, and other concerns that sell to consumers. Logically, then, capital spending is closely tied to the industrial-production cycle. To take our earlier shirt analogy a step further, during an economic boom, after a few quarters of 10% increases in shirt production, shirt manufacturers inevitably recognize the need for additional manufacturing capacity.[5] This leads them to place orders for additional shirt-making machinery and maybe even to build new shirt-producing factories. The opposite is also true: when shirt demand is flat or declining, purchases of new shirt-producing plant and equipment fall to virtually zero. Theoretically, when production capacity is relatively unused, there is no need to purchase additional capacity at all.

Capital spending is thus exposed in a highly leveraged way to the demand cycle of the economy, starting with the consumer.

Figure 7-4 shows a typical four-year cycle in the relationship between industrial production and capital spending. In most cycles, because of the time lag between order and delivery (or completion) in the plant-and-equipment sector, year-over-year increases in capital spending peak two to four quarters after those of industrial production, with a similar lag at economic troughs.

Again, let's look at the real world of the U.S. economy, as shown in Figure 7-5. We can see that in the past forty years, it does indeed work this way: in virtually every cycle, peaks and troughs in capital spending comparisons followed those of industrial production by two to four quarters.

FIGURE 7-4

Typical cycle: Capital spending rises or falls two to four quarters after industrial production

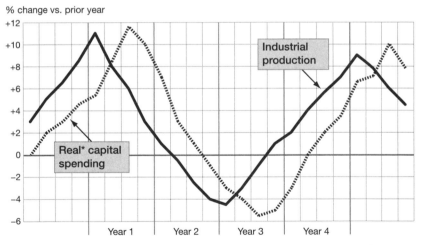

% change vs. prior year

Following strong uptrends in industrial production (solid line) and demands for services, manufacturers and service providers embark on periods of capital spending (dotted line) to build the equipment, factories, and offices that produce these goods and services.

This usually entails a lag of two to four quarters, making capital spending always a lagging sector and indicator in the economy. Therefore, it should not be used for forecasting general economic activity.

*Adjusted for inflation

FIGURE 7-5

Swings in industrial production drive changes in real* capital spending

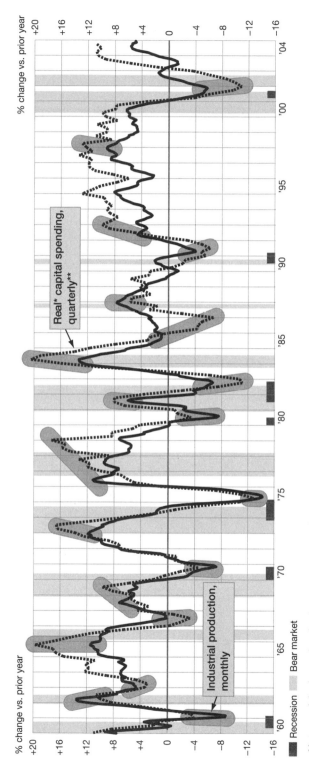

% change vs. prior year

Real* capital spending, quarterly**

Industrial production, monthly

■ Recession   ■ Bear market

Not surprisingly, peak gains in manufacturing (industrial production) are usually followed, typically two to four quarters later (shaded ovals), by peak increases in capital spending (spending on plant and equipment that increases production capacity). The relationship appears more coincident at economic troughs.

Sources: Capital spending—Bureau of Economic Analysis; industrial production—Federal Reserve Board
*Adjusted for inflation
**Includes nonresidential structures, equipment, and software under gross private fixed investment; excludes residential structures

Consumer Spending

This being the case, then capital spending also follows some consumer spending, as shown in our economic cycle chronology in figures 2-1 and 7-1. If:

- Moderate cyclical patterns in real consumer spending create volatile coincident swings in industrial production.

- In turn, volatile swings in industrial production lead cycles in capital spending.

Then, as figure 7-5 shows, as a corollary it is also true that *moderate* consumer-spending cycles lead, by two or four quarters, *more volatile* cycles in capital spending. Again, as with figures 7-2 and 7-4, figure 7-6 presents a typical example of this phenomenon.

FIGURE 7-6

Typical cycle: Major swings in capital spending lag moderate changes in consumer spending by two to four quarters

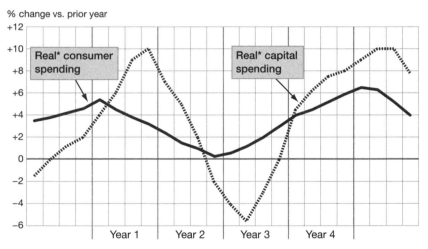

Moderate changes in consumer spending drive volatile swings in industrial production (figure 7-2), and the volatile capital-spending cycle lags these swings by two to four quarters (figure 7-4).

Consequently, as shown here, moderate changes in real consumer spending (solid line) also lead more volatile swings in real capital spending (dotted line) by two to four quarters. Though economists continue to debate this subject, the forty-year record shown in figure 7-7 leaves little doubt.

*Adjusted for inflation

Moreover, as with figures 7-3 and 7-5, our empirical look at the actual relationship between consumer spending and capital spending in figure 7-7 is clear: capital spending (spending on plant and equipment) has a volatile, lagging relationship to consumer spending. Executives and investors in capital-goods industries should view year-over-year consumer-spending comparisons as their primary leading indicator.

It's Not "Different This Time"

In the preface, I noted a common quip in the business community: the four most dangerous words in assessing economic and stock market cycles are, "It's different this time!" The reality is that, most often, it's *not* different this time.

I challenge you to carefully review the actual historical consumer-to-production, production-to-capital-spending, and consumer-to-capital-spending relationships in Figures 7-3, 7-5, and 7-7, respectively. You will find the following:

- The relationships between these three series are generally consistent in cycle after cycle in terms of sequence, lead or lag time, and magnitude. Exceptions exist, but they pale by comparison with the rule.

- The most recent downturn, which took place in 2000 to 2002, was well within the bounds of past cycles in both sequence and the growth-rate decline of each of these three primary segments of economic activity. Despite the widespread view that this latest cycle was different, when viewed empirically in the charted context of more than forty years of cyclical history in these three charts, the latest cycle appears absolutely classical.

Of course, each cycle—each period in history—will have its own unique social, geopolitical, technological, and other characteristics surrounding cyclical economic developments. However, after these factors manifest themselves in consumer spending at the front end of the cycle, the economic cause-and-effect relationships appear to remain remarkably similar from cycle to cycle.

FIGURE 7-7

Swings in real* consumer spending (PCE) drive changes in real* capital spending

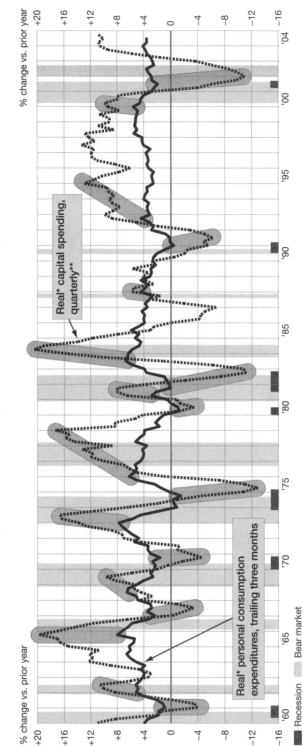

% change vs. prior year

Real* capital spending,
quarterly**

Real* personal consumption
expenditures, trailing three months

■ Recession   ■ Bear market

Consumer spending on goods and services (real PCE, solid line) triggers—usually with a 6- to 12-month lag time—business investment in the facilities and equipment that provide those goods and services (real capital spending, dotted line). Consequently, consumer spending is a highly effective leading indicator (shaded ovals) of future volatile swings in capital spending. Note that capital spending, as a laggard in the economy, remained strong during the early to mid stages of many bear markets (vertical shaded bars), possibly deceiving unwary investors into believing that economic growth was proceeding.

Source: Bureau of Economic Analysis
*Adjusted for inflation
**Includes nonresidential structures, equipment, and software under gross private fixed investment; excludes residential structures

When It Rains in Consumer Spending, It Pours in the Economy

In virtually every economic slowdown from 1960 onward, any down-turn of 3 or more percentage points in the year-over-year rate of growth in consumer spending has precipitated a far steeper slowdown in industrial production and, in turn, capital spending, usually to year-over-year declines of 4% or more at its trough. Much has been made of the unique character of the tech bubble of the late 1990s and the fact that the 2000–2002 downturn was driven by capital spending. The fact, is, however, that economic weakness first showed up in the con-sumer sector in 1999 and early 2000 and proceeded, in turn, through inventory channels into the industrial production and capital-spending sectors. When consumer spending peaked at year-over-year growth of 5.5% in 1999 and slipped to less than 3% growth as of early 2001, capital-spending growth fell to a year-over-year decline of 10%. When viewed in the context of more than forty years of cyclical economic his-tory (as shown in Figure 7-7), the sharp downturn in capital spending of 2000–2002 was not atypical after all.[6] This is not to say that the bursting of the tech bubble, as well as the World Trade Center disaster in September 2001, did not have a meaningful effect. They did. How-ever, even including these effects, the cyclical patterns of the 2000–2002 downturn appear, in figures 7-3, 7-5, and 7-7, to be within his-torical norms.

Remarkably, in most historical cycles, even after several quarters of weakening year-over-year growth in consumer spending, economists and analysts for capital-goods industries tend to maintain relatively benign forecasts of capital spending. They often fail to forecast (or *accept*) the inevitable substantial downtrend in plant and equipment spending that follows any meaningful slowdown in the growth of per-sonal consumption expenditures.

As we saw in chapter 6, it is the very nature of a lagging series to appear healthy well after its leading indicator has turned downward, and vice versa. Thus, capital spending almost always continues to thrive long after growth in consumer spending has passed its peak and has begun to decline. Conversely, following troughs and subsequent upturns in year-over-year consumer-spending comparisons, capital spending will continue to deteriorate sharply for six months or longer. Rather than use this relationship between leading and lagging indicators for forecasting purposes, the unwary forecaster typically is influenced, ipso facto, by the lagging direction of capital spending and remains positive or negative long after the rate of change in consumer spending is forecasting a reversal in fortune.

Throughout much of 2003, economists and others awaited a recovery in capital spending to "lead" the U.S. economy out of the 2000–2002 downturn. There were great cheers when, in late 2003, capital spending indeed began to recover. Fine. However, based on the consistent patterns revealed in figures 7-5 and 7-7, this should never have been in question: the upturn in consumer spending that began in early to mid-2003 virtually guaranteed that capital spending would begin to rebound. When this occurred in late 2003, capital spending was simply following its normal function of lagging relative to what happened to consumer spending before it.

The Supply-Side Debate Resolved

Despite the commonsense foundation of the causal, leading and lagging relationship between consumer demand and capital spending (as clearly documented in figure 7-7), many economists see capital spending as an equally important, if not more important, *driver* of economic cycles compared with consumer spending. The role of capital investment as a primary economic driver vis-à-vis consumer spending is an issue of major proportions, because it lies at the heart of tax policy and political debate. Stimulating the economy via tax reductions and financial incentives for businesses and wealthy individuals to invest in business capacity—in a greater degree than tax reductions for lower- and middle-income wage earners—is typically identified with the conservative political agenda. However, the capital-spending-drives-consumer-spending thesis is also prevalent among politically balanced economic commentators.

For example, this line of thinking is described by highly regarded economists Robert Heilbroner and Lester Thurow in their basic economic text, *Economics Explained.* In a chapter titled "Passive Consumption, Active Investment," the authors write as follows:

> *Investment is not only a driving and potentially destabilizing force in the economy, but its impact is magnified because of what economists call the "multiplier." The idea of the multiplier is simplicity itself. When a change in spending occurs, such as a new investment project, the money laid out for construction workers' wages, materials, and the like does not stop there. The recipients of the first round of investment spending will engage in additional spending of their own. What they buy provides new sales and hence jobs for others. And so initial bursts of spending create secondary and tertiary bursts until the effect is finally dissipated.*
>
> *Two final and very important conclusions follow from this. First, we have seen that investment is a driving, not a driven, part of the economy. To be sure, as with consumption, investment spending is also influenced by the incomes that businesses receive. Some investment follows the direction of consumer buying, especially accelerations and decelerations in consumption spending. When consumption spending rises, new factories have to be built to service it. But the distinguishing feature of investment, taken as a critical activity of the business sector, is that it is not a caboose, but an engine. It leads the economy.*[7]

This is a common view among economists, and it would lead us to believe that capital spending drives consumer spending more than vice versa and that capital spending is a more important, primary driver in the economy. However, if this were the case, cyclical uptrends and downtrends in capital spending would *lead* those of consumer spending.

However, with all due respect to Heilbroner and Thurow, there is little evidence in the typical three- to six-year business cycles presented clearly in our charts extending back to 1960, that changes in capital spending *lead* changes in consumer demand. Again let's look at figure 7-7: it shows clearly that, cyclically, year-over-year rates of change in consumer spending lead those of capital spending, and not vice versa. In doing so, figure 7-7 pretty much dispels any notion that, *at least in cyclical terms,* capital spending has a leading role in the economy. Cyclically, capital spending is the laggard; it is the caboose.

Of course, who would disagree with the contention that, on a longer-term basis, capital spending has salutary effects on economic growth? Building factories, purchasing production equipment, developing and spending on new technologies—by government and private initiatives—clearly produce jobs and spur productivity throughout the economy over longer periods of time—say, ten years or more. The appropriate question, however, is whether the effect of capital spending on economic growth is primary or secondary within the economy; does it figure importantly in economic cycles, or is it just longer-term background music? We saw in chapter 2 that capital spending *in total* amounts only to 17% of GDP (versus consumer spending, which is 70% of GDP). In addition, as Heilbroner and Thurow acknowledge, "Some investment follows the direction of consumer buying, especially accelerations and decelerations in consumption spending."[8] Logic suggests that by providing capacity to produce the goods and services sought by the 70% of the economy represented by consumer spending, capital spending is more beholden to consumer spending than vice versa. Therefore, even with its multiplier effect, it cannot—and has proven itself not to—lead the economic cycle.

Some economists may disagree, arguing that capital spending leads consumer spending in the *following* cycle by three to four years. But this would be a bit like observing at a track meet that the leading runner, who has lapped an opponent on a circular track and is now coming up behind him, is "following" him. The assertion that consumer spending virtually always drives capital spending, based on an economic proof mechanism as simple as charts, may be greeted with derision by those who see capital spending as a cyclical driver in the economy. A reasonable response will be to seek from them some form of evidence—preferably visual and comprehensible to those of us with a reasonable level of economics education but lacking advanced degrees in mathematics—that can prove their case in more than only ideological and theoretical terms. The burden of proof should be on the theorist, and not the audience.

This is not a small question, for it lies at the heart of a contentious political debate about whether tax incentives geared toward business ("investment") have a greater economic benefit than those that target consumers. From a cyclical perspective, figure 7-7 seems to offer a clear answer: consumer tax cuts achieve a greater shorter-term cyclical benefit. (This comes, however, at a cost: except in times of government surplus, personal tax cuts might otherwise be defined as "government borrowing to keep consumers spending.") From a longer-term perspective, however, the benefits of incentives to keep businesses spending on modernization and productivity cannot be denied.

The clear, sequential cause-and-effect chain from consumer spending to industrial production to capital spending provides a strong analytical base for businesses and investors whose fortunes are tied up in component industries within these sectors. Those working within the manufacturing and capital-spending sectors of the economy should thus learn to track changes in consumer spending in (cyclically) forecasting the outlook in their sectors of the economy.

Chapter 8 moves forward in our chronology of the economic cycle and shows how consumer spending, by driving manufacturing and capital spending, is also a key determinant of corporate profits and the stock market.

Consumer Spending, Corporate Profits, and the Stock Market

The consistent pattern of the demand cycle documented in chapter 7—consumer spending leads to industrial production, which leads to capital spending—encompasses more than 80% of total economic output, or GDP. That being the case, where does the stock market fit in? From a timing standpoint, are bull and bear markets closely tied to the demand cycle of the economy? Or do stock market moves result from a dizzying combination of constantly changing monetary and liquidity concerns, international issues, psychological factors, and valuation levels, with no one factor having a consistent dominant effect?

The correct answer is that although many factors—some unique to each period—affect each stock market cycle, only a few primary drivers have historically had a consistent, repeated causal relationship to bull and bear markets.

The Cornerstone of Corporate Profits

As shown in figure 8-1, the demand cycle in the economy—beginning with accelerating and decelerating year-over-year rates of change in real consumer spending and continuing through industrial production and capital spending into corporate profits—is the key driving force in bull and bear markets. I am not suggesting here that demand-cycle economics should serve as the only input to stock market forecasting, but it's a great place to start because of the surprising consistency with

FIGURE 8-1

Chronology: Consumer spending drives corporate profits and the stock market

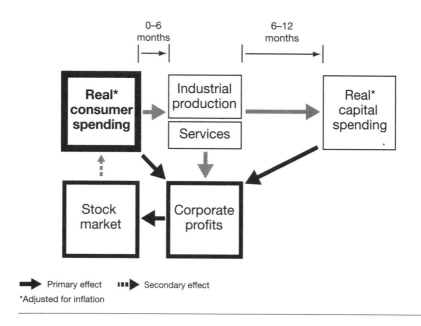

➡ Primary effect   ▪▪▷ Secondary effect
*Adjusted for inflation

which increasing and decreasing rates of change in consumer spending at the front end of the demand cycle drive corporate profit comparisons and their undeniable impact on stock market trends.

Figure 8-2 provides statistical detail regarding the length and depth of the thirteen bear markets that occurred in the fifty-four years from 1950 through 2004, representing approximately one bear market every four years. This chart shows how much stronger and longer most bull markets are than bear markets. Still, we must always remember that it takes a 33% advance in the stock market to offset a 25% decline.

Most companies and stocks are in industries that are part of the economic-cycle demand chain that begins with consumer spending and continues into industrial production and services and then into capital spending. With consumer spending itself representing more than two-thirds of gross domestic product (GDP) and driving much of the rest, consumer spending can clearly be regarded as the key driver in corporate profits.

FIGURE 8-2

Bull and bear markets, 1950–2004

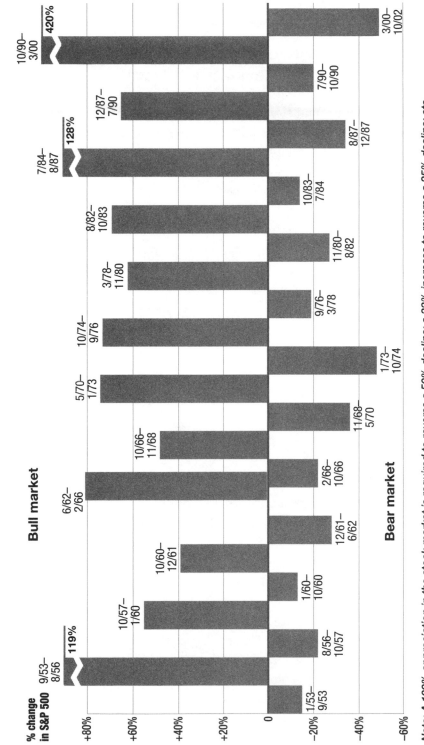

% change
in **S&P 500**

Bull market

9/53–8/56 **119%**
10/57–1/60
6/62–2/66
5/70–1/73
10/74–9/76
3/78–11/80
8/82–10/83
7/84–8/87 **128%**
12/87–7/90
10/90–3/00 **420%**

Bear market

1/53–9/53
8/56–10/57
1/60–10/60
10/60–12/61
12/61–6/62
2/66–10/66
10/66–11/68
11/68–5/70
1/73–10/74
9/76–3/78
11/80–8/82
10/83–7/84
8/87–12/87
7/90–10/90
3/00–10/02

Note: A 100% appreciation in the stock market is required to reverse a 50% decline; a 33% increase to reverse a 25% decline; etc.

_____

Consumer Spending as a
Stock Market Indicator

It is generally (and correctly) presumed that when profit growth for the majority of companies is increasing, the stock market rises, and when profit growth for most enterprises is declining, the stock market declines. Individual stocks advance and retreat as investors perceive strength and weakness, respectively, in their earnings comparisons. They are, in this regard, trees in the forest of the stock market. However, surprisingly little empirical work has been done to measure, or *time*, stock market cycles against year-over-year corporate-profit comparisons. Consequently, as with many indicators in the realm of the economy and the stock market, few investors really have a solid grasp of exactly when, in a typical cycle, the stock market begins to react to corporate profit comparisons.

The problem for investors, however, is that of predicting these earnings uptrends and downtrends—for individual companies and the stock market as a whole—far enough in advance to take advantage of earnings-driven stock movements. I believe that by carefully tracking year-over-year rates of change in real consumer spending at the leading edge of the chain of economic causes and effects, investors can gain some timing advantage.

Figure 8-3 shows how growth in consumer spending (the key driver of the economic cycle), corporate profit comparisons (represented by S&P 500 earnings per share), and the stock market interrelate in a typical cycle. Moderate swings in consumer spending (solid line) set into motion more volatile fluctuations in industrial production and capital spending, and for that reason they also result in significant swings in corporate profit comparisons (dotted line).

Note that the scale at the right is far greater than the scale at the left, suggesting far wider percentage increases and declines for S&P 500 earnings per share than for real consumer spending. Bear markets, denoted by vertical gray bars in figure 8-3, begin when the *rates of growth* in both real consumer spending and corporate profits peak— often at the same time—and end as both real consumer spending and corporate profits head for their poorest comparisons.

FIGURE 8-3

Typical cycle: Consumer spending drives corporate profits and the stock market

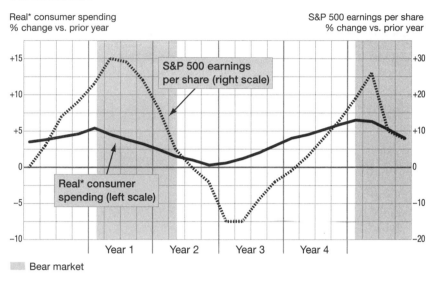

Real* consumer spending
% change vs. prior year

S&P 500 earnings per share
% change vs. prior year

Bear market

First, note the volatility of corporate profits (S&P 500 earnings per share) in the dotted line (right scale) vis-à-vis consumer spending in the solid line (left scale). In general, corporate profits are coincident with, to slightly lagging, those of consumer spending, which drives growth in many industries.

*Bear markets (vertical gray bars) typically begin when year-over-year consumer spending and corporate profit comparisons **peak** and **begin to slow**. Conversely, bear markets typically come to an end before consumer spending and corporate profit comparisons reach bottom.*

*Adjusted for inflation

Again, let's see how this has worked in the real world of the U.S. economy and stock market over the past fifty years. Figure 8-4 compares, from 1950 through 2004, year-over-year percentage changes in real consumer spending (real personal consumption expenditures) with year-over-year growth in corporate profits, as measured by earnings per share of the S&P 500's industrial stock index. As our typical-cycle example in figure 8-3 suggests, in terms of percentage change, year-over-year swings in S&P 500 earnings per share (reflected in the more volatile scale at the right) are far greater than real consumer-spending comparisons (left scale). As in each of the previous charts, the cause-and-effect relationship is compelling: moderate changes in real consumer spending, with their overwhelming effect on the economy at large, are coincident with or slightly precede extremely wide swings in corporate profits. It is only a short deductive step, then, to conclude that consumer spending, with its central role in the U.S. economy, is a key input to stock market performance.

In figure 8-4 the vertical shaded areas represent bear markets, defined here as periods in which the S&P 500 index declined by 12% or more. Unshaded areas represent bull markets.

A close look at figure 8-4 reveals that most bear markets from 1960 to 2004 were indeed closely related to slowdowns in the year-over-year rate of growth in consumer spending (shown in the solid line). In most instances, the bear markets began (see circles) when consumer spending growth reached its peak at +5% to +8% year-over-year and then began to slow.

This is an important point and needs to be repeated and amplified: most stock market declines started when the year-over-year rates of growth in the economy, starting with real consumer spending, began to slow from peak rates. By the time the year-over-year rates of growth in consumer spending had fallen halfway to their nadir, driving down corporate profits with them, most of the damage to the economy and stock market had been done.

Stated another way, if most bear markets began with the onset of a slowdown in consumer spending, then most slowdowns in consumer spending resulted, through their effect on corporate profits, in bear markets.[1] So the relationship of consumer spending to the stock market in most cycles has been surprisingly simple:

- A slowing in the rate of growth in real consumer spending from its peak produces a slowing of growth in corporate profits.

- When the rate of growth in corporate profits begins to slow from big increases to smaller gains (and eventually to declines), investor enthusiasm wanes, stock by stock.

- The collective effect of this increasing discouragement with profit comparisons produces a bear market.

At the trough, as we can see in figure 8-5, in most cases after year-over-year real consumer spending comparisons approached zero or began actually to decline, the bear market had already ended and the stock

FIGURE 8-4

Bear markets begin when growth in real* consumer spending (PCE) peaks and begins to slow

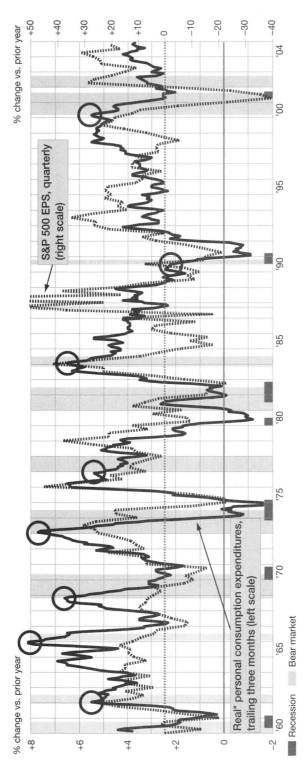

The relationship between economic slowdowns (led by downtrends in year-over-year consumer spending) and bear markets (vertical gray bars) is remarkably consistent, though not infallible, over many cycles. Most bear markets begin (see circles) when the year-over-year **rate of growth** in consumer spending is peaking, and investor and general business optimism are at their highest! Considerable courage is required to reduce investments at such times. The bear market then proceeds as profit comparisons slow.

This suggests that finding an effective discipline for forecasting (downturns in) consumer spending is essential to reducing stock market exposure, against conventional wisdom, at these junctures.

Most bear markets are largely over by the time recessions (black bars) are under way.

Sources: PCE—Bureau of Economic Analysis; S&P 500 EPS (earnings per share) (1960–4Q1989)—Bureau of Economic Analysis; S&P 500 EPS (4Q1989–2004)—Standard & Poor's
*Adjusted for inflation

FIGURE 8-5

Bear markets usually end before troughs in real* consumer spending (PCE)

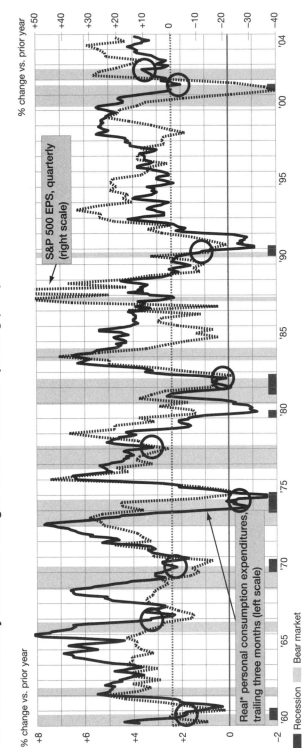

Stock market declines, designated here by the vertical gray bars, usually end—and bull markets begin—when the year-over-year rate of growth in real consumer spending, at the leading edge of corporate profits and the economic cycle, is at or approaching a trough. At such times, investor and general business pessimism is at its worst. Forecasting upturns in consumer spending provides the rationale—and therefore the courage—to go against conventional wisdom during such periods.

Sources: PCE—Bureau of Economic Analysis; S&P 500 EPS (earnings per share) (1960–4Q1989)—Bureau of Economic Analysis; S&P 500 EPS (4Q1989–2004)—Standard & Poor's
*Adjusted for inflation

market was already advancing in anticipation of the upturn. In most instances, the bear market came to an end (see circles) approximately two quarters before the trough in year-over-year consumer spending activity.

It is also clear that the periods of the fewest and shortest bear markets occurred during the early to mid-1960s, mid- to late 1980s, and the mid- to late 1990s, during the most extended periods of consumer spending growth in the history of the chart.

We can also see clearly in figures 8-4 and 8-5 the extent to which recessions—designated by the black bars at the bottom—are, for investors, a lagging and analytically useless measure of economic harm. By the time recessions occurred—much less were verified by the community of economists—the year-over-year rate of growth in economic activity in these cycles had been shrinking for some time, and the stock market declines (the vertical shaded areas) that accompanied the declining rates of growth were over.

Paul Samuelson once made a popular quip dissociating the stock market from the economy: "The stock market has predicted nine out of the past five recessions!"[2] Although this statement cleverly suggests that bear markets often erroneously indicate the onset of recession, it misses the real point: Although the decline in the economic growth rate in several downturns was not sufficient to meet the standard definition of recession (two consecutive quarters of absolute declines in real GDP), virtually every *slowdown* of 2 to 3 percentage points or more in year-over-year consumer-spending growth *did* cause a sufficient downturn in corporate profits to precipitate a bear market. Quite simply, the eventuality of a recession is not required to trigger a bear market.

Sell While the Ducks Are Still Quacking?

The coincidence of stock market declines with downtrends in the year-over-year rate of growth in consumer spending presents investors with a number of thorny issues. First and foremost, because bear markets typically begin when the year-over-year rate of growth in consumer spending is at or close to its peak, stocks are best sold when this, the largest and chronologically earliest sector of the economy, is still apparently very healthy! This poses a significant challenge, because, at such times, investors' inclinations to remain positive are overwhelming. At these junctures, only the most dedicated and disciplined evaluation of leading indicators of consumer spending will suggest that strong economic growth is coming to an end. The optimism reflected throughout 2004 and into early 2005 is a fine example of this. Economists and business-people have rarely identified and used these indicators in time to call key turning points in the economy, and few investors have effectively employed them to buy or sell stocks at the optimal time.

Conversely, most bear markets end when year-over-year economic comparisons, beginning with the consumer, are still only *approaching* their worst levels (in figure 8-5, see 1960, 1966, 1970, 1974, 1982, 1990, and 2001–2002). Consequently, investors wishing to buy in at market bottoms need to do so as economic comparisons are still deteriorating sharply. Summoning not only the rationale, but also the courage, to buy in such difficult economic times requires a clear grasp of leading indicators as harbingers of better things to come. This is especially true at a time when the dire current state of the economy, as reflected in coincident and lagging indicators, is typically leading most investors and businesspeople to despair.

Unquestionably, myriad other factors—such as price-earnings valuations, interest rates and the competitive attractiveness of bonds and other interest-bearing securities, investing institutions' cash positions, and other issues affecting equity values—play key roles in major stock market movements and in market peaks and troughs. Nevertheless, the simple fact is that the stock market almost always peaks when economic times are good and bottoms when current business conditions are terrible and approaching their nadir.

Buy Low, Sell High!

The old saw about buying low and selling high is so self-evident, so *mocking* in its obvious delusion, that the term and concept are greeted as much with derision as with good-natured humor. Veteran investors are fond of noting that stocks are one of the few commodities where the demand typically *rises* as prices go up and falls when prices decline. Indeed, we might reasonably observe that the stock market peaks only when a sufficiently large number of people have such optimism that they are willing to pay the very highest valuations for stocks. Such investors, quite at odds with the oh-so-obvious mantra of "buy low, sell high," are "buying high." Conversely, the stock market bottoms when the greatest number of shareowners are willing to sell at what proves to be the lowest prices, also quite the opposite of the "buy low, sell high" dictum.

What causes such self-damaging behavior? The answer is a relatively simple one: investors—large money-managing institutions and small shareowners alike—largely extrapolate into the future the business conditions that they perceive at the current moment: an optimistic economic outlook when the stock market is at a peak, and entrenched pessimism regarding economic prospects when the stock market is at a bottom.

In the morass of anecdotal economic commentary that investors of all types face daily, and given the lack of effective ongoing disciplines for tracking economic cycles (the raison d'être for this book), most investors find in the strength or weakness of the latest business and economic reports ample reasons for remaining, respectively, optimistic or pessimistic on the outlook for stocks. And key lagging indicators, such as capital spending and employment (or unemployment), remain favorable well after the peak in economic activity or, conversely, negative well after the trough. Therefore, they offer false solace that the economy will continue in the direction in which it was most recently headed.

Can We Learn How and When to Go Against the Flow?

In this context, what does it actually take to buy low and sell high?

- At least from a cyclical, market-timing perspective, it requires first and foremost a sufficient comprehension of the stock market's consistent relationship to the economic cycle.

- Second, we must muster the courage to sell stocks when the year-over-year rate of change in consumer spending, at the front end of the cycle, is at its best, and optimism about the economy (i.e., encouragement to be heavily invested) is ubiquitous—or, conversely, to wade into the market and purchase stocks when the world appears to be coming to an end.

Figures 8-4 and 8-5, by actually verifying the "sell-when-the-economy-is-at-peak-growth" and "buy-when-economic-growth-is-tanking" phenomena, can help supply you with that comprehension and courage.

However, clearly it is not this simple, for the investor must also recognize that today's period of strong economic growth or significant weakness may continue for long periods. How are we to know, for example, that today's 5% year-over-year growth in consumer spending is at a peak? Perhaps growth in real PCE will advance even further, to 7%, over the next twelve to twenty-four months. Thus, we need more than just the observation that consumer spending growth, as our key economic driver, is at "strong" or "weak" levels.

If we are to muster the courage to sell while the ducks are still quacking or buy when the economic downturn appears to have no end, we must find a methodology for forecasting turning points—the change in direction of growth rates of consumer spending itself. This requires us to identify the following:

- *The true leading indicators of consumer demand.* These are individuals' real hourly earnings (explored in chapter 10) and interest rates (chapter 13). But learning to obey these leading indicators when they are turning down in the face of strong business conditions is the cornerstone of having the courage to "sell high."[3]

- *Coincident indicators, such as the consumer confidence indices (chapter 9) and consumer borrowing (chapter 12).* However, these may be less useful in spotting a change in consumer spending until it is already taking place and therefore already reflected in the stock market.

- *Lagging indicators, such as employment and unemployment (chapter 11) and capital spending.* We must consciously fight their tendency to deceive us well after a change in economic direction is under way.

Coming to Grips with Our Emotions

Recognizing that bear markets inevitably begin when economic growth is at its best and bull markets almost always begin when the economic news is relentlessly bad, businesspeople and investors must learn to deal with this counterintuitive yet very real phenomenon. This holds true whether you're dealing with the stock market as a whole or with individual stocks. If you are an executive in a company that is tied to the economic cycle, you must learn to expect your stock to begin turning down when your unit growth in sales and year-over-year profit comparisons are at or near peak rates, when optimism abounds throughout your company.

This will pit your intellect (an empirical understanding of our thesis) against your emotions (your faith in the latest business conditions, often including a lagging and favorable low- unemployment picture). Conversely, your stock price will almost certainly improve rather dramatically at a time when your business is suffering significant deterioration in sales and profits, with several quarters of significant pain to come. In both cases, you and the other executives and workers are likely, at economic turning points, to be perplexed by the divergence between your stock price and your current business conditions.

The story is told of a corporate chief executive who, after finishing a glowing forty-five-minute presentation on his company's prospects at a meeting with analysts, announced that he would now be happy to take analysts' questions. An analyst in the front row raised her hand and asked, "How is business right now?" The CEO responded enthusiastically, "Business couldn't be better!" "Couldn't be better. Hmm." The analyst immediately rose, left the room, and issued a sell recommendation.

Timing the Market Versus Long-Term Buy-and-Hold

Many, indeed perhaps most, experienced investors assert that attempting to time the market is a fruitless endeavor, that buying good-quality stocks and holding them over long periods is by far the superior investment strategy. Having seen the excellent results of astute investors who have practiced investing for the longer term over several decades, I find it hard to disagree. Attempting to time the market, even with the tools I have discussed, is a tricky business (as is any mode of investing in equities).

That being said, one danger particularly facing individual investors is that of professing long-term investment goals and then acting self-destructively in the shorter term by selling after price declines when the ebb and flow of the stock market goes against them. Undoubtedly, many, even most, investors who waded into the stock market in the late 1990s did so with longer-term investment goals in mind. However, it would have been hard in 2002, with the Dow more than 30% lower and the S&P 500 down almost 50%, to convince many of these same investors, who plunged into the market only two years earlier when the Dow Jones was more than 11,000 and the S&P more than 1,500, that buying and holding is an effective long-term strategy.

The difficult reality is that many individual investors are most likely to undertake "long-term" accumulation of stocks when the economy is healthiest (close to a peak), only to become discouraged when the stock market falls drastically, leading to their selling their shares and incurring losses. The wisest approach for investors is to maintain a moderate long-term position in stocks that acknowledges favorable secular growth prospects for the U.S. economy, seeking cyclical opportunities to trim positions when the economy is at its strongest and adding to the portfolio when the outlook appears bleakest. Thus an investor can take into account as well as the longer-term growth prospects and the cyclical realities of the market.

Looking Forward: The Three Engines of Consumer Demand

Hopefully, it is clear by now that consumer spending is the cornerstone of the U.S. economy, representing the front end of the entire demand cycle of consumer spending, industrial production, and capital spending; consumer spending thus serves as the key driver of corporate profits and thereby functions also as a key stock market indicator. This raises a vital question: is there any means by which consumer spending itself, as the central economic driver, can reasonably be forecast in order to give businesses and investors a greater advance warning of vital turning points in the economic cycle and, with it, the stock market? In part III of this book, we will see, as you may already have suspected, that again the answer is yes.

III

Forecasting Consumer Spending

Understanding the Key Indicator Relationships

CHAPTER NINE

Forecasting Consumer Spending

Numbers, Not Psychology

In part II of this book we saw the large proportion of the U.S. economy represented by consumer spending and, equally important, the degree to which consumer spending drives cycles in industrial production, capital spending, corporate profits, and the stock market. Staying abreast of consumer spending and retail sales is thus a smart move for any businessperson or investor. It is even better to become a smart forecaster of future turning points in consumer demand before its uptrends and downtrends become widely evident and are working their way into business conditions and stock market expectations. That is the goal of part III of this book.

Consumer spending is subject to a wide variety of stimuli, some of them financial (wages, consumer borrowing, etc.), others fiscal and monetary (taxes and interest rates), and still others psychological (war, terrorism, political instability). Other stimuli, such as real estate values and inflation, combine these characteristics.

Even in the 1970s, however—when I first tackled the forecasting of consumer spending and retail sales—I realized that I had to resist the temptation to try taking into account so many factors that I would lose sight of the few primary drivers that, for forecasting purposes, truly counted. A compulsion to see all the factors at the same time had thwarted many others in their efforts to figure out where the consumer was headed. I sought to identify two or three causal factors that (1) were rooted in common sense and (2) could be proven to have causality over repeated cycles, without lapsing into the uncontrolled anecdotal speculation that characterizes much economic discourse today. The question is, what are the factors that count?

Forget Your Emotions and Follow the Money

Because we are all consumers, it is easy for us to believe that we have a pretty good handle on the factors that drive consumer spending—first, whether or not we and others have jobs; then how wages or income are faring compared to a year ago; then the values of our home and investments; and finally, our general confidence in the future, which may result from political and social inputs in addition to financial information. However, in forecasting consumer demand, if we use psychological inputs, we need to document them in a statistical form if we are to test their historical validity as leading indicators and keep ourselves from lapsing into unsupported hunches. It is better, then, to follow our now familiar policy of statistical empiricism and ask the key questions: What are the sources of consumer spending, which ones dominate, and how do we track them?

To do this, it will help to differentiate two different types of consumer spending power:

- *Personal income.* More than half of personal income is the wages and salaries consumers generate from their jobs. It typically comes in a weekly, biweekly, or monthly paycheck stream and, because most consumers are at lower- or middle-income wage levels, gets spent as it is received.[1] It would be foolish to think that personal income itself is not the primary driver of consumer spending.

- *Personal wealth, or non-income spending power.* This is more the result of intermediate- to longer-term changes in surplus income, investments (notably including the stock market), and home values. These sources can also shape spending, but they sit on the back burner—in consumers' bank and investment accounts—and require a conscious action on the consumer's part, such as liquidating an investment position, refinancing and borrowing against the value of a home, and so on.[2]

In sum, by far the more powerful of these two sources of spending power—particularly from a business-cycle perspective—is the ongoing flow of income directly into consumers' pockets or personal checking accounts. If you can forecast personal income—primarily wages and salaries—you will most likely be able to forecast consumer spending. Figure 9-1 shows the simple formula for all wages and salaries in the economy.

But here's where most predictions of consumer spending get tripped up. Most forecasters—economists and non-economists alike—intuitively and emotionally regard employment, or jobs, as the most important input to wages and salaries and personal income. After all, a job is the cornerstone of each individual consumer's spending power, the root of his or her economic well-being, and a cornerstone of consumer psychology. In short, we all have an emotional knee-jerk response to view employment as *the* key driver of income and psychological well-being (read consumer confidence) that makes consumer spending possible.

Although this view of employment is accurate to a certain extent, it misses the point that workers are invariably hired after the economy improves, or fired after it deteriorates, and therefore employment is always—not sometimes, but always—a lagging indicator in the economic cycle. Chapter 11 explores this phenomenon in detail. The reality is that the *wage growth of the employed* has a far greater effect on, and is a far superior leading indicator of, consumer spending. Figure 9-2 schematically illustrates this underappreciated principle.

Those who master this observation have the best chance of focusing on the real leading indicator of consumer spending: the wage gains of employed workers, as opposed to consumer psychology emanating

FIGURE 9-1

Total wages and salaries formula

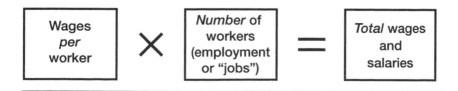

FIGURE 9-2

Wage growth, and not employment, is a leading indicator of consumer spending

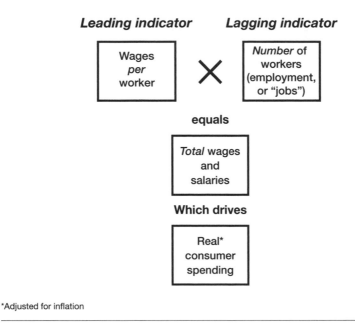

*Adjusted for inflation

from changes in employment, which remains one of the economy's notable lagging indicators. That being said, much of the discourse you will encounter in the business press and in television reportage continues to focus on consumer psychology—particularly indices of consumer confidence—so let's delve a bit deeper into this subject.

Does Consumer Psychology Count?

Any regular viewer of television news will recognize that a considerable portion of broadcast reporting on the economy consists of interviews with shoppers in stores and parking lots. Shoppers are asked about their spending plans in response to the latest reported economic stimuli. Here are some typical replies:

- "Two of my neighbors were laid off last month, so we're going to save more and spend less on Christmas presents this year."

- "With gas prices so high, we're going to stay closer to home and take a shorter vacation this year."

- "I just received my tax rebate, so I'm going to Home Depot, and we're going to build that rear deck we've always wanted."

Such samplings of individuals' sentiments at any given juncture make good television, and, to be fair, are representative of the collective mood of consumers. After all, total consumer spending is comprised of tens of millions of consumers who express their economic feelings daily in the nation's stores, restaurants, and theaters. However, these anecdotal inputs alone are not very useful as a measure of consumer psychology. Consequently, economic pundits have turned for guidance to more empirical and long-standing measures of consumer sentiment.

Although psychological inputs make great reading, filling books and articles with interesting and sometimes amusing anecdotes, they have contributed relatively little empirically or methodologically to the job of forecasting consumer spending uptrends and downtrends and the economic advances and slowdowns that follow them. Why? It is mainly because the dollars and cents consumers earn and have access to are the major input to their economic psychology. The psychology is thus the by-product, and not the driver.

Consumer Confidence Indices:
Widely Watched, but Are They Useful in Forecasting?

The two most widely heralded monthly indicators of consumer confidence are the Consumer Confidence Index (published by The Conference Board) and the Index of Consumer Sentiment (compiled by the University of Michigan Survey Research Center). The reason for these two series' popularity is simple: their very names suggest that consumer sentiment, or psychology, can be measured and that important insight into consumers' intentions for future spending will be gained.

No argument: there is value in evaluating and tracking the collective state of mind of consumers. The big question is, does this information help us predict consumer-spending trends? I have found no evidence that it does.

A core mission of this book is to put forward the view that no economic data series should be presented in a vacuum but instead should be measured empirically in relation to another series that either it is purported to *lead* or that leads *it*. Remarkably, with regard to the consumer confidence indices (among many others), we almost never see this exercise carried out by the news services that dutifully report the data, nor by the commentators who review it.

The consumer confidence indices are derived by asking consumers, who are polled monthly, a series of questions. For the Consumer Confidence Index, The Conference Board asks those polled to respond "positive," "neutral," or "negative" to the following questions (as detailed on The Conference Board Web site):[3]

- *Respondents' appraisal of current business conditions*
- *Respondents' expectations regarding business conditions six months hence*
- *Respondents' appraisal of the current employment conditions*
- *Respondents' expectations regarding employment conditions six months hence*
- *Respondents' expectations regarding their total family income six months hence*

For the Index of Consumer Sentiment, the University of Michigan Survey Research Center asks a larger number of questions touching on personal financial expectations, employment, and opinions on government economic leadership, including the following (as detailed on the University of Michigan's Web site):[4]

- *"Now looking ahead—do you think that a year from now you (and your family living there) will be better off financially, or worse off, or just about the same as now?" (Multiple choice answers include "will be better off," "same," "will be worse off," and "don't know.")*
- *"Now turning to business conditions in the country as a whole—do you think that during the next twelve months we'll have good times*

financially, or bad times, or what?" (Answers include "good times," "good with qualifications," "pro-con," "bad with qualifications," "bad times," and "don't know.")

- *"How about people out of work during the coming twelve months— do you think that there will be* more unemployment than now, about the *same, or less?" (Answers include "more unemployment," "about the same," and "less unemployment.")*

Despite the forward-looking nature of these questions, when the results of these consumer sentiment polls are charted over several decades vis-à-vis actual growth in consumer spending, they have little predictive value. The top chart in figure 9-3 traces The Conference Board's Consumer Confidence Index compared with year-over-year changes in real consumer spending (real PCE) from 1967 to 2004; it demonstrates clearly the coincident, rather than leading, relationship between the two series. The bottom chart in figure 9-3 charts the same relationship between the University of Michigan's Index of Consumer Sentiment and consumer spending and also demonstrates a lack of predictive value. There are few instances in which either of the two indices has moved sharply higher or lower *in advance of* an uptrend or downtrend in the year-over-year rate of growth in real consumer spending.

The reason is simple. First, the process of asking consumers to look forward to predict their financial circumstances and spending plans appears on the surface to have forecasting value. However, answers to questions asked today will reflect the respondents' attitudes today. A consumer who responds optimistically about her appraisal of current or future economic conditions and personal spending plans today is likely already spending at a favorable level. If three months from now that same consumer answers the same forward-looking questions in a more pessimistic manner, she will already have reduced current spending in response to the changes in conditions that led to the more negative responses.

Second, realistically, there is no reason to believe that consumers, individually or as a group, have more insight into the future than economists or businesspeople. Individual consumers, far from having a disciplined method for looking forward, are more likely to extrapolate current economic conditions. In other words, although the questions

FIGURE 9-3

Consumer sentiment surveys: Coincident, not leading, indicators

The Consumer Confidence Index

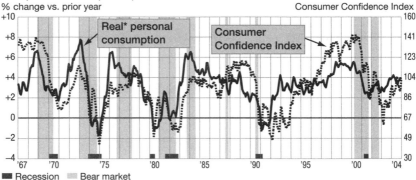

■ Recession ▨ Bear market

The Consumer Sentiment Index

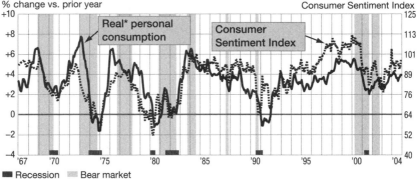

■ Recession ▨ Bear market

*The Consumer Confidence Index (compiled by The Conference Board) and the University of Michigan's Consumer Sentiment Index are based largely on questions asked of consumers regarding their expectations of future economic conditions. The indices are, however, largely coincident in their relationship to year-over-year consumer spending. This is because consumers' attitudes toward the future, manifested in answers given **today** to questions asked **today**, reflect today's economic inputs and sentiments. Neither index, therefore, has proved to have significant predictive value.*

Sources: PCE—Bureau of Economic Analysis; Consumer Confidence Index—The Conference Board; Consumer Sentiment Index—University of Michigan Survey Research Center
*Adjusted for inflation

"This is the New York 'Times' Business Poll again, Mr. Landau. Do you feel better or worse about the economy than you did twenty minutes ago?"

are predictive in nature, the respondents' attitudes and the spending of all consumers reflect conditions in effect at the time of the asking.

As with many of the economic inputs received in the press every day, the consumer confidence indices are presented with a certain degree of reportorial solemnity that seems to validate their value in forecasting consumer demand, without reporters' providing empirical backing that validates their predictive power.

Behavioral Economics: Catchy Concept, but Is It Macroecomically Relevant?

Another psychology-based realm of economic investigation that has gained considerable currency during the past decade or two has been the field of *behavioral economics*, which explores to what extent human nature affects rational economic and investment decision making. As with consumer confidence, the very name of this new field suggests that patterns of consumer or business behavior—both rational and irrational—can yield insights that are useful in forecasting the future direction of economic growth. The irrational component has been receiving a great deal of attention by economists as a means of explaining unexplainable events, such as booms and crashes, in the stock market. Much of this work was pioneered by Daniel Kahneman and J. Tversky, who won the Nobel Prize in 2002 for their *prospect theory*, which explores aspects of sentiment in financial and investment decision making.

However, much behavioral economics analyses appears to be *situational*—that is, used to evaluate decisions on pricing or risk and other choices made by individual (or groups of) consumers and businesspeople. These include narrow questions regarding marketing, financial, and policy problems, such as varying pricing alternatives on goods and services, individuals' financial decision making, and responses to changes in tax policy. We must not—as some economics writers have—confuse these narrower questions with the broader need to develop working disciplines for forecasting the macro economy and the stock market. Few of these studies have moved the ball forward in providing convincing and ongoing methods that a typical business manager, investor, or policy maker might sufficiently understand to put to pragmatic use in forecasting. If the theorist is not able to show that the hypothesis and method would have provided consistent and useful guidance to economic developments in past cycles, we are left with the question, How does this help me, in a disciplined and systematic manner, to figure out where the economy is headed next year?

For economic theorists, the thrill of the chase and the potential for intellectual recognition may of themselves be sufficient reward, but businesspeople and investors need a concrete system for tracking where they are in the economic cycle and where they may be headed. Although behavioral economics will undoubtedly continue to prosper in its work on highly specific human-response situations within the economy, it addresses a need quite different from our quest for a nontheoretical, statistically empirical, comprehensible discipline for forecasting consumer spending and other economic activity at both the macro and the industry level.

Putting psychological analyses behind us, let's now move forward to evaluate how consumers' real wages can be used effectively to forecast uptrends and downtrends in consumer spending at the front end of the economic cycle.

CHAPTER TEN

Real Earnings

The Powerhouse of the Economy

We have established several important principles that allow us to separate the wheat from the chaff in forecasting consumer spending, which, as we saw in part II, is the front end of the business cycle:

1. *Soft* inputs, such as the consumer confidence indices and ad hoc observations regarding consumer psychology, have not proven helpful in forecasting uptrends and downtrends in consumer spending. Putting aside personal hunches and emotions in predicting the next turning point, we must stick with the numbers that define consumers' actual incomes, or spending power. These indicators consist primarily of wages (hourly earnings) and salaries and deserve our first and greatest attention when we project consumer demand.

2. Employment (jobs) lags changes in the economy, so we must remove it from our calculations in forecasting consumer demand. As emotionally attached as we may be to the subject of jobs, we must put these feelings aside when forecasting.

3. As shown in figure 10-1, this leaves us with a focus on spending power per worker as the most important and, historically, by far the most helpful leading indicator of consumer-spending uptrends, downtrends, and turning points.

The key determinant of growth in unit consumer spending is the *unit purchasing power*, or *real wages*, of the 93% to 96% of the workforce that is employed (given an unemployment rate of 4% to 7%), rather

FIGURE 10-1

Chronology: Real hourly earnings drive consumer spending, corporate profits, and the stock market

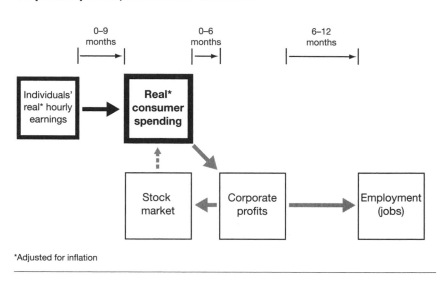

*Adjusted for inflation

than marginal changes in the *number of employed* (or the *unemployment rate*). Think about it: the total number of employed persons in the United Sates in 2004 was approximately 139 million. Most had held jobs (had not become unemployed) throughout the previous three years. Changes in the rates of increase in their spending power are a far more potent factor in most instances than a 1 or 2 percentage point increase in the number of unemployed.

In this chapter, we will see how the *real average hourly earnings* series published by the Bureau of Labor Statistics provides the measurement we need of the purchasing power of those employed. In doing so, this series serves as the single most reliable leading indicator of consumer spending and consequently also is one of the better predictors of the general direction of the economy and the stock market.

How Personal Income Drives Consumer Spending

But before focusing on the real average hourly wage series, we should look at the source of U.S. consumers' income. *Personal income—all* income generated by individuals—totaled $9.7 trillion in the United States in 2004. By far the largest component of this was wages and salaries of $5.4 trillion, representing 56%. All other sources, combined, of personal income received by individuals in the United States were far less significant. Figure 10-2 shows the flow from personal income to consumer spending in the most simplistic terms (2004 data).

Subtracting personal tax and other nontax payments of $1.1 trillion from total personal income of $9.7 trillion, disposable personal income (income after taxes) in the United States in 2004 was $8.6 trillion. Of this, $8.2 trillion, or 95%, flowed into consumer spending. Excluding a few miscellaneous items, this left a scant $102 billion added to savings, representing a *saving rate* of only 1.2% of disposable personal income.[1] This rate is rate in 2004 was the lowest in history, and contrasts sharply with that of most other developed countries, where much higher percentages of income are saved.

What stands out here is the importance that wages and salaries—at $5.4 trillion and 56% of overall personal income—play in relationship to total consumer spending of $8.2 trillion. Recall the analogy in a chapter 9 endnote of the stream of personal income flowing into the pond of consumer spending *power*, which in turn flows out into the lower stream of actual consumer spending. Figure 10-3 provides a

FIGURE 10-2

Wages, personal income, and real* consumer spending (PCE), 2004

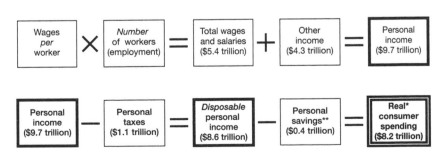

Sources: Earnings—Bureau of Labor Statistics; PCE—Bureau of Economic Analysis
*Adjusted for inflation
**Personal savings + personal interest payments + personal current transfer payments

FIGURE 10-3

Personal income: The wellspring of consumer spending, 2004

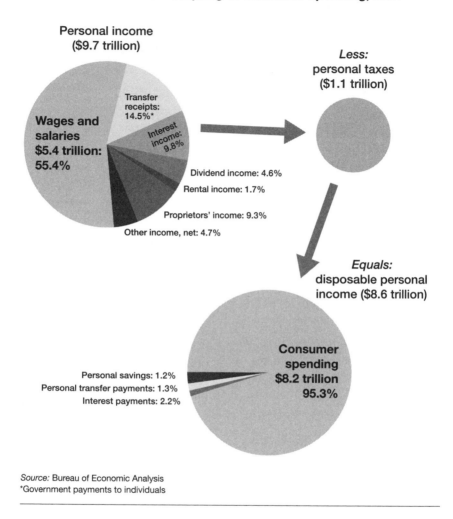

Personal income
($9.7 trillion)

Less:
personal taxes
($1.1 trillion)

Wages and salaries $5.4 trillion: 55.4%

Transfer receipts: 14.5%*

Interest income: 9.8%

Dividend income: 4.6%

Rental income: 1.7%

Proprietors' income: 9.3%

Other income, net: 4.7%

Equals:
disposable personal
income ($8.6 trillion)

Consumer spending $8.2 trillion 95.3%

Personal savings: 1.2%
Personal transfer payments: 1.3%
Interest payments: 2.2%

Source: Bureau of Economic Analysis
*Government payments to individuals

visual sense of the relative importance of wages and salaries within personal income and its relationship to consumer spending.

Wages and salaries represent the preponderance of spending power flowing directly into consumers' pockets and checking accounts. In forecasting, we must give precedence to wages and salaries over *wealth* factors, such as stock portfolios and home values, which require a specific liquidation decision and transaction on the consumer's part.

Real Average Hourly Wages: The Winning Indicator

The best measurement of individuals' unit purchasing power through wages and salaries is the Bureau of Labor Statistics' average hourly earnings series, which tracks average hourly wages for all hourly non-supervisory workers, representing 64% of all employment in the United States in 2004. Although this series does not incorporate supervisory workers and upper-echelon executives, it has proven over the years to be a generally effective measurement for tracking wage growth for a large portion of the working population, the *ongoing employed*, exclusive of the lagging effects of changes in *the number of* employed.

However—and this is important—an extra step is required. The economy is always forecast in real, or unit, terms, adjusted for inflation—for example, *real* GDP, *real* PCE (consumer spending), and so on. And of course, industrial production is reported as an index measured in units, and employment, one of the most closely watched of all economic data series, is inherently a nominal series (the number of workers). So to forecast real consumer spending, we must use *real* average hourly wages; to do this, we must deflate (divide) them by the personal consumption expenditures (PCE) deflator, the consumer price inflation index most widely accepted by government bureaus and economists. This calculation yields real average hourly earnings, the most effective measure of unit spending power of the vast majority of the population that remains employed even in an economic downturn.

In my estimation, real average hourly earnings is the most effective single leading indicator of consumer spending. I have tracked this series on a monthly basis since identifying its predictive qualities in the mid-1970s.

In figure 10-4, the solid line traces year-over-year percentage changes in average hourly earnings in nominal (dollar) terms from 1965 through 2004. Changes in year-over-year *real* average hourly earnings—average hourly earnings growth minus the effects of consumer price inflation as measured by the PCE deflator (the shaded areas between the two lines)—are depicted in the dotted line. This series, with the effects of inflation removed, is our best measurement of the purchasing power of individuals' hourly earnings. You can see here that

FIGURE 10-4

How inflation affects growth in real* average hourly earnings

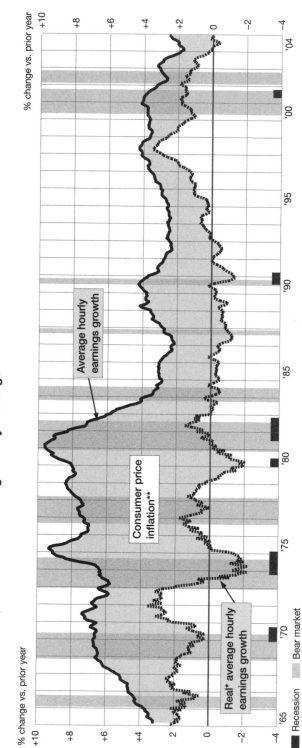

% change vs. prior year

Changes in consumer price inflation have an often significant effect in reducing average hourly earning gains (in dollar terms—solid line) to real average hourly earnings, or individuals' **unit purchasing power** (dotted line).

Source: Hourly earnings growth—Bureau of Labor Statistics; PCE deflator—Bureau of Economic Analysis
*Adjusted for inflation
**Personal consumption expenditure (PCE) deflator

individuals' year-over-year real average hourly earning comparisons over the past forty years fluctuated in a band between +4% and −2%, with consumer price inflation being the most volatile factor in these comparisons.

Now let's take a look in figure 10-5 at how real average hourly earning comparisons lead consumer spending in a typical cycle. The dotted line represents year-over-year real average hourly earnings comparisons, and the solid line denotes year-over-year growth in real consumer spending. As we saw in figure 10-4, the typical year-over-year range for real average hourly earnings comparisons is −2% to +4%. However, year-over-year swings in real consumer spending (as we have seen in earlier charts) are somewhat greater, typically ranging from zero to +6%.

FIGURE 10-5

Typical cycle: How real* average hourly earnings lead real* consumer spending

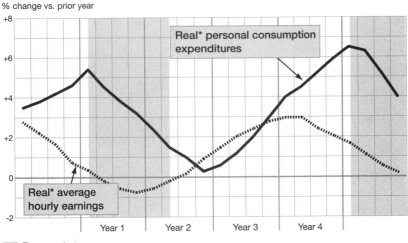

% change vs. prior year

Bear market

Changes in individuals' year-over-year real average hourly earnings (dotted line)— usually ranging from −2% to +3%—have typically been a reliable indicator of broader swings in real consumer spending (solid line). And because stock market declines have often correlated with the early stages of consumer-spending slowdowns, real hourly earnings have also been a useful leading indicator of stock market direction, particularly before bear markets.

*Adjusted for inflation

Usually, real hourly wage comparisons begin to slow six to twelve months *before* the peak in consumer-spending growth, often as a result of rising inflation caused by the strong consumer spending itself. After some months, consumer-spending growth slows in response to the diminished purchasing power, as shown in year 1 of our typical cycle in figure 10-5. This slowdown normally continues for a year or longer until the reduced consumer demand results in lower inflation, with real average hourly earnings comparisons then starting to recover (year 2 in figure 10-5). This recovery, in turn, results in a rebound in consumer-spending growth and a return to the top of the cycle (year 3). This process is usually circular, as diagrammed in figure 10-6. [2]

Our hypothetical charts of a typical cycle are fine and dandy, but now, in figure 10-7, let's look at actual year-over-year real average hourly earnings changes in the U.S. economy from 1965 through 2004; figure 10-7 compares them with real consumer spending (remember, more

FIGURE 10-6

The consumer spending, inflation, real* hourly earnings circle

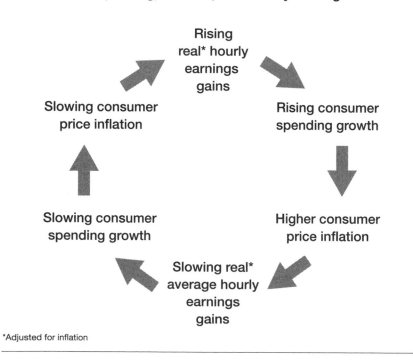

*Adjusted for inflation

124

FIGURE 10-7

Real* hourly earnings: Best leading indicator of real* consumer spending (PCE) downturns

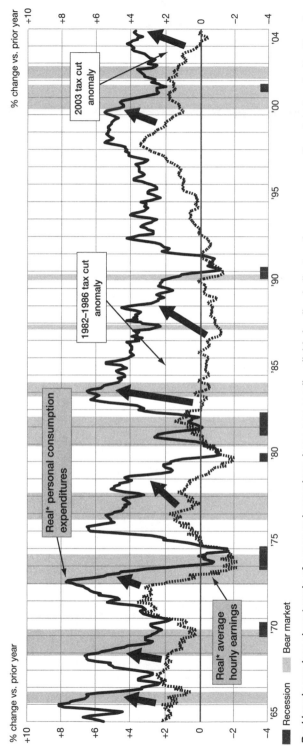

Real hourly earnings downtrends of a year or longer have been a generally reliable leading indicator of consumer-spending downtrends. Real hourly earnings gave particularly notable advance warning of the 2000–2002 economic downturn.

Real hourly earnings are reported on a pretax basis. Therefore, in the mid-1980s and 2003, strong gains in consumer spending despite slowing real earnings were an anomaly reflecting federal tax cuts in those periods.

Sources: Earnings—Bureau of Labor Statistics; PCE—Bureau of Economic Analysis
*Adjusted for inflation

than two-thirds of the U.S. economy) to see whether real hourly earnings predict the key turning points.

Note that I present this same chart four times in this chapter—it is that important—with different notations and observations each time.

The dotted line in figure 10-7 represents year-over-year growth in individuals' real average hourly earnings, and the solid line is year-over-year real consumer spending in aggregate. Take a good, hard look to see whether the direction of the dotted line—upward or downward—is in fact a good forecaster of the direction of the solid line. I think it is. The arrows in this chart highlight the repeated instances in which a downtrend of six to nine months or more in year-over-year real hourly earnings comparisons warned of a forthcoming downturn for consumer spending in general.

Figure 10-8 is the same chart, but with the arrows now indicating periods during which an uptrend in real average hourly earnings foretold a coming recovery in consumer-spending growth.

To be sure, real average hourly earnings (the dotted line) throws us an occasional head fake, moving first in one direction and then in another before settling into a clear trend.[3] There is not much to be done about this. However, in the main, when real hourly earnings comparisons are headed up or down for six months or longer, real consumer spending follows. And when we get a significant divergence in direction between the two, it is real hourly earnings that tell us that a new direction—a turning point—is about to occur for consumer spending.

I must highlight one important issue in dealing with the real average hourly earnings series: the hourly earnings on which it is based are in *pretax* terms. This means that the occasional effects of government tax cuts or tax increases on year-over-year unit purchasing power comparisons are not reflected in the real hourly earnings data. For example, the two major tax cuts implemented by the Reagan administration in 1982 and 1986 kept consumer spending increasing at a strong rate of 3% or greater throughout the mid- and late 1980s despite year-over-year declines in (pretax) real average hourly earnings. This prevented a consumer-spending slowdown that almost certainly would otherwise have occurred, given how poor the underlying real earnings comparisons were. In this case, to have followed the real average hourly earnings series alone would have resulted in greatly

FIGURE 10-8

Real* hourly earnings: Best leading indicator of real* consumer spending (PCE) upturns

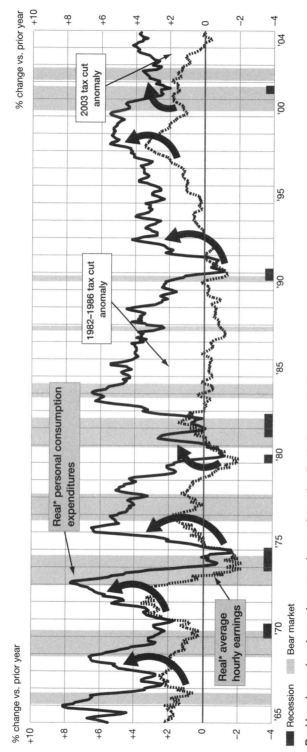

*Real hourly earnings have also proved a consistent leading indicator of **advances** in consumer spending.*

Real hourly earnings are reported on a pretax basis. The apparent anomaly of strong growth in real consumer spending despite slowing real hourly earnings in the mid to late 1980s and in 2003 is attributable to the 1982/1986 and 2003 tax cuts.

Sources: Earnings—Bureau of Labor Statistics; PCE—Bureau of Economic Analysis
*Adjusted for inflation

underestimating consumer-spending strength resulting from these tax cuts.

The most recent example, of course, was the Bush administration's tax cuts of 2003. Similarly, although real hourly earnings comparisons slowed from mid-2003 through early 2004, growth in real consumer spending actually accelerated, reflecting the extra dollars in consumers' pockets resulting from the tax cut. Conclusion: real average hourly earnings comparisons are an excellent leading indicator of consumer spending growth *except* when major changes in taxes result in a significant alteration of after-tax income.[4]

The Remarkable 2000–2003 Experience

Never has the real hourly average earnings series proven more effective as a leading indicator than before the 2000–2002 economic and stock market downturn. For much of 1998, growth in real hourly earnings was unusually strong, exceeding 3% year-over-year. This resulted from hourly earnings growth of more than 4% in 1998, at a time when inflation had fallen to only 1% (see figure 10-4). However, growth in real hourly earnings slowed continually throughout 1999 and 2000, as rising inflation (attributable to increasing energy prices)—vis-à-vis stable to slightly slower wage gains—eroded growth in purchasing power. Throughout late 1999 and early 2000, the continuous slowdown in real hourly earnings comparisons virtually shouted—based on the historical relationship between real earnings and consumer spending—that a consumer-led economic slowdown was at hand. The period of warning was a good deal longer than normal, providing more than ample time for anyone monitoring real earnings to turn negative on consumer spending, the economy, and the stock market as early as mid- to late 1999—but no one was watching this series!

Extraordinary stock market profits for a large proportion of Americans—the much heralded "wealth effect" resulting from the technology, general economic, and stock market boom of the late 1990s—*postponed,* but did not prevent, the inevitable effects of slowing real hourly earnings, which drove the sharp slowdown in consumer spending growth that began in mid-2000 and continued throughout 2001.

Inevitably, as we learned in chapters 7 and 8, this drove even more pre-cipitous declines in industrial production, capital spending, corporate profits, and the stock market.[5]

Recognition of the predictive qualities of real average hourly wages should have led business managers to reduce their inventories and operating expenses, and investors to reduce their stock portfolios, well before the curtain fell on the economic and stock market boom of the 1990s. Indeed, I remember being chided by friends over my bearish-ness throughout 1999 and early 2000, but I was rewarded as I sat out the economic and stock market bloodbath that followed.

Equally impressive was the positive signal flashed—in the face of rampant pessimism—by real hourly earnings through much of 2001, as lower inflation drove rising gains in real earnings for most of 2000 and the first half of 2001. By early September 2001, even before the World Trade Center tragedy on September 11, the sharp slowing in the economy had most observers convinced that further declines in con-sumer spending were at hand. And yet, rising gains in real wages were telling us throughout 2001 that the spending power of the typical employed worker was now accelerating. And remarkably, in the face of a national tragedy of the greatest proportion, real consumer spending turned right around during the first half of 2002 and—against all expectations—accelerated. The stock market dutifully followed, rising 21% from its low ten days after September 11 to an interim peak in early January 2004. Consumer spending accelerated in 2002, despite rising unemployment and the steepest declines in consumer confi-dence in more than a decade. All this tells how powerful real average hourly earnings are as a leading indicator of real consumer spending.

As I write, in early 2005, real hourly wage comparisons have contin-ued to slow significantly, reflecting rising prices for fuel and some other commodities. Furthermore, the 2003 tax cut has passed its anniversary and no longer is adding to spending-power comparisons. When com-pared with the greater than 4% gains in real consumer spending in the first half of 2004, this slowdown in real hourly wage comparisons clearly suggests a forthcoming downturn in consumer spending growth and all that follows it—a classic negative divergence in which the lead-ing indicator is heading sharply lower while the series it typically leads is thriving, sending a strong warning signal.

There are times when leading indicators such as real average hourly earnings are moving sideways and can be considered equivocal. However, when they are pointed unequivocally in a higher or a lower direction, they should also be regarded, and followed, unequivocally. This appears to be one of those times.

How Employment and Borrowing Leverage Real Wages

Over the years, I have also found the relationship between year-over-year changes in real average hourly earnings and real consumer spending to be remarkably helpful in understanding the dimension of a cycle, both its magnitude and duration. Figure 10-9 helps us visualize this: note that real consumer spending (the solid line) is almost always growing at a faster year-over-year pace than the underlying real average hourly earnings of individuals (the dotted line).

This differential, represented by the highlighted space between the two lines in figure 10-9, consists primarily of two things: (1) growth in employment—that is, the number of individuals receiving wages (hourly earnings)—and (2) growth in consumer borrowing, which is an additional nonwage source of consumer spending power. In other words, these two sources of incremental spending power "leverage up" the growth of underlying hourly earnings of employed individuals into a higher rate of growth in aggregate real consumer spending. As real hourly earnings rise at the beginning of a cycle and consumer spending itself begins to grow at a faster rate, the effect of stronger consumer spending works its way through the economy, and employment and consumer borrowing begin to pick up. This leads to the strongest part of the cycle, when the accelerative effect of growth in employment and consumer borrowing—typically 3 to 4 percentage points—is at its highest.

However—and this is important—this differential inevitably disappears at the end of each cycle (see the circles in figure 10-9) when growth in employment and increases in consumer borrowing disappear; this results in a rapidly falling rate of growth in real consumer spending as it returns to the underlying rate of growth in real hourly earnings of the employed.[6]

FIGURE 10-9

Growth in employment and borrowing "leverages up" real* hourly earnings

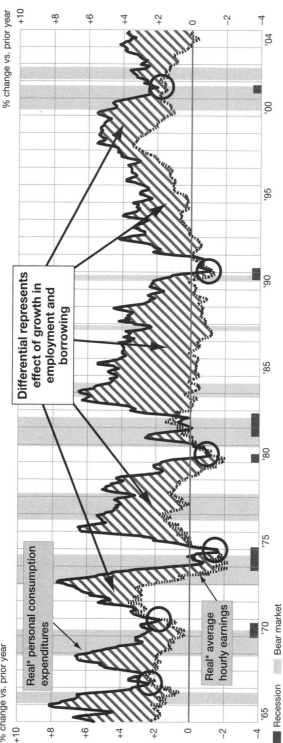

% change vs. prior year

Differential represents effect of growth in employment and borrowing

Real* personal consumption expenditures

Real* average hourly earnings

 Recession   Bear market

The differential between the real earnings growth of individual consumers (dotted line) and aggregate real consumer spending (solid line) is comprised mainly of (1) growth in employment (consumers receiving income) and (2) additional funds generated for spending by consumer borrowing. This differential swells during the early and middle stages of a typical consumer-spending cycle. However, in the late stages of each economic and consumer-spending downturn, year-over-year growth in both employment and borrowing typically returns to "zero." This results in aggregate consumer-spending growth falling to the underlying rate of growth in individual consumers' real wages (see circles).

Sources: Earnings—Bureau of Labor Statistics; PCE—Bureau of Economic Analysis
*Adjusted for inflation

As figure 10-9 shows, this differential expanded and then disappeared in each of the six consumer-spending cycles starting in 1960. Consequently, at the end of every cycle, the year-over-year rate of growth in real consumer spending—aggregate spending by all consumers—fell to the underlying rate of growth in the real earnings of individuals (marked by circles) at the end of each of these cycles. This decrease typically resulted in steeper declines in consumer-spending comparisons than widely anticipated in economists' forecasts. We might as well ask ourselves whether this will be the case again in 2006 or 2007.

The Core Role of Inflation

The circular relationship between the rate of growth in consumer spending (and general economic growth), inflation, and individuals' real wages is hardly a new concept. This phenomenon is associated with the thinking of John Maynard Keynes and the concept of *demand-pull* inflation. This classical economic thesis has been the cornerstone in recent years of Federal Reserve Board policy during periods of strong economic growth to cool off the economy by raising interest rates as a means of slowing consumer demand in order to thwart rising inflation.

Inflation is, without question, the most important of all economic indicators (excluding, of course, real GDP itself). And, as you can see in figure 10-4, consumer price inflation is usually more volatile than hourly wage increases in determining real average hourly wages. However, we tend too often to look at inflation per se, without relating it to the preinflation growth in wages whose purchasing power it reduces. In other words, the cornerstone role of the real-wage effect is often overlooked.

A Useful Stock Market Indicator

I learned long ago that almost every stock market decline in the past four decades has been closely related to a deceleration in the year-over-year rate of growth in unit consumer spending. To repeat this book's central mantra, year-over-year uptrends and downtrends in unit consumer spending drive year-over-year industrial production, capital spending, and corporate profits and are therefore a key factor in the direction of the stock market. Real hourly earnings, as an often effective leading indicator of consumer spending, therefore also serve as a useful leading indicator of the direction of the stock market.

I ask you to indulge me by looking one more time at the chart you've now seen three times—this time with a set of notations related to the stock market. Figure 10-10 verifies the contention that downtrends in year-over-year growth in real average hourly earnings (highlighted in the ovals), as a reliable leading indicator of downturns in consumer spending, have also typically preceded bear markets (the vertical gray bars) by various periods and with varying degrees of clarity.[7] In short, a slowdown in real hourly wage comparisons is often a clear signal to reduce exposure to the stock market. Uptrends in real average hourly wages have also been useful, but not as consistently reliable, in signaling new bull markets.

Real Hourly Earnings: The Real Thing

Although it is an important signal of future trends in unit consumer spending, the real average hourly earnings series is, surprisingly, one of the less noticed indicators in economic commentary. It possesses neither the drama of unemployment nor the speculative mystery of the Fed's interest-rate decisions. The general and business press almost never include the monthly report of real hourly earnings in their commentary, and this measure is seldom used by economists as a cornerstone indicator in forecasting consumer spending and the economy. Most casual observers of the economy don't even recognize its existence. However, as the charts in this chapter clearly demonstrate, it is perhaps the most effective leading indicator of unit consumer spending, which represents more than two-thirds of all economic activity and drives much of the rest of the economy. The real hourly earnings series is, in short, one of the most important of all economic forecasting tools.

FIGURE 10-10

Real* hourly earnings: A useful leading indicator of stock market declines

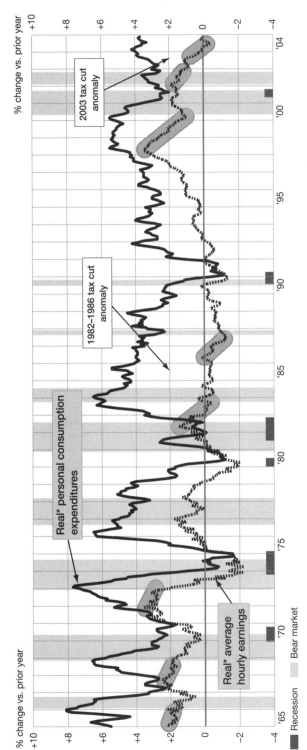

% change vs. prior year

Slowing year-over-year real* hourly earnings growth—a generally reliable leading indicator of forthcoming downturns in year-over-year consumer spending (solid line), followed by the economy in general—has also been a signal of forthcoming declines in the stock market (vertical gray bars).

Real* hourly earnings are reported on a pretax basis. The apparent anomaly of strong growth in real consumer spending despite slowing real hourly earnings in the mid to late 1980s and in 2003 is attributable to the 1982/1986 and 2003 tax cuts. This also helped prevent significant bear markets during these periods.

Sources: Earnings—Bureau of Labor Statistics; PCE—Bureau of Economic Analysis
*Adjusted for inflation

Chapter 11 addresses employment and its paradoxical relationship with consumer spending. On the one hand, employment is driven by and lags consumer spending, but on the other hand, it has some impact on consumer spending through its effect on incomes. This chicken-and-egg relationship is one of the most interesting and problematic aspects of the evaluation of economic cycles.

CHAPTER ELEVEN

Employment and *Un*employment

The Economy's Deceptive Laggard

If you have a job, you're much more likely to go to the store and buy things and therefore help drive consumer spending and the economy. So jobs (or employment) drive the economy, right?

But you also know that when the economy turns down, employers start to lay off workers, and they rehire only after business (the economy) gets better. So the economy (two-thirds of which is consumer spending) drives jobs, right?

Wait. Which is it?

Actually, both statements are true. But the latter is a far more powerful causal relationship in defining how the economic cycle unfolds, as shown in figure 11-1. Uptrends and downtrends in the economy always lead, and employment follows. Understanding which comes first and which goes later is essential to correctly perceiving the course of the economy and staying above the fray as others lose their way.

Employment: Separating the Personal from the Pragmatic

Earlier in this book, we described the importance of recognizing employment and unemployment as lagging rather than leading indicators. This was essential as we established the importance of staying focused on real hourly earnings of the ongoing employed (rather than employment-affected data) as the best leading indicator of consumer

FIGURE 11-1

Chronology: Consumer spending drives employment, not vice versa

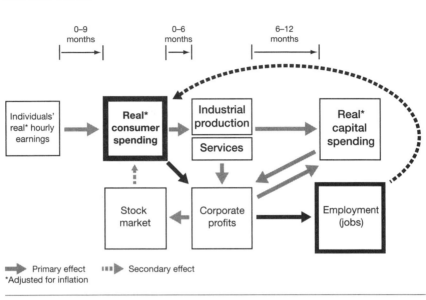

spending. This chapter documents and explores the lagging role of employment so that we can keep it in the proper perspective.

Regardless of our political beliefs or economic views, we all see employment and jobs as the cornerstone of collective and personal well-being. After all, everyone feels personally the emotional and economic difference between being employed (having a job) and being unemployed (being jobless). Being employed implies economic well-being and the ability to buy life's necessities—and even, perhaps, luxuries—whereas unemployment often suggests personal deprivation and, not infrequently, desperation. So it is not surprising that most of us personalize strong employment as a harbinger of better economic times and see lower employment (i.e., rising unemployment) as a sure signal of tougher times ahead. Unfortunately, however, this is one of the most common and harmful mistakes a businessperson or investor can make in attempting to forecast economic events.

Please don't get me wrong: we should not interpret this empirical observation of the lagging role of employment as insensitivity to the subject. But we should not let our emotions on the subject of jobs

"I don't <u>like</u> six per-cent unemployment, either. But I can live with it."

muddle our pragmatic, analytical understanding of employment's lagging role as an economic indicator.

I experienced three economic cycles, from the mid-1960s through the mid-1970s, before fully realizing this. In cycle after cycle, I would hear forecasters assure us far past the peak rate of growth in the economy that strong employment figures (usually reported as "lower unemployment" or "lower jobless claims") ensured stable growth in consumer spending and the economy in general for the foreseeable future—only to have an economic downturn suddenly appear despite the favorable job picture. Conversely, well after an economic trough, concerns over a weak job market or a "jobless recovery" would make me hesitate to participate in the upside.

After falling prey to the same mistake a number of times, I decided to subject employment data to the same test (year-over-year charting) used with every other putative economic cause-and-effect relationship in this book. The results of this empirical test were clear: sequentially, employment uptrends and downtrends follow, rather than lead, those of consumer spending and the broad economy. In a typical cycle (figure 11-2), the peak rate of growth in employment follows the peak in consumer-spending growth by six to twelve months. At the bottom, the time lag appears to be slightly less, perhaps three to six months.

As always, I am not asking you to accept this as a theoretical assertion; the actual data from 1960 through 2004 are contained in figure 11-3. The consistency of the consumer-spending-leads-employment relationship is so clear in figure 11-3 that it leaves little room for argument: employment is a lagging indicator, and the use of any employment-based case as a primary rationale for forecasting consumer demand and the economy is likely to be flawed.[1]

FIGURE 11-2

Typical cycle: Employment lags real* consumer spending (PCE)

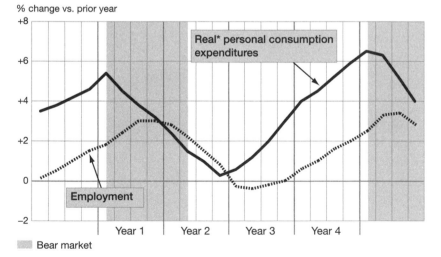

% change vs. prior year

In a typical cycle, U.S. employment moves between year-over-year increases of 2% to 3% at economic peaks, and zero growth or slight declines at economic troughs. Employment advances and slowdowns nearly always follow, rather than lead, those of consumer spending.

*Adjusted for inflation

FIGURE 11-3

Employment's lagging relationship to consumer spending (PCE)

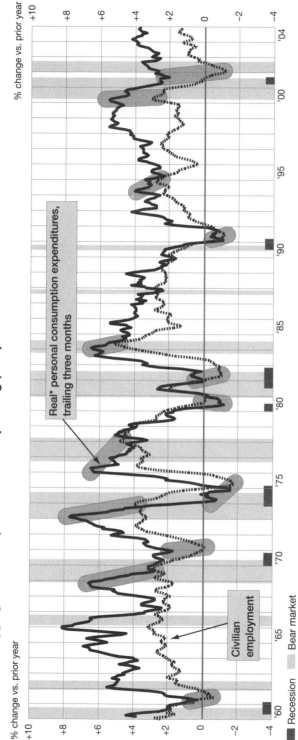

% change vs. prior year

Real* personal consumption expenditures, trailing three months

Civilian employment

■ Recession   ▨ Bear market

*Over many cycles, employment growth has proved to be a **lagging** indicator of consumer spending, typically peaking a year after consumer spending and bottoming six to twelve months after the trough in consumer demand. It is evident in this chart that peaks and troughs in employment follow, rather than lead, those of consumer spending. This suggests that even though employment does have some secondary causality in driving consumer demand, it should never be used as a **primary** indicator in forecasting consumer spending.*

Sources: Employment—Bureau of Labor Statistics; PCE—Bureau of Economic Analysis
*Adjusted for inflation

The Chicken and the Egg

When we put social sensibilities aside, it is not difficult to grasp the logic of employment's lagging role. Workers are almost always fired from jobs after business gets worse and are hired after business rebounds from a downturn. The primary causality, and therefore chronology, is that consumer spending drives employment. Perhaps the best way to characterize the circular, chicken-and-egg relationship between consumer spending and employment is to say that consumer spending, because of its cornerstone role in the economy, represents 75% of the forces driving employment, whereas employment comprises only 30% of the forces driving consumer spending; individuals' real hourly earnings, as we saw in Chapter 10, are a far bigger driver. It is a perfect example of the asymmetrical circular causality described in chapter 6 and diagrammed in figure 11-4.

Thus, even though employment is one of the three key drivers of consumer spending, it is actually a lagging indicator and therefore deceptive for those who see it as forward-looking and predictive. If we understand this, we will gain a much clearer view of economic events,

FIGURE 11-4

Asymmetrical circular causality

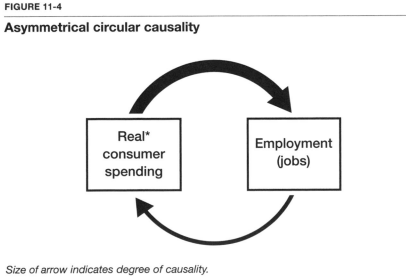

Size of arrow indicates degree of causality.
*Adjusted for inflation

even while others stay positive past economic peaks and pessimistic long after the troughs.

Mastering the Unemployment Rate

Few observers of economic data monitor employment in terms of year-over-year percentage change as shown in figure 11-3; instead, they focus instead on the widely reported *unemployment rate*. This is understandable because of the unemployment rate's significant role as a sensational and emotional indicator that is the subject of evening news broadcasts and newspaper reports. Not surprisingly, the unemployment rate, too, is a lagging indicator.

Again, let's look at a typical cycle. Figure 11-5 shows how the unemployment rate behaves vis-à-vis consumer spending, the front end of

FIGURE 11-5

Typical cycle: The unemployment rate *follows* consumer spending (PCE)

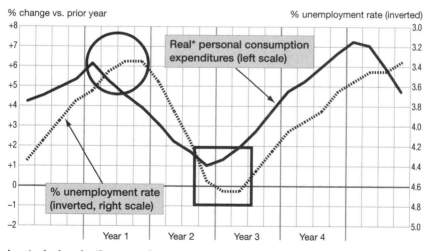

In a typical cycle, the unemployment rate—presented here on the inverted right scale—is most favorable (lowest/inverted) two to four quarters after the peak in consumer-spending growth (see circle), after an economic downtrend is well under way. Conversely, the unemployment rate is usually at its worst (highest/inverted) three to six months after consumer spending and the economy in general have begun to improve (see square).

*Adjusted for inflation

the business cycle. We need to pay extra attention to the format of this chart, which is a bit more complex than our earlier typical-cycle charts due to its two different scales. Growth in consumer spending is measured on the left scale, as in previous charts. However, the scale for the unemployment rate on the right side of the chart is shown inverted, because a low unemployment rate matches up with a strong economy, and a high unemployment rate is consistent with a weak economy. As shown, in each case, the unemployment rate follows the turning point in consumer spending.

Again, this is not theoretical. As with earlier charts, we can find the same proof by viewing the historical data from 1960 to 2004 as presented in figure 11-6. It is not overstating to say that unemployment's lagging role is indisputable: throughout this period, the unemployment rate reached its lowest (i.e., most favorable) levels well after consumer spending had peaked and begun to slow down, and the unemployment rate peaked (lowest in the inverted presentation on the chart) well after consumer spending bottomed and turned upward. In short, the unemployment rate told us not where consumer spending was *headed* but rather where it had *been*.

It is useful to understand the leading role of individuals' real hourly earnings in driving consumer spending and the economy, but ironically it is almost equally helpful to master the lagging character of employment data (and the unemployment rate) in the day-to-day flow of economic news. Why? It's because this empowers us to sit above the fray as many others follow employment data and remain positive far past economic peaks or pessimistic well after economic troughs.

The Unemployment Rate: An Effective Stock Market Tool

Now we will explore one of the most interesting, and potentially lucrative, of all the economic and investment cause-and-effect relationships: that of the stock market and the unemployment rate. We saw in chapter 10 that bear markets usually begin when the year-over-year rate of increase in real consumer spending, at the front end of the business cycle, peaks and begins to slow. And we've seen in figure 11-6 that the lagging unemployment rate typically reaches its most encouraging

FIGURE 11-6

The unemployment rate's lagging relationship to real* consumer spending (PCE)

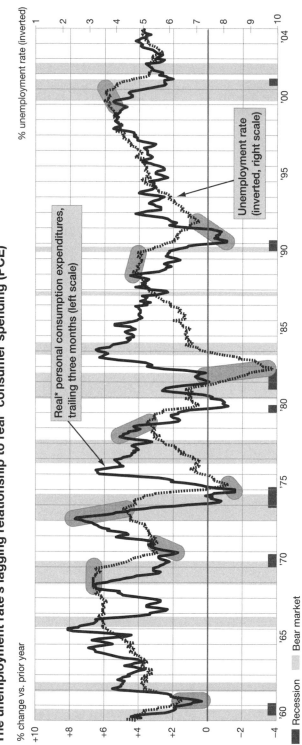

% change vs. prior year

% unemployment rate (inverted)

Real* personal consumption expenditures, trailing three months (left scale)

Unemployment rate (inverted, right scale)

*The unemployment rate (dotted line), shown **inverted** here (see right scale), typically reaches its most favorable (lowest/inverted) level a year or more after the peak in year-over-year consumer-spending growth (solid line). It reaches its most alarming (highest/inverted) levels well after consumer-spending growth has reached its trough and has begun to recover.*

Recession   Bear market

Sources: Unemployment—Bureau of Labor Statistics; PCE—Bureau of Economic Analysis

*Adjusted for inflation

(i.e., its lowest) level well after these peaks in consumer demand have passed, and therefore as much as a year into the economic slowdown and the bear market. In other words, during the first year of an economic slowdown and bear market, for those who fail to perceive its lagging character, a low unemployment rate provides false hope that the recent weakening in the economy will be moderate and short-lived.

Then comes the cruelest twist for the unwary: a year or more into the slowdown, after a good deal of the damage to business and the stock market has already been done, the unemployment rate finally capitulates, following the economic cycle first and begins to turn sharply upward. This event throws a major scare into businesses and investors, who now begin to fear that a further economic unraveling is in store; it happens at exactly the wrong time, when most of the downside in the cycle is, in fact, behind us, and the informed businessperson and investor would be wiser to seek signs of the upturn.

Figure 11-7 shows what this phenomenon looks like in a typical cycle. Please bear with me. This chart has several moving parts:

- Year-over-year growth in consumer spending, denoted by the solid line and measured in the left scale

- The unemployment rate, shown by the dotted line and relating to the inverted scale on the right

- A bear market, denoted by the vertical gray bar

The circle in the chart shows how the bear market typically ends only after a significant increase in the unemployment rate (moving *lower* on the inverted right-hand scale) leads investors to throw in the towel on stocks after having endured most of the bear market.

Again, we can test the thesis by looking at the actual numbers, as they unfolded from 1960 through 2004, in figure 11-8. The circles in this chart mark the unemployment rate at the time each of the bear markets in the vertical gray bars came to an end. We can see clearly that most bear markets ended only after an upturn (remember: moving downward in the chart, given the inverted unemployment scale) of 1 or more percentage points in the unemployment rate sent shivers down the spines of businesspeople, economists, and investors. This scare

FIGURE 11-7

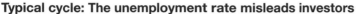

Typical cycle: The unemployment rate misleads investors

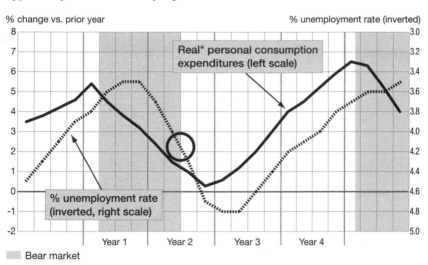

■ Bear market

Bear markets (vertical gray bar) usually begin when consumer-spending growth (solid line) peaks and begins to slow. However, favorable (low) unemployment continues well past this point, encouraging unwary investors to believe in a strong economy as the bear market deepens. Then, a year or more into the bear market, unemployment begins to worsen sharply, leading to belated and misplaced pessimism, setting the stage for the end of the bear market (see circle).

*Adjusted for inflation

almost invariably helps to create the final selling that marks the stock market bottom and the beginning of a new bull market.

When all those around you are distraught for the wrong reason, allowing themselves to be swayed by a lagging indicator such as unemployment, you will be well served by putting that indicator into its proper sequential perspective. At such junctures, investors who have a firm grasp of the unemployment rate's deceptive lagging qualities as an economic indicator might, instead, advantageously purchase stocks. Why? There are two reasons: the more reliable leading indicators of consumer spending and the economy, such as real average hourly wages, are by then already turning upward; and there is comfort to be gained from the fact that misguided pessimism among others based on

FIGURE 11-8

The unemployment trap: Unemployment and the bear market

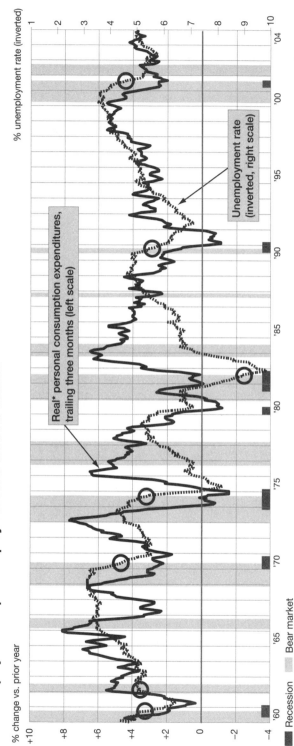

As a substantially lagging indicator, the unemployment rate appears favorable (lowest/inverted) well after consumer-spending growth has peaked and the bear market (vertical gray bars) has been under way for some time. Bear markets typically end when the unemployment rate finally worsens significantly, increasing by 1% or more (see circles). This may reflect a selling crescendo spurred by misplaced fears that higher unemployment is a sign of an even poorer economy ahead. Those who understand unemployment's lagging—and therefore deceptive—nature will avoid this trap.

Sources: Unemployment—Bureau of Labor Statistics; PCE—Bureau of Economic Analysis
*Adjusted for inflation

the unemployment rate and recent business conditions is playing itself out in climactic selling of stocks, minimizing further risk!

The bear market of 2000–2001 was classic in this regard. With the economy having slowed throughout late 2000 and 2001, the S&P 500 as of September 10, 2001—the day before the World Trade Center tragedy—had already fallen 28% from its peak in 2000. The unemployment rate, after fostering false security by remaining under 4.0% throughout 2000, as of August 2001 increased to 4.9%; this rise confirmed investors' worst fears, with few economists or analysts picking up on the improvement in individuals' real hourly earnings that had been occurring throughout 2001.[2] Although the stock market fell another 11% in the three weeks after September 11, it then rallied 21% by early January 2002 as an interim recovery in the economy developed. The recession of 2001 was already over, and, although the stock market did have a secondary downturn in mid- to late 2002, the sharp increase in the unemployment rate of 2001 proved to be the economic straw that broke the back of business and investor sentiment at exactly the wrong time.

A Simple Formula for Consumer Spending

Chapter 9 presented the diagram repeated here in figure 11-9 to describe how (leading) real wages of employed workers multiplied by (lagging) employment—that is, the number of workers—equals (coincident) aggregate wages and salaries, the largest component of personal income.

Given this, if we were simply to add (1) the year-over-year percentage increase in individuals' real hourly earnings and (2) the year-over-year percentage increase in employment, the sum might largely explain—that is, approximate—the year-over-year growth in aggregate real (unit) consumer spending at any given time. The simple formula for this equation is shown in figure 11-10.

Figure 11-11 presents a simple comparison of the *combined* year-over-year increases of real hourly earnings and employment (dotted line) with year-over-year increases in real consumer spending (solid line) from 1965 to the present. From the close fit between these two

FIGURE 11-9

Wage growth, and not employment, is a leading indicator of consumer spending

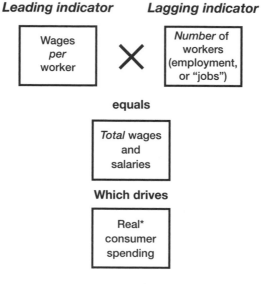

Leading indicator   *Lagging indicator*

Wages per worker   ×   *Number* of workers (employment, or "jobs")

equals

Total wages and salaries

Which drives

Real* consumer spending

*Adjusted for inflation

FIGURE 11-10

Hourly earnings growth and employment growth, combined, produce growth in consumer spending

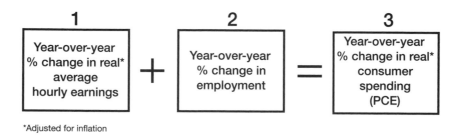

1
Year-over-year % change in real* average hourly earnings

+

2
Year-over-year % change in employment

=

3
Year-over-year % change in real* consumer spending (PCE)

*Adjusted for inflation

150

FIGURE 11-11

Combined year-over-year increases in employment and real* earnings growth approximate growth in real* consumer spending (PCE)

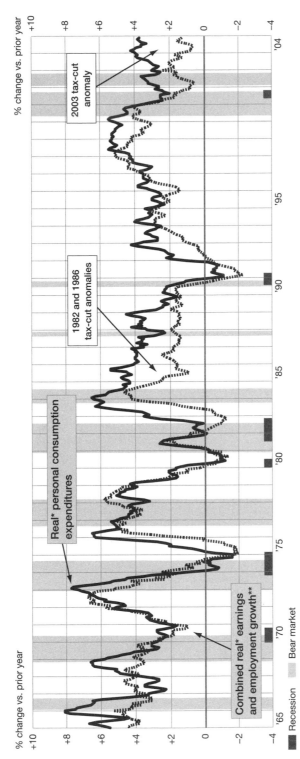

Adding the year-over-year rate of increase in real* average hourly earnings (wages **per** worker) to the year-over-year rate of increase in employment (**number** of workers) approximates the combined effect that these two "engines of consumer demand" have on consumer spending. The sum of these series (dotted line on chart) closely matches the uptrends and downtrends in consumer spending (solid line). This suggests that these two economic inputs—real hourly earnings (leading) and employment rate (lagging)—combine to account for a preponderance of the advances and declines in the consumer-spending cycle. Because real average hourly earnings is a pretax series, however, tax cuts can create anomalies (see 1982 and 1986, and 2003).

Sources: Employment—Bureau of Labor Statistics; PCE—Bureau of Economic Analysis
*Adjusted for inflation
**Year-over-year % increase in real wages plus year-over-year % increase in employment

lines in figure 11-11, it is clear that these two dominant engines of consumer demand, combined, do indeed explain most of the vacillations in year-over-year consumer spending growth over the past four decades. The differences that exist between these two lines are largely attributable to the following factors:

- The real average hourly earnings series is based only on hourly nonsupervisory workers, who represent 64% of total employment in the United States. This leaves 36% of employment unmeasured (although real hourly earnings are probably a satisfactory proxy for the remainder).

- The real average hourly earnings series is measured on a pretax basis. Therefore, any changes in tax law and tax rates alter the series' after-tax effect on consumers' unit purchasing power. Tax cuts in 1982 and 1986 explain much of the difference between the lines in the mid- to late 1980s, as does the 2003 tax cut for the most recent period.

- As employment growth rises and falls, it is difficult to determine the mix of incomes being gained or lost and their statistical impact on year-over-year changes in consumer spending.

- These two series do not take into effect the often significant impact of consumer borrowing, the third major engine of consumer demand. Consumer borrowing is discussed in more detail in appendix A.

These caveats notwithstanding, the fit between the two lines in figure 11-11 over many decades is an impressive and, even for economically astute readers, a surprising one.

In the next three chapters we evaluate the undeniable, but often mysterious, role of interest rates as yet another important driver of consumer spending at the front end of the business cycle.

CHAPTER TWELVE

Interest Rates, Inflation, and the Economic Cycle

The next three chapters move outside the realm of income- and employment-driven consumer spending into the world of interest rates and the role of the Federal Reserve Board in managing them. We are in an unusual period of low interest rates and rapidly increasing borrowing in all three major economic sectors: government, business, and consumer. These chapters look at three related but separate subjects:

- Applying the ROCET approach to determine whether interest rates are an effective leading indicator of consumer spending and therefore the economy at large

- The long-term relationship between interest rates and the stock market, and implications for investors for the rest of this decade

- The role that this decade's rising federal deficits may play in this outlook

Economists, investors, and businesspeople obsessively track and speculate on the activities of the Federal Reserve Board and, since 1987, of Alan Greenspan, its highly respected but often controversial chairman. In the broadcast and print media, the Fed and Greenspan are frequently lauded or blamed for the nation's economic successes and failures, as are the Fed's perceived effects on the stock market. One can hardly overstate the extraordinary mystique accorded by the business and investment communities to "what Alan Greenspan is going to do" at the next Open Market Committee meeting.

"Honey, Alan Greenspan Lowered the Fed Funds Rate!"

Right or wrong, it has been universally accepted that one of the most powerful determinants of economic growth or stasis is Federal Reserve Board action with regard to interest rates. Until a few years ago, this action typically was manifested in the Fed's manipulation of the *discount rate*, the interest rate at which member banks borrow from the Fed. The discount rate over many decades played a major role in determining the level at which major banks set their *prime rate*—that is, the lending rate charged to their best and most creditworthy, or prime, customers. The role of the discount rate, however, has recently been passed to the *federal funds rate*, often shortened to *fed funds rate*.[1]

The Fed's actions with regard to the discount rate or the fed funds rate give rise to a chain of interest-rate effects that are eventually reflected in consumer borrowing of various types. Thus, as shown in figure 12-1, these interest rates are key determinants of certain types of consumer demand.

FIGURE 12-1

Chronology: Interest rates are an additional indicator of consumer spending

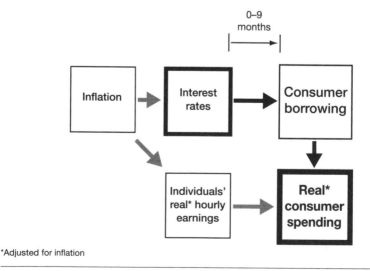

*Adjusted for inflation

"And please let Alan Greenspan accept the things he cannot change, give him the courage to change the things he can and the wisdom to know the difference."

A number of commentators even suggest that the Fed's mere act of lowering or raising the fed funds rate has such a salutary or negative publicity effect through the nation's news media and financial markets that it immediately affects consumer expectations and therefore spending. This is unlikely: none of us personally, as consumers, nor any of our friends or colleagues, has ever read the morning newspaper and exclaimed, "Honey, Alan Greenspan lowered the fed funds rate!" and headed to our nearest electronics store to purchase a television. Nonetheless, as lower or higher interest rates work their way into the cost of consumer borrowing for consumer products and services, there is an unquestionable impact on consumers' propensity to borrow and consume.

Do Interest Rates Really Drive Consumer Spending?

Let's step back and again subject the relationship between Fed policy and consumer spending to our two now familiar tests. First, is the hypothesis logical? Does it make common sense to hypothesize that advances and slowdowns in consumer spending are largely responsive to interest rate changes set in motion by the Fed and, if so, over what time frame? Second, when we chart historic changes in the discount rate (and more recently the fed funds rate) with year-over-year rates of change in consumer spending over a number of decades, can we discern that a clear relationship in fact exists?

The best way to administer the commonsense test is (1) to identify which sectors of consumer demand are sensitive to changes in interest rates and (2) to evaluate the extent to which these and other sectors are demonstrably affected by these changes.

Housing is the first of two major sectors of consumer spending that are, without question, significantly affected by interest-rate changes. According to the Bureau of Economic Analysis, owner-occupied housing accounted for 15% of personal consumption expenditures in 2004. Clearly, mortgage payments—a significant portion of the cost of ongoing home ownership—are tied to interest rates, although in varying degrees, based on (1) whether the mortgage is fixed or variable rate and (2) the proportion (in the overall mix of mortgages) of the most recent fixed-rate mortgages at any given time. (Interest payments on older fixed-rate mortgages are not affected.)

The second major sector of consumer spending affected by interest rates is the purchase of automobiles. In 2004, total motor vehicles and parts, including purchases of new and used automobile and noncommercial light trucks, accounted for 6% of PCE. As seen clearly in recent years, consumers' purchases of automobiles can be greatly impacted by interest rates charged on automobile loans. Interest rates charged by banks and other financial institutions on such loans are likely to rise and fall with interest rates elsewhere in the economy. However, interest rates charged by automobile manufacturers and dealers may fluctuate to a far greater extent, based on sales promotions. This is especially true on the downside, when a slow economy creates panic among car producers to increase demand. (An example are the loans made at 1% and even 0% annual percentage rates by some producers in 2002. In these instances, the automobile manufacturer absorbs the loss on unprofitable interest rates and includes it in the sticker price.) Even in these extreme cases, a low underlying fed funds rate enables low interest charges that would be impossible in a more normal interest-rate environment.

Beyond the housing and automotive sectors, there is the relatively large pool of higher-priced purchases—many of which are *discretionary*, or postponable—such as home furnishings (including furniture, televisions, computers, and other electronics), jewelry, boats and sporting goods, and the like, as well as leisure services such as vacations. In many cases, loans for such goods and services are obtained directly from the retailer or manufacturer or from a bank or other financial institution. Undoubtedly, rising and falling interest rates—ultimately based on increases and decreases in the fed funds rate, the prime rate, and other bellwether interest rates—stimulate or retard, respectively, demand for such goods and services. In 2004 these categories accounted for about 7% of total personal consumption expenditures.

But taken together, the foregoing areas of potentially interest-rate-sensitive consumer spending in 2004 accounted for only about one-third of total PCE.

It would be a stretch to suggest that other large segments of consumer spending have a high degree of sensitivity to interest rates. For example, food at home (about 7% of consumer spending) and eating out (5%) cannot be considered to be interest-rate-sensitive because they are not the subject of consumer borrowing. The same is true of other large nondiscretionary segments of consumer spending, such as medical expenses (17%) and education (2%). Even expenditures on such discretionary categories as clothing, entertainment, and toys, can hardly be considered to be sensitive to interest rates even though they may be paid for with credit cards.

This raises an interesting question: if a great deal of consumer spending in retail venues (stores, restaurants, travel, and places of entertainment) is paid for by consumers using major credit cards such as American Express, MasterCard, and Visa as well as proprietary retailers' cards, would this also not tend to increase the short-term sensitivity of spending to interest rates? Here, the answer is no, for two reasons.

157

First, a great many consumers pay off their credit card debt within a month (essentially using the credit card as a tool of convenience). Second, the annual charges on such credit—usually ranging from 12% to 20% annual percentage rates—are so much higher than the prime rate that the card issuers typically do not change these rates in response to the underlying discount rate or fed funds rate.

What the Charts Show

Now it's time to "go to the videotape," to see whether a predictive relationship in fact exists between interest rates and consumer spending. Despite the above, the answer seems to be yes, even though less than half of consumer spending appears to be sensitive to interest rates.

As you look at Figure 12-2, again I ask you to slow down a bit, take a deep breath, and carefully wrap your mind around the presentation of the data. It is one of the most difficult charts in this book because some of the information is presented in a counterintuitive way. But it is one of the most important in predicting the course of the economy.

Figure 12-2 applies our ROCET method to tracking interest rates. The dotted line shows *year-over-year changes* in (as opposed to absolute levels of) the discount or federal funds rate. This series is compared with year-over-year growth in real consumer spending (the solid line) from 1966 through 2004. So that you can best see their relationship, the scale at the right showing the discount or federal funds rate is inverted to show how declining (moving upward on the chart) interest rates stimulate rising real consumer spending growth and how rising (moving downward on the chart) rates lead to slowing consumer spending. Logically, the greater the year-over-year decline in interest rates, the greater the stimulus to consumer spending; the greater the increase in interest rates, the greater the suppressing effect on consumer spending.[2] Take your time in digesting this chart. Mastering the two lines and their scales will be worth the effort.

Figure 12-2 reveals that year-over-year advances in the discount or fed funds rates (when the dotted line moves *downward* on the inverted scale) have consistently appeared to presage slowdowns in growth in consumer spending (the solid line). Conversely, a declining discount or

FIGURE 12-2

The discount or fed funds rate as a leading indicator of real* consumer spending (PCE)

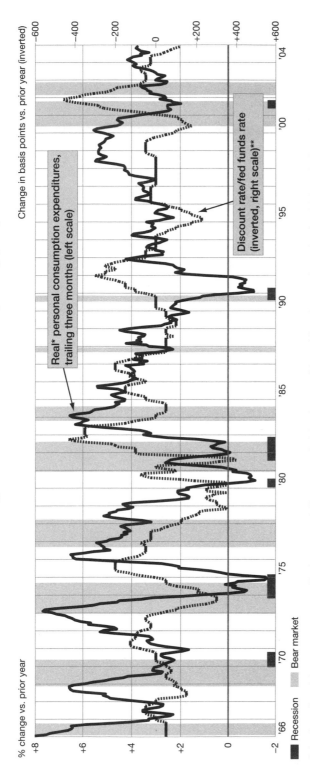

It is clear that rising year-over-year Fed-managed discount or fed funds rates (dotted line, inverted on chart), which make borrowing more costly, have typically led slowing growth in consumer spending (solid line). Conversely, falling discount or fed funds rates, which make borrowing easier, have almost always presaged upturns in consumer spending. The leading/lagging relationship between interest rates and consumer spending is remarkably consistent (with the exception of the mid-1980s to 1990s).

Sources: PCE—Bureau of Economic Analysis; Discount/fed funds rates—Federal Reserve Board

*Adjusted for inflation

**Discount rate until year end 2000, fed funds rate thereafter

fed funds rate (again, inverted so that it moves upward on the chart) appears to have led almost every major advance in consumer spending over the past forty years, often by as much as twelve to eighteen months. The only significant anomaly was in the early 1990s. As a leading indicator of consumer spending, year-over-year rates of change in interest rates—represented here by the discount or fed funds rate—rank close to real average hourly wages in efficacy.

Inflation and Interest Rates: The Key Link

This raises an important question: if, as described earlier, roughly two-thirds of all consumer spending is not financially or even psychologically related to fluctuations in interest rates (or, for that matter, to Federal Reserve Board policy), how do we explain the correlation between consumer spending and the discount or fed funds rate? It is not because the cost of borrowing is higher or lower but rather because the discount rate, or more recently, the fed funds rate, is closely tied to inflation, which directly impacts real earnings (consumers' unit purchasing power) and therefore consumer spending. This is a case like that described in chapter 6: because A drives both B and C, B and C appear to be more directly linked than may actually be the case.

Inflation is the key moving force in real hourly wages (which I have identified as the primary driver of real consumer spending) as well as of interest rates. This creates the impression that interest rates and consumer spending are more closely connected than perhaps they really are. Figure 12-3 is a chronological schematic that shows the relationship between inflation, interest rates, and consumer spending.

In its efforts to manage the economy with stable, moderate growth, the Federal Reserve Board responds to two key influences: (1) the current rate of economic growth and (2) inflation. When either appears to be too high, the Fed applies the brakes by raising the discount or fed funds rate; and when economic growth sags badly (typically accompanied by reduced inflation), the Fed stimulates the economy by lowering the discount or fed funds rate.[3]

Figure 12-4 shows how close the relationship between consumer price inflation (as measured by the PCE deflator) and the discount or

FIGURE 12-3

Inflation drives consumer spending in two ways

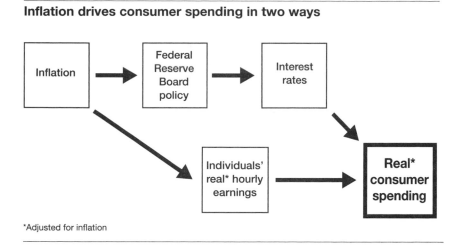

*Adjusted for inflation

fed funds rate (as set by the Fed) has been.[4] Over the past four and a half decades, since 1960, every major uptrend and downtrend in inflation has been paralleled by the Fed's raising and lowering the discount or fed funds rate, typically with a slight lag.

This helps explain why, even though two-thirds of consumer spending arguably is not interest-rate-sensitive, the fed funds rate (as presented in figure 12-2) *appears* to be a reliable predictor of year-over-year changes in consumer spending. It is not the discount or fed funds rate, or interest rates themselves, that is the primary driver of consumer spending. Rather, it is because the hidden hand of inflation—the key driver of interest rates—has a causal effect not only on interest rates but also, more importantly, on consumers' unit purchasing power.

Understanding this interwoven relationship between inflation, consumers' real earnings, interest rates, and consumer spending puts us in a stronger position to forecast consumer spending. We can now appreciate that real earnings and interest rates, with their common dependence on rising or falling inflation, are key drivers to be monitored in predicting consumer demand.

Chapter 13 looks at how this relationship plays out in the stock market. We will also derive important clues about the investment outlook for the second half of this first decade of the new century.

FIGURE 12-4

Inflation drives interest rates

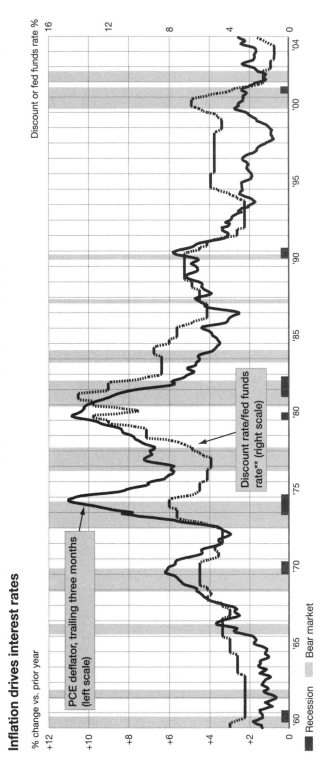

 Recession   Bear market

Consumer price inflation, represented here by year-over-year increases in the personal consumption expenditures deflator (solid line), is closely watched by the Federal Reserve Board. It is clear from this chart that the Fed's setting of the discount or fed funds rate is responsive to changes in the rate of inflation.

Sources: PCE—Bureau of Economic Analysis; Discount/fed funds rates—Federal Reserve Board

*Adjusted for inflation

**Discount rate until year end 2000, fed funds rate thereafter

CHAPTER 13

Interest Rates and the Stock Market

A Concerned Look Forward

If there is a consistent relationship between inflation, interest rates, and consumer spending, then there is necessarily also a multifaceted connection between interest rates and the stock market. Figure 13-1 illustrates this principle. Although it may come as no surprise, you will benefit by applying the ROCET method to tracking interest rates and their effects on the ebb and flow of the stock market.

Interest rates affect the stock market in two important ways: (1) by their effect on the rate of overall economic growth and, consequently, on corporate profits and (2) by their effect on stock valuations (price-earnings ratios).

In chapter 8, we saw that rising and falling rates of growth in consumer spending, at the leading edge of the economic cycle, are the key driver of corporate profit comparisons and therefore of bull and bear stock markets. Because rising and falling interest rates are one of several key inputs to consumer spending, they therefore can also be considered a key determinant of the stock market from the point of view of economic momentum.

Furthermore, it is widely understood that when interest rates rise, the attractiveness of bonds and other income-yielding investments rises, reducing the comparative appeal of stocks' dividends and earnings yields and thereby causing stock valuations (price-earnings ratios) to decline. Conversely, falling interest rates make alternate investments less attractive and cause stocks' price-earnings ratios to rise.

FIGURE 13-1

Chronology: Interest rates as a leading indicator of consumer spending and the stock market

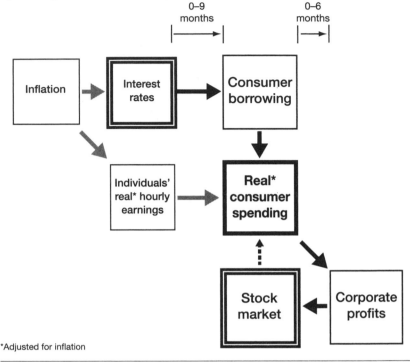

*Adjusted for inflation

This chapter takes a separate look at each of these two issues. Charting them is a significant aid in understanding major stock market trends.

Interest Rates, Consumer Spending, and Bear Markets

Figure 13-2 repeats figure 12-2, which shows that year-over-year changes in the discount rate or fed funds rate (the dotted line, inverted, using the right scale) lead year-over-year changes in unit consumer spending (real PCE; shown in the solid line, using the left scale). But here, we concentrate specifically on the consequent connection between interest-rate changes and stock market movements over more than four decades.

FIGURE 13-2

Rising discount/fed funds rates: A harbinger of bear markets

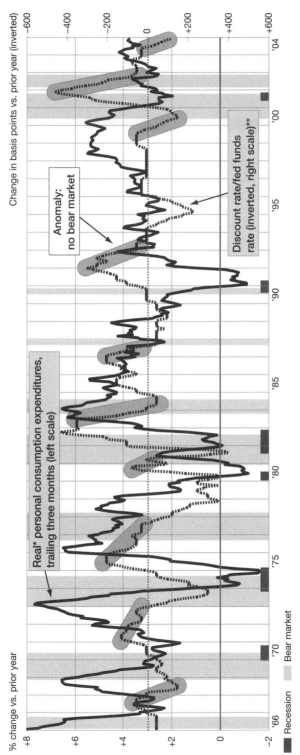

% change vs. prior year

Change in basis points vs. prior year (inverted)

Anomaly:
no bear market

Discount rate/fed funds
rate (inverted, right scale)**

Real* personal consumption expenditures,
trailing three months (left scale)

Recession   Bear market

We saw in chapter 8 that bear markets typically begin when the year-over-year rate of growth in consumer spending (solid line) peaks and begins to fall. As shown in the shaded ovals, rising interest rates (dotted line, inverted, right scale), because they have been effective leading indicators of consumer-spending slowdowns, also are an effective indicator of approaching bear markets (vertical gray bars).

Sources: PCE—Bureau of Economic Analysis; Discount/fed funds Rate—Federal Reserve Board

*Adjusted for inflation

**Discount rate until year end 2000, fed funds rate thereafter

In this case, I have used shaded ovals to highlight those instances over the past four and a half decades in which the year-over-year rate of change in the discount rate or fed funds rate began to increase sharply (remember: *declining* on the inverted scale in this chart): in 1967–1968, 1971–1972, 1975–1976, 1980–1981, 1983, 1987, 1999–2000, and 2002. In each instance in figure 13-2, the onset of a higher discount or fed funds rate was the harbinger of a coming downturn in the rate of growth in consumer spending (followed by the economy in general) and a clear forerunner of a stock market decline, as denoted in the vertical gray bars. The only anomaly was in 1992–1993, when the year-over-year discount or fed funds rate comparison rose and a bear market did not ensue. It is a good bet that, when the fed funds rate is increasing year-over-year at a rising pace for six months or more, a difficult stock market is at hand. As I write in early 2005, the steady march of higher interest rates throughout 2004 and into 2005 appears to have been sending such a signal.

Interestingly, falling interest rates are somewhat less reliable in pointing the way to bull markets, predicting stock market advances sufficiently early in perhaps only half of the instances.

Stock Valuations: Where Interest Rates Go . . .

But interest rates have an even more direct effect on stock prices. Even casual observers of the stock market recognize that there is an inverse relationship between interest rates and stock valuations. We typically value stocks based on their price-earnings ratios: stock A selling at $40 per share with earnings per share of $2.00 has a price-earnings ratio of 20 times. But another, equally important, way to look at this is that stock A's *earnings yield*—its earnings per share as a percentage of the stock price—is 5.0%. This earnings yield represents one measure of theoretical return to the owner of the stock, just as interest received is the key measure of return to bondholders.

Clearly, if interest rates on bonds and other financial instruments that compete with stocks as investments were to, say, double. Stock A's earnings yield, to be competitive, would also have to roughly double, to 10%. This would mean that in order for the earnings yield to stay competitive, the floor price would have to fall by about 50% to $20 per share.

Essentially, therefore, when interest rates rise significantly over longer periods of time, price-earnings valuations on stocks fall commensurately. This means that despite growing profits, stock prices may advance only minimally during such periods as declines in price-earnings valuations offset growth in earnings.

This is exactly what happened between the early 1960s and 1981–1982, when the 10-year Treasury yield (considered a cornerstone interest rate in the economy) rose from only 4% to an unprecedented 14% (see figure 13-3). During this twenty-one-year period, the following occurred:

- The secular rise in interest rates resulted in increasingly depressed price-earnings valuations on stocks.

- The S&P 500 stock price index over 21 years rose only 81%, from a 1961 average of 66.27 to a 1982 average of 119.71. This represented an average annual return (excluding dividends) of only 2.9%.

- The frequency and duration of bear markets (the vertical gray bars in figure 13-3) were significant, with bear markets occurring every 2½ to 4 years and typically lasting one year or longer.

In contrast, the 10-year Treasury yield between 1982 and 2003 fell from over 14% to approximately 4%. During this twenty-one-year period, the following occurred:

- Declining interest rates resulted in a long-range improvement in price-earning valuations of stocks.

- The S&P 500 rose a stunning 706%, or an annual average of 10.5%.

- Bear markets were far less frequent and of shorter duration.

Clearly, the underlying upward or downward trend of interest rates over longer periods makes a major difference in stock market returns to investors.

FIGURE 13-3

Long-term interest-rate changes and the stock market

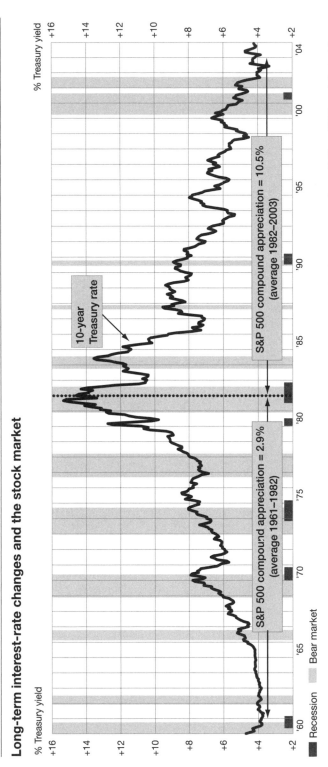

Because of the inverse relationship between interest rates and stocks' price-earnings ratios, rising interest rates from 1960 to 1982 contributed to a compound annual appreciation of only 2.9% in the S&P 500 Index. Conversely, falling interest rates from 1982 to 2003 were a major long-term stimulus to the stock market, helping produce compound annual growth in the S&P 500 of 10.5%. Note that bear markets from 1960 to 1982 were more frequent and longer, whereas from 1982 to 2003 they were less frequent and shorter in duration.

Sources: PCE—Bureau of Economic Analysis; Treasury rate—Federal Reserve Board

A Problematic Outlook

However, investors in this first decade of the new millennium face a daunting prospect with regard to interest rates and their likely effect on stock valuations over the coming decade. Three bellwether interest rates—the discount rate (in recent years, the fed funds rate), the prime rate, and the 10-year Treasury yield—are close to their lowest level in more than forty years (see table 13-1).

The fed funds rate—the interest rate that to a large extent acts as a foundation for all other interest rates up the line—bottomed at only 0.98% in 2003 and has risen to 2.8% at this writing. One conclusion appears to be unavoidable: the short-term and long-term potential for a further lowering of this base interest rate is minimal; if interest rates change significantly, the only prospect is an increase. Today's low interest rates are reflected in price-earnings ratios that are high by historic standards and therefore vulnerable.[1]

Rising interest rates are more likely to hinder stock market and valuation performance, perhaps significantly, in the years ahead. Offsetting stimuli for a rising stock market will have to come from other quarters—for example, solid economic growth resulting in a strong increase in corporate profits—to produce longer-term gains in equity prices. Clearly, the stock market of the middle and late part of this decade is facing an inherent interest-rate disadvantage.

In his recent book *Bull's Eye Investing* (John Wiley & Sons, 2004), John Mauldin, with impressive clarity, details the long history of stock

TABLE 13-1

Three bellwether interest rates

Interest rate	1961 average	1982 average	2003 average	As of 4/15/05
Discount/fed funds rate*	3.0%	11.0%	1.1%	2.8%
Prime rate	4.5	14.9	4.1	5.8
10-year Treasury yield	3.9	13.0	4.0	4.5

*Discount rate in 1961 and 1982; fed funds rate in 2003 and 2005

market cycles and the relationship between interest rates, price-earnings ratios, and stock prices. Using an analysis developed by Jeremy Grantham, founder of Grantham, Mayo, Van Otterloo Advisors, a prominent Boston investment management firm, Mauldin outlined historic ten-year stock market returns based on quintiles ranging from highest to lowest overall stock market price-earnings ratios at the beginning of the ten-year periods. Not surprisingly, he found that ten-year returns were by far the lowest in periods that began in years with the highest price-earnings ratios, such as those of 2004 and 2005.

Quite simply, the prospect for rising interest rates from the low base of 2004 and 2005 poses a significant risk to stock market performance over the second half of this decade. Investors, therefore, would do well to approach this period with some caution vis-à-vis the more favorable interest-rate environment that characterized the previous two decades.

In chapter 14, we will see how the growing federal deficit may very well exacerbate potential interest-rate increases faced by businesses and investors in the years ahead.

The Link Between Federal Deficits and Interest Rates

It has been my purpose throughout this book to provide a common-sense empirical methodology for business managers, investors, and others to use in tracking economic relationships as a means of forecasting. I have not offered specific conclusions on key economic policy issues. However, one hotly argued policy debate fits nicely into the ROCET approach of assessing economic cause and effect: whether fluctuations in the federal deficit, and the federal government borrowing that results from them, have a meaningful effect on interest rates.

This debate has been intense since 2002 because of growing concern that the federal deficit, which appears certain to reach record levels during the middle years of the first decade of the 2000s, will drive interest rates sharply higher over the next several years. Those who favor major tax cuts (primarily Republicans), with their shorter-term effects of driving the federal deficit higher, argue (not surprisingly) that there is little proof that federal government borrowing is the, or a, key driving force in interest rates. In contrast, those who oppose large-scale tax cuts (primarily Democrats) see large federal deficits not only strangling the federal government's spending power and stifling social programs, but also as the harbinger of higher interest rates that will surely stifle the economic growth that the tax cuts were designed to stimulate.

By taking a charted look at annual borrowing increases vis-à-vis interest rates over the past four and a half decades, we can gain some insight into this debate. Three questions lie at its heart:

- If interest rates are the price of money, does sharply higher federal government demand for capital strain the debt market's ability to supply it, leading to higher interest rates?

- In this process, does new federal government debt, being the highest quality and most negotiable of all debt forms, crowd out other debt issuers, with an aggravating effect on nongovernment rates of interest?

- Or are too many other factors at work even to attribute fluctuating interest rates to overall changes in borrowing levels?

The press commentary surrounding this debate has been largely anecdotal and devoid of statistics. Papers in economic journals have tracked historical interest-rate data against a number of inputs, including federal government borrowing, using complex mathematical formulas.[1] However, both the methods and the conclusions have failed to gain traction with business or investor audiences. The question is therefore still unresolved.

In assessing the issue of a possible relationship between the federal deficit and interest rates, we must resist the temptation to compare past years' federal deficits alone with changes in interest rates. Interest rates for the economy reflect the demand for money for the economy as a whole, and not just the federal government's demand for capital via federal debt. It is, therefore, illogical to expect interest rates to reflect only federal government borrowing without taking into consideration the borrowing (capital needs) of state and local government, individuals, and corporations. If we are to test the thesis that interest rates, as the price of (borrowed) money, respond to the levels of new borrowing, we must take into account the total demand for borrowed funds by all significant borrowers combined: the federal government, state and local governments, individuals, and businesses.

Figure 14-1 provides a useful perspective on the composition of total domestic nonfinancial debt.[2] At the end of 2004, federal government debt represented only 18% of all total domestic nonfinancial debt. This proportion was down significantly from 23% and 27% at the end of 1990 and 1994, respectively, a bloated level of federal debt that followed the increase in government deficits resulting from tax cuts in the mid- and late 1980s. State and local governments accounted for

FIGURE 14-1

Composition of total domestic nonfinancial debt, 2004

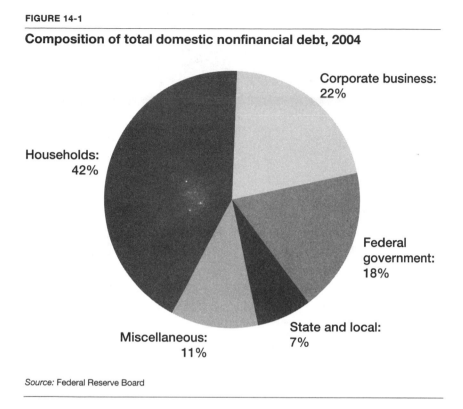

Corporate business: 22%

Households: 42%

Federal government: 18%

Miscellaneous: 11%

State and local: 7%

Source: Federal Reserve Board

another 7%, with total government debt thus being 25% of all national debt. Debt held by households (individuals) was the largest component, accounting for 42%, and corporate business debt represented 22%.[3] Clearly, the federal government is only one among several large borrowers seeking funds in the debt markets.

The Smoking Gun in Deficits and Interest Rates

Although there is little evidence that federal government debt alone has a defining effect on interest rates, the rate of growth in total domestic nonfinancial debt—*all* national debt—clearly does.

Figure 14-2 traces year-over-year percentage increases in total domestic nonfinancial debt vis-à-vis the prime rate from 1960 through 2004, and a convincing causal relationship emerges: virtually every uptrend and downtrend in the rate of growth in total borrowing in the economy

FIGURE 14-2

Increases in total domestic nonfinancial debt drive the prime rate

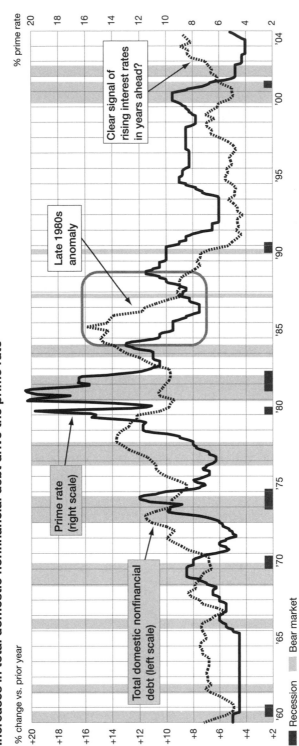

Over most of the 40-plus years since 1960, rising year-over-year increases in total domestic nonfinancial debt (dotted line) have led—typically with a one- to three-year lag—to higher interest rates, represented here by the prime rate (solid line). Conversely, slowing growth in total domestic nonfinancial debt has usually resulted—with a similar lag—in lower interest rates. One notable anomaly in this relationship was the mid- to late 1980s.

If this relationship holds true in the future, the sharp increase in total domestic nonfinancial debt that resulted in part from the growing federal deficit of the mid-2000s seems almost certain to lead to higher interest rates in the current decade.

Source: Federal Reserve Board

from 1960 to the early 2000s—with the exception of the period from 1985 to 1988—appears to have precipitated, within one to three years, a rise or fall, respectively, in the prime rate. The chart credibly suggests that accelerations and decelerations in the combined growth of federal government, state and local government, corporate, and individual debt indeed usually determine the direction of interest rates.

Again, as we've seen in numerous other charted cause-and-effect relationships in this book, the ROCET method—charting the year-over-year *rate of change* in the relevant series—reveals predictive qualities in the relationship that might otherwise be missed.

Figure 14-3 presents the same analysis with regard to year-over-year changes in total domestic nonfinancial debt vis-à-vis uptrends and downtrends in the interest rate on 10-year Treasury bonds. (This interest rate is driven by market forces as much as by the Federal Reserve's historic setting of the discount rate or the fed funds rate.)

Clearly, we should not simply overlook the significant 1985–1988 anomaly in the relationship between the rate of growth in total domestic nonfinancial debt and interest rates. Although U.S. interest rates typically are less subject to external forces due to the sheer size of the economy, vacillations in our balance of payments, as other nations purchase or sell U.S. debt, can have an effect. As with most of the charts throughout this book, the predictive relationship between increases in our total national debt and the direction of interest rates, though not perfect, is persuasive.

2005–2010: Higher Interest Rates Lie Ahead

Both sides in the current debate over deficits and their relationship to interest rates are right to some extent. Those who argue that federal deficits alone are not the sole determining factor in the direction of interest rates can rightly assert that the federal government is only one of several issuers whose combined growth in borrowing determines the direction of interest rates. However, opponents of massive ongoing tax cuts appear to have an even stronger case. When the federal government increases its borrowing at an unusually rapid pace, its effect on the increase in total domestic nonfinancial debt is likely sufficient to

FIGURE 14-3

Increases in total domestic nonfinancial debt drive the 10-year Treasury yield

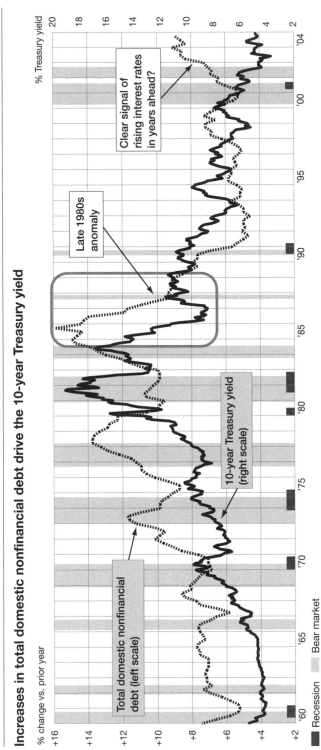

With modest variations, the same cause-and-effect relationship between growth in total domestic nonfinancial debt and the Prime Rate shown in figure 14-2 holds true here with the 10-year Treasury rate. It is also driven by financial market forces, primarily supply and demand for U.S. government debt.

Source: Federal Reserve Board

drive interest rates higher. That appears to be the likely outcome in this decade.

The current situation is a case in point. As outlined in table 14-1, total domestic nonfinancial debt in 2000 increased only 4.9% over the prior year, at a time when the federal government was running a surplus sufficient to offset higher household and corporate borrowing. However, federal borrowing swelled to well over $350 billion in 2003 and 2004, and is probably headed higher in 2005 and beyond.

Furthermore, in part because of the 2003 federal tax cuts, state and local governments appear to be on the verge of their greatest need for debt financing in history. As table 14-1 indicates, a combined increase in federal, state, and local borrowing to $450 billion or more ($350 to $400 billion federal, and $100 to $120 billion state and local), added to a recent norm of over $1.7 trillion in borrowing by corporations, individuals, and miscellaneous, is pushing the year-over-year rate of growth in total domestic nonfinancial debt to 8% or more, a rate not experienced

TABLE 14-1

Increases in total domestic nonfinancial debt, by component, 2000–2004

(Dollar amounts in billions)	2000	2001	2002	2003	2004
Total domestic nonfinancial debt (beginning of year)	**17,269.9**	**18,118.5**	**19,237.1**	**20,554.7**	**22,249.5**
Increase vs. prior year					
Federal government	(295.9)	(5.6)	257.6	396.0	362.6
State and local government	15.5	105.8	143.9	117.8	115.4
Total government	**(280.4)**	**100.2**	**401.4**	**513.8**	**478.0**
Household	570.8	622.9	734.1	863.8	1,032.7
Corporate business	354.4	228.6	28.9	169.8	240.1
Nonfarm, Noncorporate	192.9	156.4	145.3	151.2	168.2
Farm business	10.9	10.5	7.8	7.7	12.3
Total private	**1,129.0**	**1,018.4**	**916.2**	**1,192.5**	**1,453.2**
Total domestic nonfinancial debt	**848.6**	**1,118.6**	**1,317.6**	**1,706.3**	**1,931.2**
Total domestic nonfinancial debt (end of year)	**18,118.5**	**19,237.1**	**20,554.7**	**22,261.0**	**24,180.7**
% increase vs. prior year	**4.9%**	**6.2%**	**6.8%**	**8.3%**	**8.7%**

since the late 1980s. This is reflected in the sharp upturn in year-over-year rate of growth in total domestic nonfinancial debt reflected in figures 14-2 and 14-3.

The upward trajectory of year-over-year increases in total debt during the past two years, if continued into the future, represents a classic divergent lead/lag pattern (see chapter 6) vis-à-vis recent record low interest rates; thus, a further major advance in interest rates is indicated. With the latest federal funds rate still less than 3% as of early 2005, the Federal Reserve Board has limited tools with which to offset an interest-rate rise if the demand for borrowed funds increases sharply. An anomaly of the mid-1980s variety is possible, but the consistent predictive relationship in figures 14-2 and 14-3 makes it a strong bet that interest rates in the next few years are headed higher, with federal-deficit-driven borrowing a major contributing factor. Clearly, the potential effect on overall economic growth and stock market valuations is problematic.

Part III has explored how certain economic data series can be used effectively to forecast uptrends and downtrends in consumer demand, giving us an advantage in predicting the course of the economy and the stock market at large. Of nearly equal importance, we have seen which indicators lag and mislead and should therefore be avoided. Part IV looks at how we can employ this methodology and some of these key economic cause-and-effect relationships to improve forecasting of the business cycle for individual industries and even companies.

IV

From Theory to Practice

*Applying the Charting Discipline
to Your Own Forecasting*

CHAPTER 15

Forecasting for Your Own
Industry or Company

In parts II and III, we established that there are consistent, repeating cause-and-effect macroeconomic relationships that exist between three major sectors of the economy: consumer spending, manufacturing (industrial production), and capital spending (plant and equipment). We also learned that there are generally reliable leading indicators of primary uptrends, downtrends, and turning points in consumer spending itself. Therefore, forecasting consumer spending can help businesses and investors see around economic corners.

Understanding this chain of economic cause and effect can, I believe, help businesses and investors to predict macroeconomic uptrends and downtrends, or at least understand them better as they occur rather than belatedly react to them.

Is Forecasting at the Micro Level a Realistic Prospect?

This raises an important issue. For business executives working or investing in specific industries, is it possible to drill down beneath the macroeconomic surface and use the analytical charting techniques we have explored at the macroeconomic level to forecast the demand cycle in economic subsectors or individual industries? For example, might a manufacturer of machine tools—metal stamping and cutting equipment—in the capital-spending sector forecast its sales by charting, as a leading indicator, consumer spending (personal consumption expenditures) on durable goods or, more specifically, sales in retail stores of metal-intensive products, such as automobiles and appliances? Or might a manufacturer of cardboard boxes chart consumer spending on durable and nondurable goods combined—products typically shipped in boxes—as a leading indicator of demand for cardboard box production?

Analysts and investors also need to forecast more accurately the business cycle trends for specific industries. A good deal of the outperformance or underperformance of individual stocks in any given year is tied to those stocks' industry groups' *relative* performance within the economy at any given stage of the cycle. In other words, for much of the time, the stock performance of, say, JC Penney or DuPont relative to the market will depend on the performance within a given period of the retailing or chemical industries, respectively, vis-à-vis other economic sectors.

Each company, depending on whether it is in the consumer spending, manufacturing, or capital spending sector of the economy, has a predictable position within the sequence of each cyclical uptrend or downtrend. It is vital, therefore, for analysts and portfolio managers at brokerage houses and institutional investment firms to, in addition to evaluating individual company prospects, forthrightly recommend owning or avoiding specific industries based on these sequences during economic and stock market cycles. This analysis requires an attempt to get ahead of the curve in identifying major cyclical uptrends and downtrends for entire industries before these trends are perceived by the stock market as a whole. With hundreds—indeed thousands—of brokerage and money-management firms attempting to do this, it is difficult to gain an edge.

One important additional advantage of enhanced industry-specific cyclical timing should not be overlooked. Even when it is not possible to forecast an industry's ups and downs before they actually occur, any insights gained, via clear charting, into the dimension (degree of advances and declines) and duration of historic cycles for the industry will prove exceptionally valuable. Most business managers and investors have yet to master even an empirical grasp of how several decades of past economic cycles have played out in their own industries.

Which Industries Lend Themselves to This Approach?

At the outset, we must recognize that not all industries lend themselves to cyclical analysis. Again, as in all economic relationships depicted throughout this book, common sense must be our guide in determining which industries are suited and which are not.

- Some industries are far more subject to unpredictable domestic and international political events than to cyclical economic inputs. These include defense (manufacturers of military aircraft, munitions, etc.) and energy (international oil companies such as Shell and ExxonMobil). For such companies, armed conflicts or interruptions of supply abroad may have far greater effects on company fortunes over a multiyear period than does demand in the United States.

- Some of the largest industries serving consumers' nondiscretionary social needs—such as health care, pharmaceuticals, and education—are inherently noncyclical. They are driven more by demographics, consumer needs that aren't postponable, and, to a certain extent, changes in legislation and government programs. Such industries are not to a meaningful degree captive to cyclical economic variables.

- Other industries, including several in the consumer-spending category, are subject to some extent to economic variables but are driven to a much greater extent by new fashions or entertainment-related trends, or "hits." These include, to varying degrees, such industries as women's apparel, athletic footwear, and entertainment companies (movies, recorded music, television).

- Still other industries are on such rapid growth curves that, during their highest-growth phases, the effect of economic cycles is not visible on their operating results. Such industries are often technology-based. Examples are computers and software during the late 1980s through mid-1990s and the biotechnology sector during the past decade.

Nevertheless, a great many industries—ranging from finished-product businesses (such as major appliances or office furniture) to basic commodity industries (such as steel and chemicals)—are subject to cyclical economic forces and are therefore good subjects for the forecasting methodologies described here. In all instances, the application of good old-fashioned common sense, combined with a detective mentality, will take us a long way in applying our chart-based forecasting methodology to broad industrial sectors (e.g., retail sales in general), specific segments (e.g., home improvement retailers), or even individual companies (e.g., The Home Depot, Lowe's).

Why Aren't Companies Themselves Forecasting More?

Few of the major industrial companies in the United States have serious in-house economic forecasting disciplines. Instead, most rely on the anecdotal inputs described in chapter 1. An important question emerges here: with all the statistical material available, why don't more of these companies (not to mention the professional investment analysts who follow them) attempt to develop the charting-based, predictive disciplines I am suggesting?

The answer seems clear: the historic paucity of credible macro-economic forecasts—and, equally important, forecasting disciplines—has generated an atmosphere of forecasting apathy among companies and investors. In short, the lack of reliable and comprehensible forecasting at the macro level has sapped the analytical will of those with the most to gain at the micro level.

It is time for companies to return to the drawing board and establish reasonably simple forecasting disciplines, such as those set forth in this book, to reeducate themselves regarding the forecasting possibilities. As with the macroeconomic series reviewed in parts II and III, the charting process must emanate from, and stand the test of, two key questions:

- Is a possible predictive relationship between a chosen economic data series and the target industry's or company's sales rooted in common sense? Intuitively, might one reasonably expect a cause-and-effect relationship to exist?

- After the two series have been charted over repeated past economic cycles, is a predictive relationship clear (albeit with occasional imperfections) to the chart reader's eye?

To test such assumptions, it is vital to adhere to the key charting disciplines reviewed in chapter 5:

- Chart on a year-over-year basis to avoid the seasonal adjustment and quarter-to-quarter volatility, or noise, that can obscure valid underlying trends.

- Where necessary, present data on a monthly rolling "trailing-three-months" basis rather than individual-month basis. This practice also reduces excess noise and enhances chart-reading clarity.

- If the two series being charted have widely different amplitudes (degrees of change), use two scales (right and left) to better compare the two lines.

- Provide horizontal grid lines to facilitate the perception of rates of change, and vertical grid lines to clarify time periods.

- Provide sufficient space to accommodate visually the several decades of data encompassing a sufficient number of cycles.

Such seemingly small details are important in ensuring the clarity that is essential to determining whether sought-after long-term cause-and-effect relationships between two series indeed exist. It is easy to do this by using data-gathering services and data-manipulation and visual tools found in widely available computer software. Companies and investors have no excuse for not pursuing this technique.

Microeconomic Detective Work: Two Case Studies

With these chart-enhancing rules in mind, we're ready to embark on the intellectually gratifying and potentially rewarding task of determining (1) what series we wish to forecast (the industry or company sales in need of forecasting) and (2) what series we can use most effectively as a leading indicator.

Let's put ourselves in the shoes of Mary, a planner for the plastics division of Apex Chemicals, who has been asked to develop a discipline for forecasting demand for her division's products. In the Federal Reserve Board's annual and monthly tabulation of industrial production, Mary might select a target series that most closely matches her division's output—perhaps "chemical production" or, better, the "plastics materials and resin" subcategory.[1]

With plastics in broad use throughout consumer spending and the economy in general, Mary, using the ROCET approach, might reasonably chart year-over-year changes in real (unit) consumer spending on all durable and nondurable goods (the driver of product demand at the front end of the economic cycle) versus the selected plastics materials and resin industrial production series, as shown in figure 15-1. And, indeed, a clear relationship emerges: figure 15-1 shows that, for more than forty years, year-over-year rates of change in plastics materials and resin production are usually coincident with, or sometimes lagging, consumer spending, and they exhibit the same inventory-driven volatility as most production series (note the larger right-hand scale).

Mary now has, in a single chart, an empirical look at her industry's typical cyclical behavior in economic cycles over the past forty-plus years. Although executives at Apex Chemicals probably already had an intuitive sense of the volatility of their plastics and resin business over the years, figure 15-1 likely provides an illuminating and empirical grasp of their business sector's behavior vis-à-vis the macro economy over many years.

Importantly, Mary's forecasting prospects might be enhanced by using the historic sales data of Apex Chemicals itself, either total company sales or sales by division or category (the latter details are probably not available to those outside the company).

Another case: John is a senior planner at the Amalgamated Carpet Company and has been assigned to forecast the outlook for sales of carpeting. Knowing that the greatest single stimulus to demand for carpeting is people moving into new homes, John obtains an economic series known as "housing turnover." This is the sum of (1) sales of new homes, as reported monthly by the Census Bureau, and (2) sales of existing one-family homes, as reported monthly by the National Association of Realtors.[2] This series essentially represents the number of

FIGURE 15-1

Consumer spending and industrial production of plastics materials and resin

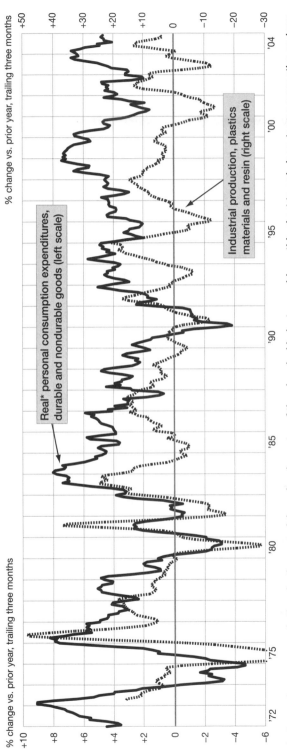

% change vs. prior year, trailing three months

% change vs. prior year, trailing three months

Real* personal consumption expenditures, durable and nondurable goods (left scale)

Industrial production, plastics materials and resin (right scale)

A planner in a company in the plastics materials and resin sector of the chemical industry could use this chart to gain long-term perspective on how cyclical changes in the rate of growth of consumer spending on durable and nondurable good affect this sector's demand and manufacturing cycle. Note the much greater range of the right-hand scale. Clearly, moderate uptrends and downtrends in consumer spending (solid line, left scale) result—via the swelling and ebbing inventories in distribution pipelines—in much greater swings in the production of plastics materials and resin (dotted line, right scale).

Sources: PCE—Bureau of Economic Analysis; Industrial production—Federal Reserve Board
*Adjusted for inflation

homes, new and previously occupied, into which new families are moving. Because new floor coverings are needed in almost all such moves, common sense suggests this indicator as a possibly important leading indicator of demand for new carpeting.

Figure 15-2 tracks year-over-year percentage changes in housing turnover (note: solid line, left scale) with sales of floor-covering stores (dotted line), which is part of the monthly retail sales series reported by the Department of Commerce.

This chart presents a convincing leading-indicator relationship: up-trends, downtrends, and turning points in housing turnover are followed, twelve to eighteen months later, by similar trends in the sales of floor coverings. For an even more relevant picture, John might realistically plot Amalgamated Carpet's own order rates or sales vis-à-vis housing turnover. John could even pursue this analysis on a geographic basis: if Amalgamated Carpet operated primarily in the southeast portion of the United States, John could obtain housing turnover data for the Southeast as his leading indicator.

FIGURE 15-2

Housing turnover leads sales of floor-covering stores

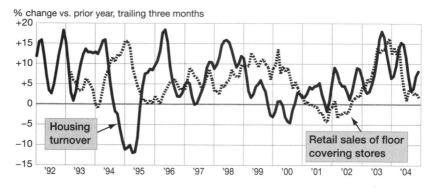

% change vs. prior year, trailing three months

Economic detective work: because most carpeting must be customized, almost every move into a new home generates demand for the product. Therefore, a planner for a carpeting retailer can use housing turnover—the number of households moving into new and previously occupied homes—as a valuable leading indicator. This chart shows that year-over-year upturns and downtrends in housing turnover (solid line) usually lead carpet demand at retail (dotted line) by about six to eighteen months. Note: The lead time in recent years has been somewhat shorter.

Sources: Housing turnover—National Association of Realtors, U.S. Census Bureau;
Retail sales—U.S. Census Bureau

This example also tells us that, in searching for leading indicators, executives in and analysts of specific industries need not feel constrained solely to macro government data. Hundreds of trade associations—such as the National Board of Realtors, the American Machine Tool Distributors' Association, and the Association of Home Appliance Manufacturers—as well as quasi-governmental bodies release monthly and quarterly data that may be useful as leading indicators (causes) of individual industry sales trends (effects). The opportunities for developing a disciplined, empirical approach are significant.

Most businesspeople will recognize that little organized thought or effort is given to forecasting demand trends in their lines of business. Similarly, investors will note the paucity of careful investigation, based on comprehensible and historical statistical cause and effect, in analysts' reports. However, the opportunities for such analysis are virtually endless, suggesting great opportunities for businesspeople and analysts who are industrious enough to put these tools to use.

Start with Deductive Reasoning, Finish with a Chart

Mary's and John's examples show that good results are likely if the forecaster is willing to engage in a bit of deductive reasoning. Housing turnover—the number of single-family homes changing hands—proved itself (in figure 15-2) to be an excellent leading indicator of year-over-year carpeting demand; it is also, in general, a solid predictor for many home-related consumer goods. However, forecasters of home décor and improvement products might intuit that the statistical effect of homes changing hands varies considerably based on the nature of the home-related product. For example, in almost all instances when a single-family home changes hands, the new occupants might be expected to purchase new carpeting or draperies and other window coverings. These products require a certain degree of customization and are seldom brought from a previous home. Thus, one might expect housing turnover to be an excellent leading indicator for these products, as it proved to be for carpeting. On the other hand, purchasers of a new home are far more likely to bring with them home furnishings such as chinaware, glassware, and silverware. These home categories would thus be less subject to the housing-turnover cycle and more likely to be tied to leading indicators that affect consumer spending in general.

Simple deductive reasoning goes a long way in giving us a starting point for developing a charted historical cause-and-effect relationship. If the relationship can be shown visually to exist, it may prove rewarding in predicting the business demand cycles for a specific industry or even the sales of an individual company.

Consumer Spending and Retail Sales

In my role as retail-industry analyst for more than twenty years at Goldman Sachs, one of my key responsibilities was to attempt to forecast the direction of sales in U.S. retail stores. Would retail sales accelerate, providing a favorable backdrop for the performance of stocks such as Wal-Mart, Federated Department Stores, and Gap, or was the sales outlook bleak, with a likely opposite effect?

Early in my analytical career, I learned that I could not rely on economists' forecasts of consumer spending and retail sales. Often, these forecasts were too late in spotting economic turning points to be useful in taking advantage of stock market moves, which discount, in advance, changing economic directions. By the time higher-than-expected or lower-than-expected sales or profits were reported, or even hinted at, by the companies, stock prices already amply reflected the new direction.

Total retail sales in 2004, as compiled by the Department of Commerce, were $3.5 trillion, representing 43% of all consumer spending (personal consumption expenditures) of $8.2 trillion. This number includes sales in retail outlets of all types, including not only the conventional retail stores where we all shop regularly—such as supermarkets, department stores, discount stores, apparel stores, and hard-goods specialty stores—but also automotive dealerships, restaurants and bars, travel agencies, and other businesses selling goods and certain services directly to consumers. Table 15-1 shows the major segments of retail sales in 2004.

Almost all major retailers, most of which are publicly owned, report sales on a monthly basis. Most report not only total sales increases (including the contribution of stores opened during the past year) but also their *comparable-store* sales—that is, sales increases of stores open

TABLE 15-1

Components of retail sales, 2004

(Dollar amounts in billions)	Amount	% of total
General merchandise stores*	$ 501.1	14.3%
Furniture and appliance stores	197.6	5.6%
Clothing and accessory stores	189.2	5.4%
Sporting goods, hobby, book, and music stores	79.9	2.3%
Office supply and stationery stores	25.0	0.7%
Gift, novelty, and souvenir stores	14.7	0.4%
Total GAF store sales:	**$ 1,006.8**	**28.7%**
Motor vehicles and parts stores	878.7	25.0%
Food and beverage stores	496.8	14.2%
Building material, garden, and supply stores	301.6	8.6%
Gas stations	319.4	9.1%
Nonstore retailers**	231.8	6.6%
Health and personal care stores	204.8	5.8%
Miscellaneous	67.8	1.9%
Total retail sales	**$ 3,508.4**	**100.0%**

Source: U.S. Census Bureau, Department of Commerce
*Includes department stores, discount department stores, warehouse clubs, supercenters, and other
**Includes catalogs and Internet

during both the current sales period and the comparable period a year ago. Not surprisingly, on a short-term basis, stocks of retailers react favorably or unfavorably when these monthly sales reports exceed or fall short of expectations.

Most of the retail stores we associate with suburban highways and shopping centers fall into the category the Department of Commerce calls *GAF stores*, or general merchandise, apparel, and furniture and appliance stores. Conventional department and discount stores fall into this category. Examples are Macy's, Sears, JC Penney, Wal-Mart, Target, and Kohl's. Also included are apparel specialty stores, such as Gap and Talbots, hard-lines retailers such as Circuit City and Best Buy, and specialty stores such as Toys "R" Us and Bed Bath & Beyond. GAF store sales in 2004 totaled $1.01 trillion and included most of the relevant large-scale retail chains in the United States. The discount stores and "supercenters" of Wal-Mart, America's retail giant, alone accounted for an estimated $192 billion, or 19% of this total.[3]

In the mid-1980s, in an effort to better forecast GAF store sales, my research team and I developed our *Goldman Sachs GAF Store Sales Forecast*

Index, a leading indicator designed to predict the direction of sales growth in the nation's major retail stores. The index was comprised on a 50/50 basis of the following:

- Year-over-year increases in real average hourly wages, which, as documented in chapter 10, has proven to be a generally reliable indicator of overall consumer spending.

- Year-over-year increases in housing turnover, that is, the number of houses changing hands. As seen earlier, this statistic is an excellent leading indicator of sales of home-related products, such as furniture, carpeting, window coverings, appliances, electronics, and the like.

Figure 15-3 tracks the Goldman Sachs GAF Sales Forecast Index (solid line) vis-à-vis year-over-year changes in GAF store sales (dotted

FIGURE 15-3

Goldman Sachs GAF Store Sales Forecast Index: An effective leading indicator for general merchandise sales

The Goldman Sachs GAF Store Sales Forecast Index (solid line, left scale)— comprised 50/50 of real average hourly earnings and housing turnover—has proved to be an excellent leading indicator of retail sales of GAF (general merchandise, apparel, and furniture and appliance) stores, as reported monthly by the Department of Commerce (dotted line, right scale). This was particularly true preceding the downturn of 2000–2001 and the short recovery that followed (although the index was coincident, rather than leading, in the retail recovery of 2003).

Source: Goldman Sachs research
*Adjusted for inflation

line) from 1981 to 2004. Clearly, the GAF sales forecast index served as a generally accurate leading indicator of sales in the nation's major retail chains during this period. Nearly every uptrend and downtrend in GAF store sales from 1981 to 2004 was foreshadowed by an uptrend or downtrend in the index. (The sales downtrend of 2002, an exception, was coincidental. The sales uptrend of 2003, resulting largely from the federal tax cut, was also anomalous.)

As a check against the government data, we at Goldman Sachs also constructed our own tabulation of retail chain-store sales. Our Goldman Sachs *Retail Composite Comparable-Store Sales Index* was comprised of a weighted calculation of the combined monthly comparable-store sales increases of more than thirty retailers. Figure 15-4 presents the GAF store index versus the Goldman Sachs composite. Again, we see the index's excellent predictive qualities.

FIGURE 15-4

Goldman Sachs GAF Store Sales Forecast Index versus retailers' comparable-store sales

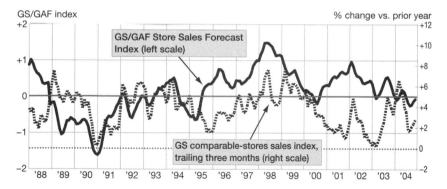

The Goldman Sachs Comparable-Stores Sales Index (dotted line, right scale) is a weighted compilation of sales growth in existing stores (excluding stores opened during the latest twelve months) for more than thirty major U.S. retailers. The GAF Store Sales Forecast Index (solid line, left scale) has generally proved to be a reliable predictor of sales trends for these companies as well (see commentary in figure 15-3).

Source: Goldman Sachs research

From Theory to Practice

Forecasting Individual Companies: Wal-Mart

Logically, given the strong record of the Goldman Sachs GAF sales fore-cast index in forecasting uptrends and downtrends in overall GAF store sales, it stands to reason that the index may also be valuable in predicting the sales trends of individual large companies within GAF store sales.

Figure 15-5 tracks the index (solid line, left scale) from 1987 to the present vis-à-vis Wal-Mart's comparable-store sales (dotted line, right scale) during the same period. Although Wal-Mart's comparable-store sales through 1992 increased steadily at 10% or more, the company's comparable-store sales thereafter were more closely related to the cycli-cality of overall GAF store sales. Consequently, as figure 15-5 shows, the GAF sales forecast index proved a generally reliable predictor of uptrends and downtrends in Wal-Mart's comparable-store sales per-formance beginning in 1994.

FIGURE 15-5

Goldman Sachs GAF Store Sales Forecast Index versus Wal-Mart's comparable-store sales

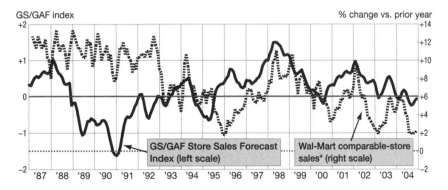

Until 1992, comparable-store sales for Wal-Mart (dotted line, right scale), the nation's largest retailer by far, grew steadily by 9% to 14%. However, in the past 10+ years, Wal-Mart's sales have become more closely linked to overall retail-industry trends. Consequently, the Goldman Sachs GAF-Store Sales Forecast Index (solid line, left scale) has now proved to be a good leading indicator of comparable-store sales for Wal-Mart.

Sources: Goldman Sachs research, Wal-Mart Stores Inc.
*Total company domestic sales

So again we see that the same cause-and-effect charting method that we applied to macroeconomic series also can work on specific industry sector such as GAF store sales, and even with sales comparisons of individual companies. This opens up a new set of possibilities for two groups: (1) executives of such companies, who can better match inventories and expenses to business levels if they can improve their advance forecasting, and (2) analysts and investors who are charged with trying to predict cyclical turning points for companies in which they are investing. This is no small matter: successful forecasting disciplines for businesspeople and investors have been almost totally lacking.

Forecasting Individual Companies: Lowe's and The Home Depot

We saw earlier that housing turnover, representing the number of families moving into new homes, logically has a strong predictive relationship with sales of carpeting and other home-related items. The same is true of the relationship between housing turnover and sales of home improvement, or DIY (do-it-yourself), retailers such as Lowe's and The Home Depot. Obviously, when families move into new homes, their needs during the first year for such large-ticket items as carpeting, window coverings, ladders, lawn mowers, and paneling for the basement are unusually high.

Figures 15-6 and 15-7 track year-over-year percentage changes in housing turnover vis-à-vis comparable-store sales of Lowe's and The Home Depot, respectively. The predictive relationship with Lowe's sales for more than a decade has been remarkable. Until 1992, The Home Depot's comparable-store sales growth (like Wal-Mart's sales in earlier years, before it became more closely related to the economy) was stable at more than 10%; however, beginning in 1993, housing turnover also has served as an effective forecaster for The Home Depot's sales (the relationship was more coincident in the latest three years, 2002 through 2004).

Manufacturing and Capital Spending

For manufacturers of most consumer goods, it should be possible to identify broad categories or specific subclassifications within personal

FIGURE 15-6

Housing turnover leads Lowe's same-store sales

Families moving into new homes typically purchase furnishings and undertake home improvement projects. Therefore, housing turnover is a solid contributor to—and a leading indicator of—sales of building materials and supplies (do-it-yourself or DIY) stores, such as Lowe's and The Home Depot. This chart proves that housing turnover has been a generally reliable predictor of Lowe's comparable-store sales trends (less so in 2003 and 2004 because of the federal tax cut). Often, year-over-year charting can be used with great success to forecast sales of individual companies.

Sources: Housing turnover—National Association of Realtors, U.S. Census Bureau; Sales—Lowe's Cos.

FIGURE 15-7

Housing turnover leads The Home Depot's same-store sales

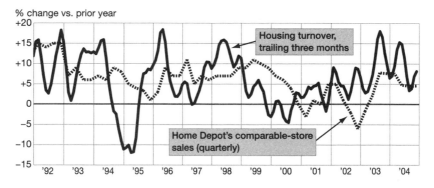

As with Lowe's, housing turnover has proved a generally reliable forecaster of comparable-store sales trends for The Home Depot.

Sources: Housing turnover—National Association of Realtors, U.S. Census Bureau; Sales—The Home Depot, Inc.

consumption expenditures or retail sales series as leading indicators of the cyclical outlook for the companies' own products. (See appendix C for categories of data series from the Bureau of Economic Analysis.)

Just as housing turnover proved to be a good leading indicator of retail sales of floor-covering stores (figure 15-2), it is also a solid predictor of sales for companies that manufacture the same products. Figure 15-8 tracks housing turnover vis-à-vis industrial production of carpeting and furniture back to 1968 and finds a good predictive fit. The industrial production series for carpeting and furniture is a volatile one, but clearly it follows uptrends and downtrends in housing turnover. The chart provides a welcome perspective on both the degree and the duration of historical cycles in both categories.

Similarly, producers of capital goods—those that build factories and offices or manufacture the machinery and equipment that goes in them—can track consumer spending or retail sales of certain types of goods as leading indicators for their business. Figure 15-9 charts year-over-year consumer spending on durable goods vis-à-vis industrial production of metalworking machinery, the metal-stamping, -bending, and -forming equipment that is used in the production and assembly of such durable consumer goods as cars, appliances, and the like.

Again, the logical cause-and-effect relationship between sales of a consumer product and orders to build the factories and equipment (capital spending) needed to produce it manifests itself in a clear leading or lagging relationship. Thus, producers of factories and equipment can use consumer spending on the product in question as a harbinger of the cyclical outlook for their sectors of capital spending.

Even a capital-goods sector as seemingly removed from consumer spending as engines, turbines, and power transmission equipment can be forecast by monitoring the dominant leading role of consumer spending within the economy, as shown in figure 15-10. The reason is simple: as advances and slowdowns in consumer demand ratchet their way into the production of consumer goods and services—and, in turn, demand for the buildings and machinery that provide them—demand for the power-producing equipment that supports all this economic output follows.

FIGURE 15-8

Housing turnover and industrial production of carpeting and furniture

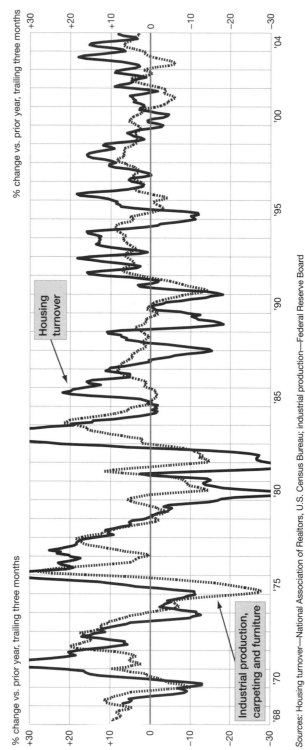

Sources: Housing turnover—National Association of Realtors, U.S. Census Bureau; industrial production—Federal Reserve Board

FIGURE 15-9

Real* consumer spending (PCE, durable goods) and industrial production of metalworking machinery

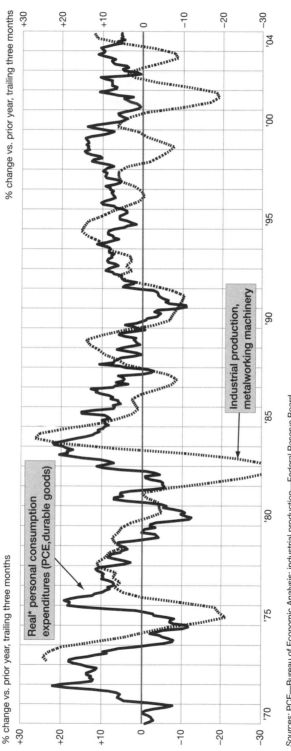

% change vs. prior year, trailing three months

% change vs. prior year, trailing three months

Real* personal consumption expenditures (PCE, durable goods)

Industrial production, metalworking machinery

Sources: PCE—Bureau of Economic Analysis; industrial production—Federal Reserve Board
*Adjusted for inflation

FIGURE 15-10

Consumer spending and industrial production of engine, turbine, and power-transmission equipment

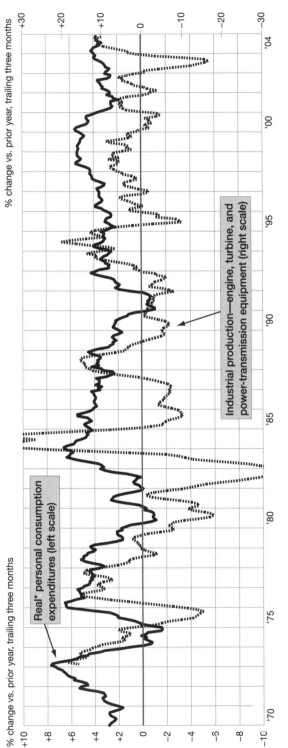

Sources: PCE—Bureau of Economic Analysis; Industrial production—Federal Reserve Board

*Adjusted for inflation

So as we can see, applied deductive reasoning, supported by empirical documentation in the form of charts, in many cases can reveal forthcoming turning points in companies' demand cycles. For a business manager, it can provide a bit of needed lead time for the company to alter business plans in time to avoid overproduction at business peaks or avoid excess cutting of staff at cyclical bottoms. But even when the microeconomic cause-and-effect relationships are coincident rather than leading, a look at a twenty-, thirty-, or forty-year history of the economic cycle as it manifests itself in a business will be highly educational; it certainly is preferable to the merely instinctive sense of business fluctuations that most executives rely on. Executives and investors will benefit significantly from observing and measuring empirically the repeated patterns and sequences that manifest themselves in their industries cycle after cycle, over many decades.

CHAPTER 16

Making Economics Happen

We have journeyed together through a number of important economic precepts, multiple economic cause-and-effect relationships, and a daunting assortment of charts. Some of these, although clearly accessible to readers having economic or business knowledge, require close attention to master. We recognize by now that monitoring and analyzing a series A and series B, bear markets, and recessions all together—even in a simplified charted format—requires serious concentration. But without charts explaining, and then documenting, historical relationships as the basis for the future, this book's exploration of the historic sequence of economic and stock market cycles as the basis for forecasting would represent theory alone and thus would be much less credible.

My purpose in this book has been to demystify the economic cycle and the stock market's historically consistent relationship to it. The key findings can be summarized as follows:

- We have learned to define and monitor economic cycles in a new way, tracking year-over-year rates of change (ROCET) rather than the more conventional approaches of tracking either levels (absolute increases versus absolute declines) or volatile and confusing quarter-to-quarter rates of increase. This new method allows us to observe cycles visually over many decades with new empirical clarity and understanding.

- This new approach demonstrates that economic indicators have moved in a surprisingly similar sequence from cycle to cycle over many decades. Figure 16-1 shows the schematic, "The Chronology of the Economic Cycle," first presented in chapter 2. My hope is that I have been able to prove that this sequence of economic indicators in fact manifests itself as presented. Armed with this new, clearer picture of the sequential consistency of economic and stock market cycles and an improved approach for monitoring them, we can get ahead of the curve in economic forecasting.

- We have seen that the stock market's relationship to the economic cycle—in our new way of tracking it—is sufficiently consistent that, ideally, we can learn to buy and sell more effectively as we predict key economic turning points.

- Applying what we have learned at the macroeconomic level to microeconomic levels empowers us in at least attempting to forecast for individual industries or even companies. We need no longer assume that, as a business managers, we are economically challenged when it comes to projecting our own demand cycle.

These findings will help us put the confusing array of economic reports that confronts us every day into an empirical discipline and an analytical perspective.

If we are business managers, putting this book's precepts to work will require us to select the data series we wish to forecast or, at least, better comprehend: the company's sales, the price of paperboard cartons, consumer spending overall, and the like. We will then select the causal factors (independent variables) that we believe are logically associated with the company's data series. Then we will chart the two—percentage changes year-over-year—on a single graph.

In most cases we will find the needed data through the company or organization itself or on the appropriate Web site. And Microsoft's Excel program, the most widely distributed statistical management software, will be sufficient—even to those who have only a passing mastery—for us to produce charts of enough clarity to get the job done. It's relatively easy, and, I promise, it will be stimulating and enjoyable—and, quite possibly, lucrative.

FIGURE 16-1

The chronology of the economic cycle

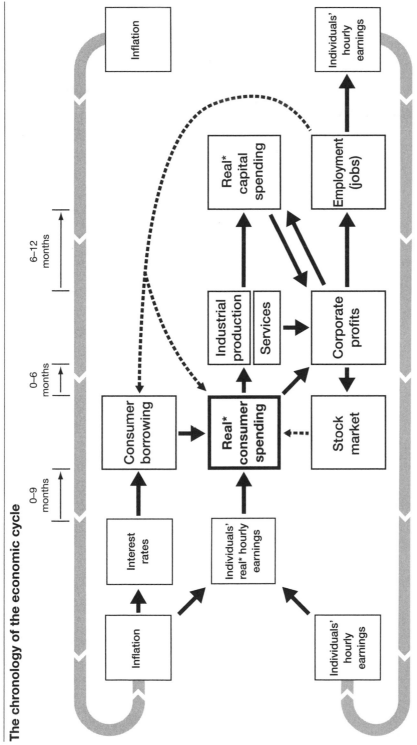

| 0–9 months | 0–6 months | 6–12 months |

Inflation

Interest rates

Individuals' real* hourly earnings

Individuals' hourly earnings

Consumer borrowing

Real* consumer spending

Industrial production

Services

Stock market

Corporate profits

Real* capital spending

Employment (jobs)

Individuals' hourly earnings

Inflation

Primary effect

Secondary effect

*Adjusted for inflation

A New Economic Perspective

There is no truly simple path to understanding the economy, but neither should we yield to the temptation of thinking that nothing is to be done. I hope I have been able to provide you with an approachable methodology that steers a course between two undesirable poles:

- Receiving at face value forecasts that emanate from abstruse economic theories or econometric models that are impossible for everyday users to comprehend, and that have not proved particularly accurate

- Rote acceptance of the daily flow of anecdotal and conflicting economic reports and predictions leading to unsupported hunches that often merely extrapolate the latest trend

If I have been successful in this, you are now better prepared to evaluate economic news as you receive it.

Late in the writing of this book, I spotted the headline "As Businesses Step Up Spending, Some See a Just-Right Economy" in the March 8, 2005 business section of the *New York Times*. The article stated, "But a wide variety of indicators now suggest that the economy is in a sweet spot: business investment is soaring, inflation appears more moderate than a few months ago; employment is climbing, even if real wages are not. Many economists have raised their growth forecasts for the year, from about 3.5 percent to 4 percent or higher." One economist quoted in the article stated, "It's clear that businesses have begun to believe that it's time to add to spending and time to hire." Another offered, "The amazing thing is that it [heightened business activity] is almost across the board in every type of equipment." One month later, in early April, the stock market fell 5% within two weeks, and economists and investors broadly began expressing fears of a slowing economy.

Based on our new understanding of sequences in the economic cycle, we should now be better prepared to evaluate this optimistic assessment. We have learned that business investment, or capital spending (chapter 7), and employment or unemployment (chapter 11) are lagging indicators that appear strongest late in the cycle, telling us where the economy has been but not where it's going. And we learned in chapter 10 that real average hourly earnings (real wages) is a leading indicator, usually telling us where consumer spending and the rest of the economy are headed. Thus, the information in the article—strength in capital spending and employment, combined with a slowdown in real earnings—is consistent with the circumstances we have seen historically at the *tail end* of periods of economic growth, when caution, and not optimism, is warranted.

Having observed what leads and what lags, in charts covering four or more decades of economic history, our ability to evaluate economic reports such as this one has been greatly enhanced.

It Begins with Econ 101

In my view, the teaching of economics needs to include a more pragmatic approach, encompassing some of the precepts I have explored here. Beginning as well as advanced students need to know more about the relationships between key macroeconomic data series, especially how these series have played out against each other over time.

Every former economics student will remember the exhaustive study of theories such as the price elasticity of demand or the marginal productivity of labor, accompanied by theoretical graphs illustrating the result of a on b when x is converging with y. However, most of these textbook graphs lack numerical scales and are only used to demonstrate theory. Few of them express actual relationships between macroeconomic data series or go on to document how well these theories have manifested themselves in the real world of historical economic data. Introductory economics courses seldom teach macroeconomic forecasting based on a down-to-earth understanding of economic cause-and-effect relationships.

Don't get me wrong. It is undeniable that a thorough education in the rich history of economic theory is imperative for all those who wish seriously to study economics. But it is also essential, whether at the beginning, master's, or doctoral level, for students to learn to gather and manipulate current data *with a level of simplicity and commitment to comprehension* that facilitates its use in the real world of policy, business, and investments. To teach even beginning economics without instructing the student in the pragmatic use of the economy's rich historical database is tantamount to teaching physics or chemistry without a lab. Often, those who have studied economics at the undergraduate level or in business schools feel—and openly lament—a lack of learning and perspective that they can apply in their lives after graduation.

Hopefully, this book will open wider the door to including in the teaching of economics a practical, empirical base for evaluating economic data series in the real world.

Without question, we can improve our understanding of the economy and stock market and, perhaps for the first time, gain a firm sense of context on where we are in the cycle, how we got here, and where we're headed. I hope the information in *Ahead of the Curve* will influence the way you think about the economy and the stock market in the future.

APPENDIX A

Credit: Consumer Spending's
Swing Factor

Given the central role played by consumer spending in determining the course of the economy and the stock market, we need to grapple with the often significant effect of consumer borrowing in accelerating or decelerating consumer demand. The importance of consumer borrowing is implicit in chapter 12's discussion of the relationship between interest rates and consumer spending. Recall that figure 10-9 presents the combined effect of growth in employment and consumer credit in leveraging up growth in individuals' real hourly earnings to considerably greater growth in aggregate real consumer spending.

However, the effects of borrowing, or credit, on consumer spending are usually coincident. As a result, they do not assume the same importance in forecasting as do such leading indicators as individuals' real average hourly earnings and the interest rates that drive credit itself. We have thus accorded consumer borrowing back-burner status here. It is, nevertheless, an interesting subject within the economy.

We are a nation of borrowers. We saw earlier, in chapter 10, that our national savings rate, which represents total saving minus total borrowing (*dis-saving*), is lower than that of most other developed countries. Debt and borrowing play a paradoxical role in our national economic life. We know that relentless borrowing by the largest sectors of our economy—consumers, corporations, and government—relative to that of our international trading partners, is a dangerous trend that can have harmful consequences. Still, borrowing is an unusually powerful driver of consumer spending and therefore of the economic

209

demand chain of consumer spending, production, and capital spending reviewed in chapter 7. If American households were actually to pay off a considerable portion of their debts by reducing their consumer spending, the shorter-term negative consequences for demand in the economy would be considerable.

For the purpose of analyzing the effects of credit on consumer spending, I here focus on installment credit and exclude home mortgages and home equity loans. Most consumers undertake mortgages—and home equity loans—to purchase or enhance their largest asset, a residence. Unlike most consumer assets, a home is amortized over a long period, and only its carrying costs (interest payments) are considered part of day-to-day consumer outlays. The significant reduction in mortgage interest rates (along with other interest rates) during the late 1990s through 2003 led to high numbers of homeowners refinancing their mortgages.

Many consumers significantly reduced the carrying costs of their mortgages, and that increased their spending power for other purposes. Others substantially increased the size of their mortgages, maintaining the same total mortgage carrying costs as before but adding greatly to their overall financial resources. Some of these incremental funds were spent on enhancing the mortgaged residences; others were saved or invested; and still others undoubtedly found their way into overall consumer spending. This latter portion is difficult to document and track and, I believe, is of marginal use in forecasting, so we'll leave this subject for others to study.

Borrowing's Effect on Consumer Spending: A Misunderstood Issue

Borrowing is an important additional source of consumer spending power that has a generally coincident effect on consumer demand. Normally, consumers borrow only for immediate purchase of goods and services or to repay other outstanding consumer loans. For our purposes, the term *consumer borrowing* refers to installment credit, as reported by the Federal Reserve Board. Installment credit is comprised of two categories: revolving credit, which consists primarily of consumer credit cards; and nonrevolving credit, which includes credit often geared to specific types of purchases and often granted directly from financial institutions to consumers (such as loans for automobiles, appliances, travel, and home improvement).

I believe that many economists and business writers err in their basic approach to assessing credit data and its effect on growth in consumer spending. As with many other economic indicators, much fuss is made about the actual *level* of outstanding consumer debt either in absolute terms or relative to consumers' aggregate disposable personal income (their capacity to support debt payments). However, the actual absolute level of outstanding consumer debt *lags* year-over-year changes in consumer spending, because outstanding cumulative debt rises and falls as the rate of growth in borrowing itself increases or declines during consumer-spending advances and slowdowns. Cumulative borrowing is highest at the end, and not the beginning, of the cycle and therefore has little value as a leading indicator.

Understanding Credit's Impact: It's the "Change in the Change" That Counts

We have reached another of those points in the unraveling of the economy where I must urge you to pause and slowly, carefully wrap your mind around a key unintuitive point, if you are to understand the effect consumer borrowing has on consumer spending: in any given year, it is the *new borrowing* that adds to consumer spending in that year *alone*. However, to understand the effect of borrowing on *year-over-year growth* in consumer spending and the economy, we must calculate the effect of this year's new borrowing (change in debt) versus last year's new borrowing (change in debt). It is the "change in the change" of outstanding debt—that is, the *second-derivative* change—that must be measured in assessing consumer credit's effects on year-over-year growth in consumer spending.

The error in most economic analysis is a tendency to look at the *level* of outstanding installment debt at any given time or, perhaps, the net increase in outstanding debt in a given year. However, if the analysis does not include *this* year's change in debt compared with *last* year's change in debt, the effect on year-over-year consumer spending comparisons and general economic growth is missed.

An Individual Example

We can best grasp this concept by first understanding the mathematical impact of consumer credit on the spending of an individual consumer. In table A-1, I have constructed a four-year model of the effect consumer credit has on the spending of John, a mythical consumer whose net take-home pay, after taxes, is static at $40,000 per year over a four-year period.

At the beginning of year 1, John's installment debt is $20,000, the result of borrowing he undertook in past years. During year 1, John borrows $1,000. Thus, his outstanding debt during the year increases 5%—from $20,000 at the beginning of the year to $21,000 at the end. His spending power during the year is thus $41,000 ($40,000 take-home pay after taxes plus $1,000 he obtained by borrowing).[1]

During year 2, John, feeling optimistic about his economic circumstances, decides to take a two-week cruise vacation. During the year he borrows an additional $5,000, increasing his debt by 24%—from $21,000 to $26,000. His total spending for the year is thus $45,000, a 10% increase over the prior year.

TABLE A-1

The role of credit: An individual example

	Year 1	Year 2	Year 3	Year 4
1. Net wages	$40,000	$40,000	$40,000	$40,000
Outstanding debt				
2. Beginning of year	$20,000	$21,000	$26,000	$29,000
3. End of year	21,000	26,000	29,000	29,000
4. Increase in debt (net borrowing during year)	$ 1,000	$ 5,000	$ 3,000	—
5. % increase	5%	24%	12%	—
6. Total spending power (#1 + #4)	$40,000	$45,000	$43,000	$40,000
Increase (decrease) versus prior year	—	$5,000	$(2,000)	$(3,000)

It is in year 3 that we see most clearly the tricky effect of consumer borrowing on consumer spending. This year, still feeling comparatively well off, John borrows an additional $3,000. His total outstanding debt increases *yet another 12%*—from $26,000 to $29,000. For most observers of economic trends, this expression of continuing economic confidence through borrowing would seem to be highly favorable. However, John's new borrowing (his increase in outstanding debt) has increased only $3,000 in year 3 versus $5,000 the year before, and his total spending power actually has *fallen* 4%— from $45,000 to $43,000.

In year 4, John sees the economy beginning to weaken and decides not to borrow at all; his debt level at the end of the year is thus $29,000, the same as at the beginning of the year. Consequently, his spending power in this final year falls an additional $3,000, or 7%, back to $40,000 as he seeks at least to maintain his "balance sheet" at existing levels.

John's example provides an important insight into the effect of credit on national consumer spending that is generally missed by economic observers. John increases his debt by 45% (from $20,000 to $29,000) during the four-year period but nevertheless experiences declining purchasing power during the final two years. Even as John continues to borrow to maintain a higher rate of spending, if he borrows (increases his debt) less in any year than in the year before, his spending power actually declines.

Measuring the Real Effect of Credit on the Economy

To apply this principle in calculating the macroeconomic effect of advancing or declining consumer borrowing on year-over-year consumer spending growth, we can use the following formula:

- Net increase in installment debt outstanding this year (contribution to this year's consumer spending)

- Minus net increase in installment debt outstanding last year (contribution to last year's consumer spending)

- Equals effect on year-over-year change in consumer spending

- Divided by last year's consumer spending

- Equals percentage-point impact of installment credit on year-over-year consumer-spending comparisons

Using this formula, figure A-1 compares the percentage-point effect of installment borrowing on year-over-over consumer-spending comparisons (dotted line) with year-over-year increases in unit consumer spending itself (solid line) from 1961 through 2004. As we can see, the swing effects typically are dramatic, ranging from a positive stimulus of 2 percentage points at periods of peak consumer-spending growth to a reducing effect equivalent to 2 percentage points at troughs. I have provided year-over-year real personal consumption expenditures for comparison so that you can ascertain where in the consumer-spending cycle the positive or negative effects of installment borrowing were at their greatest.

It is clear in figure A-1 that consumer borrowing vacillates rather frequently from adding 1 to 2 percentage points to (year-over-year) consumer-spending growth, to subtracting 1 to 2 percentage points from (year-over-year) consumer-spending growth. In general, although borrowing clearly is affected by interest rates, it increases most when employment growth in the economy is at its strongest and consumers have the economic confidence to take on additional debt; borrowing has its most negative impact when job-based economic confidence is low.[2]

This has two implications:

- The strong employment (job-confidence) input to borrowing gives it coincident to lagging characteristics.

- Accelerating or slowing borrowing most often *combines* with strong or weak employment growth either to: (1) leverage up underlying real average hourly earnings growth into much greater increases in consumer spending or (2) fall back to year-over-year declines, thereby actually subtracting from total consumer spending growth falling to or below the rate of underlying real earnings growth. This phenomenon is clear in figure 10-9.

Because of consumer borrowing's coincident-to-lagging nature, it is best to view it as an interesting but secondary input in the process of sequencing and forecasting the economy.

The volatile effect of consumer credit on year-over-year real* consumer spending (PCE)

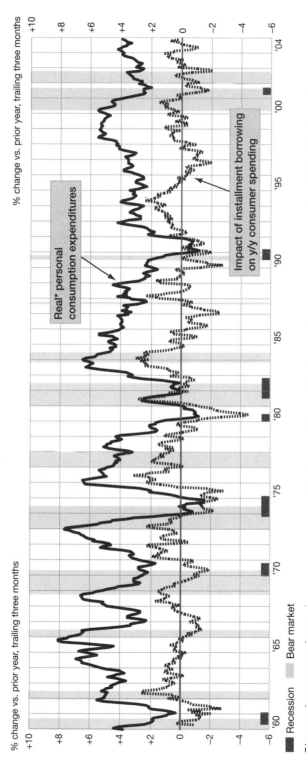

Changes in consumer borrowing on a year-over-year basis may add or subtract as much as two percentage points (dotted line) to real* consumer-spending growth (solid line) and are somewhat volatile. These effects are coincidental and have little forecasting value.

Sources: PCE—Bureau of Economic Analysis; Installment credit—Federal Reserve Board

*Adjusted for inflation

Does Charting Economic Cause and Effect Work Outside the United States?

Throughout this book, I have applied a commonsense, cause-and-effect charting methodology to the tracking of successive stages in the surprisingly consistent chronology of U.S. economic cycles. This approach was an outgrowth and an integral part of my efforts as an analyst on Wall Street to see around economic corners in predicting uptrends and downtrends in the retailing industry and other sectors of the U.S. economy. Over several decades, I have often been asked whether the consistency in the U.S. economy as reflected in our charts also pertains to foreign economies.

For perspective on the sizes of the other major economies in the world relative to that of the United States, table B-1 compares twenty of the world's largest economies in 2003 gross domestic product, consumer spending, and population; GDP and consumer spending also are presented in per-capita terms. The United States is far and away the world's largest economy in both gross domestic product and consumer spending, with Japan a strong second in both measures. Only seven countries exceeded $1 trillion in gross domestic product, and these seven, according to World Bank data, accounted for $24.2 trillion, or over two thirds of the world's total gross domestic product. In 2003, the United States and Japan together accounted for over 40% of all consumer spending globally.

An interesting way to look at consumer spending by country is to break it into its two component parts: population and consumer spending per capita. Figure B-1 does this in chart form. You can see

TABLE B-1

GDP and consumer spending of countries with largest GDPs, 2003

	Population (millions)	GDP ($ billions)	Consumer spending ($ billions)	Per capita	
				GDP	Consumer spending
United States	291	$11,004	$7,761	$37,811	$26,667
Japan	128	4,296	2,440	33,653	19,117
Germany	83	2,405	1,419	29,144	17,200
United Kingdom	60	1,799	1,134	30,208	19,038
France	60	1,763	978	29,306	16,257
China	1,292	1,417	636	1,096	492
Italy	57	1,472	883	25,626	15,374
Canada	32	870	492	27,479	15,528
Spain	41	842	487	20,497	11,854
Mexico	104	639	438	6,131	4,207
Korea	48	608	326	12,711	6,823
India	1,065	529	340	497	320
Netherlands	16	513	253	31,703	15,653
Australia	20	509	304	25,477	15,193
Brazil	179	506	287	2,828	1,605
Russian Federation	144	430	214	2,985	1,483
Switzerland	7	322	195	44,941	27,269
Belgium	10	305	166	29,309	15,964
Sweden	9	302	147	33,640	16,391
Austria	8	256	139	31,679	17,177
Total	**3,655**	**$30,786**	**$18,769**		

Source: Global Insight

that the United States and Japan are the two countries where the combination of population and per-capita spending is the greatest.

Of course, the economies of each of these twenty countries encompass most or all of the economic data series that we have discussed for the United States: consumer spending, capital spending, industrial production, retail sales, corporate profits, employment, a stock market, and the like. However, the definitions, calculations, and sampling methods vary greatly from country to country, and in many cases economic data cannot be reliably compared. To apply the full arsenal of

Appendix B

Consumer spending in major countries, 2003

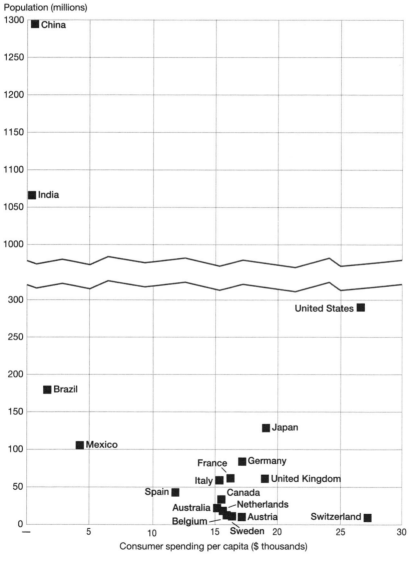

Population (millions)

Consumer spending per capita ($ thousands)

Source: Global Insight

219

charted cause-and-effect relationships we have presented for the United States to each of the other major economies would require its own book for each one, and I will leave to others the task of more completely dealing with charted cause and effect in each of these economies.

Nevertheless, a cursory look at some of the primary indicators of economic growth in key foreign countries suggests that some—but not all—of the cause-and-effect relationships that I have documented as working dependably in the U.S. economy are also key in other major developed countries such as Canada, Germany, France, Japan, and the United Kingdom. Intuitively, however, we might well expect these relationships to be somewhat less reliable outside the United States than they are here, for several reasons. First and foremost, the sheer size of the U. S. economy and its primacy in the world throughout the second half of the twentieth century have insulated it to some extent from economic developments abroad, in mature foreign economies as well as in less developed markets. This is, of course, in relative—and not absolute—terms. Economic developments abroad *do* have an effect on the U.S. economy. However, in the United States, the effects of external developments relative to total gross domestic product, given the sheer size of the U.S. economy vis-à-vis those of the rest of the world, are smaller.

Second, the U.S. economy is, on a net basis, relatively self-sufficient. In 2003, total U.S. exports were equivalent to only 11% of GDP, and imports were at 16%. Although the United States thus had a trade deficit equal to 5% of GDP, neither of the two components—exports or imports—was nearly as large, relative to GDP, as in the other most developed countries. Therefore, even significant changes in exports or imports are likely not large enough to break the cause-and-effect relationship between U.S. consumer spending on goods and the domestic industrial production of most of those goods, as shown in chapter 7.

However, for countries where exports are much larger relative to gross domestic product—countries such as Canada, France, and Germany (see table B-2)—a sharp slowdown in foreign demand for their exports might result in a weak manufacturing sector even when domestic demand was strong. Consequently, the cause-and-effect chain from consumer spending to industrial production, capital spending, corpo-

TABLE B-2

Exports and imports, percentage of GDP, 2004

| | % of gross domestic product | | |
	Exports	Imports	Trade surplus (deficit)
United States	10.0%	15.2%	(5.2)%
Canada	38.2	33.8	4.4
France	25.9	25.4	0.5
Germany	38.0	32.9	5.1
Japan	13.1	11.2	1.9
United Kingdom	24.7	28.0	(3.3)

Sources: Global Insight

rate profits, employment, and even the stock market would be broken.

Third, the U.S. dollar is the recognized currency standard in the world, with a number of other currencies pegged to it. True, there are times when declines in the dollar against the yen or the euro and other key currencies have raised concern; a good example is 2003–2005. However, relative to the giant U.S. economy, currency fluctuations of the dollar have had only marginal effects on U.S. economic cycles vis-à-vis the domestically driven cause-and-effect chain explored throughout this book.

A Charted Look Outside the United States

With these caveats in mind, let's take a look, in summarized form, at some of the same cause-and-effect relationships explored in this book as they relate to the largest and most developed economies. In general, the cause-and-effect chain extending from consumer spending to industrial production to capital spending in the United States also holds true in Canada, Germany, Japan, the United Kingdom, and France, albeit it with significant variations in lead and lag times. Clearly, the lagging nature of employment and unemployment vis-à-vis consumer spending—so counterintuitive for casual observers of the economy—also is the case in each of the developed economies.

I have found it more difficult, unfortunately, to obtain pure measurements of real average hourly earnings (removing the lagging effects of the workweek and employment) as a means of finding strong leading indicators for consumer spending outside the United States. A full discovery of the application of this book's simplified economic tracking methodology to each of these countries would require a separate volume for each. Hopefully, readers who are interested in applying this book's methods to other economies will advance this process.

Canada

Figure B-2: The relationship between consumer spending and industrial production in Canada closely parallels that in the United States (see figure 7-3). Growth in unit consumer spending in Canada over the past four decades has typically peaked at 5% to 8% and bottomed at –2% to +2%. Cycles in industrial production are roughly coincident and far more volatile, a result of inventory growth during cyclical upturns and shrinkage during contractions.

Figure B-3: Canadian capital spending, as in the United States, follows the advances and declines of industrial production, although the lag is somewhat less pronounced than its U.S. counterpart (figure 7-5). The capital spending sector in Canada also appears to be somewhat more volatile.

Figure B-4: Uptrends and downtrends in Canadian capital spending, more volatile and frequent than in the United States, appear to be roughly coincident with, to slightly lagging of, consumer spending in Canada. Both series, however, may be closely tied to their U.S. counterparts.

Figure B-5: As with unemployment in the United States, the Canadian unemployment rate (inverted in figure B-5) cyclically lags consumer spending advances and slowdowns, usually by one to two years. It also appears to be secularly higher than that of the United States.

France

Figure B-6: French cycles in consumer spending, ranging from year-over-year peaks of approximately 4% to troughs near zero, appear more similar in scope and frequency to those of the United States than to those of Germany, the United Kingdom, and Japan. French industrial production exhibits a volatility vis-à-vis consumer spending that is similar to that of the other major developed countries, suggesting the same inventory-cycle effects as in other countries.

Figure B-7: Capital spending cycles in France typically have followed those of industrial production by one to four quarters, a lag relationship quite similar to that experienced in the United States.

Figure B-8: Given capital spending's lagging relationship to industrial production in France, it also lags French consumer spending in a manner very similar to that of the United States. Based on almost three decades of evidence in this chart, those forecasting the capital-spending sector in France should monitor consumer spending as their favored leading indicator.

Figure B-9: Unemployment in France, as in all of the major developed economies we have surveyed, cyclically follows the trend of consumer-spending growth at the front end of the French economy. This proves yet again that, from a cyclical perspective, an economy's consumer spending is a far more powerful driver of employment (jobs) than vice versa.

Germany

Figure B-10: The relationship between consumer spending and industrial production, with industrial production coincident and more volatile than consumer spending, also holds true in Germany. However, the cyclical swings in both series, including the volatility of industrial production to consumer spending, are considerably less than in the United States.

Figure B-11: In most instances, capital spending advances and declines in Germany appear coincident to, to only slightly lagging of, cyclical swings in industrial production.

Figure B-12: As a result of the lower volatility of consumer spending, industrial production, and capital spending, the historical cyclical relationship between consumer spending and capital spending in Germany is far more coincident and less volatile than in the United States or Canada.

Figure B-13: As in the United States and Canada, the German unemployment rate follows cyclical uptrends and downtrends in consumer spending. Figure B-13 shows clearly the long-term increase in the German unemployment rate, attributed by most commentators to that country's exceptionally generous social and labor legislation.

Japan

Figure B-14: Japanese consumer spending from the 1980s through the early 1990s was far less cyclical than that of the United States. However, unit consumer spending in Japan has become more volatile since the mid-1990s, with a clear overall slowing trend. Industrial production in Japan has also become far more volatile, with steeper and more frequent year-over-year declines. This likely reflects a migration of other economies' import demands to other Asian countries. In general, Japanese industrial production appears, cyclically, to be less linked to its consumer demand than is the case in other major developed economies.

Figure B-15: As in Germany, capital spending in Japan appears to have a far more coincident relationship to industrial production than in the United States.

Figure B-16: Consequently, the relationship between consumer spending and capital spending in Japan is less clearly a lagging one than in the United States.

Figure B-17: Throughout the 1980s and early 1990s, the continuous strength of Japanese consumer spending, accompanied by generally solid gains in industrial production and capital spending, resulted in an unemployment rate of 3% or less. However, Japanese unemployment has since undergone a decade-long rise (remember: the unemployment rate is inverted in the chart) to more than 5%. As in the other major developed economies, unemployment (and employment) trends have followed—and not led—those of consumer spending.

United Kingdom

Figure B-18: Following rather frequent and volatile cycles from the 1960s through the 1980s, British consumer spending has enjoyed a period of sustained strength in the late 1990s and early 2000s. Industrial production in the United Kingdom has, with the exception of the 1970s, been far less volatile relative to consumer spending than in the United States. This may reflect the fact that imports are much higher in proportion to consumer spending and GDP, reducing the inventory-cycle accelerator between consumer spending and industrial production.

Figure B-19: Cyclical peaks and troughs in capital spending in the United Kingdom appear to lag slightly those of industrial production. British capital spending also appears to be somewhat more volatile than the capital-goods sector in other major developed countries.

Figure B-20: The volatility of British capital spending and its coincident to lagging relationship to consumer spending is apparent here. However, the swings in British capital spending are of such dimension and frequency that forecasting it based on consumer spending trends (as works well in the United States) would appear to be difficult.

Figure B-21: As with virtually every other developed economy, the U.K. unemployment rate follows, rather than leads, advances and declines in consumer spending. The United Kingdom has enjoyed a decade-long reduction in its unemployment rate beginning in 1993, and this is certainly attributable in part to the steady growth in British consumer spending during that same period.

Clearly, figures B-2 through B-21 suggest that the cause-and-effect relationships for the United States documented throughout this book have parallels in other major developed economies, albeit with significant

variations of lead and lag times as well as volatility. These charted relationships reflect only the surface of more complex economic
factors that differ from country to country. Nevertheless, the charts
themselves represent a starting point from which those interested in
simplifying the tracking of economic cycles using the ROCET approach
and understanding economic cause and effect can begin a journey of
exploration.

FIGURE B-2

Canada: Real* consumer spending and industrial production

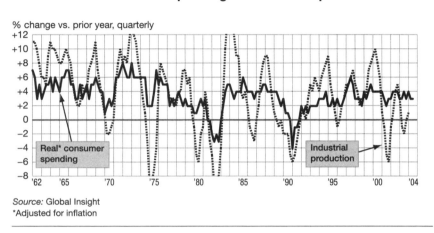

Source: Global Insight
*Adjusted for inflation

FIGURE B-3

Canada: Industrial production and real* capital spending

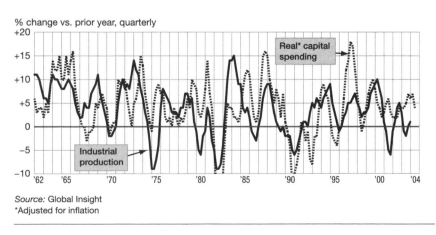

Source: Global Insight
*Adjusted for inflation

Appendix B

FIGURE B-4

Canada: Real* consumer spending and real* capital spending

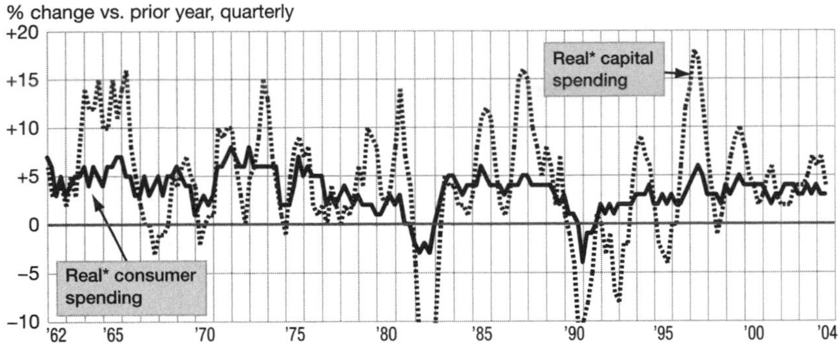

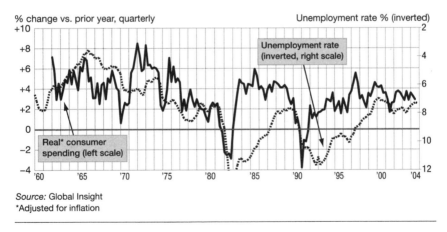

% change vs. prior year, quarterly

Source: Global Insight
*Adjusted for inflation

FIGURE B-5

Canada: Real* consumer spending and the unemployment rate

% change vs. prior year, quarterly   Unemployment rate % (inverted)

Source: Global Insight
*Adjusted for inflation

FIGURE B-6

France: Real* consumer spending and industrial production

% change vs. prior year, quarterly

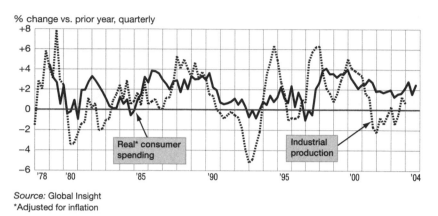

Source: Global Insight
*Adjusted for inflation

FIGURE B-7

France: Industrial production and real* capital spending

% change vs. prior year, quarterly

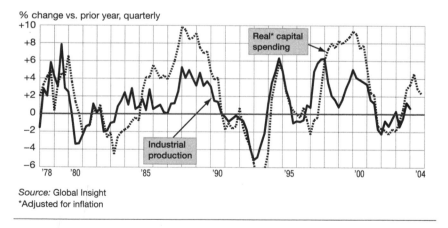

Source: Global Insight
*Adjusted for inflation

FIGURE B-8

France: Real* consumer spending and real* capital spending

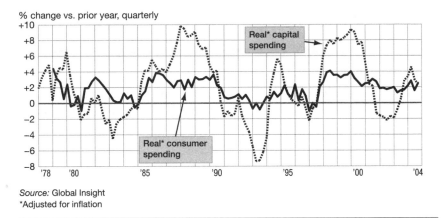

% change vs. prior year, quarterly

Source: Global Insight
*Adjusted for inflation

FIGURE B-9

France: Real* consumer spending and the unemployment rate

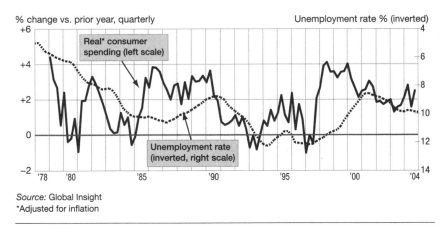

% change vs. prior year, quarterly   Unemployment rate % (inverted)

Source: Global Insight
*Adjusted for inflation

FIGURE B-10

Germany: Real* consumer spending and industrial production**

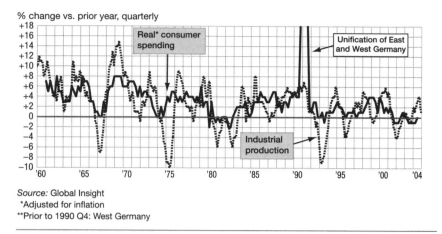

% change vs. prior year, quarterly

Source: Global Insight
*Adjusted for inflation
**Prior to 1990 Q4: West Germany

FIGURE B-11

Germany: Industrial production and real* capital spending**

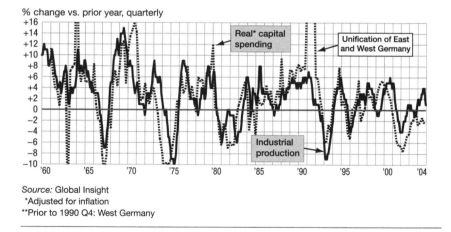

% change vs. prior year, quarterly

Source: Global Insight
*Adjusted for inflation
**Prior to 1990 Q4: West Germany

FIGURE B-12

Germany: Real* consumer spending and real* capital spending**

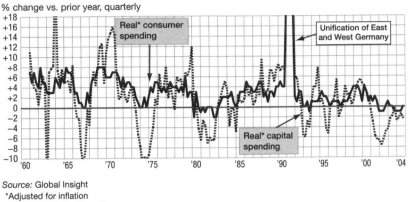

Source: Global Insight
*Adjusted for inflation
**Prior to 1990 Q4: West Germany

FIGURE B-13

Germany: Real* consumer spending and the unemployment rate**

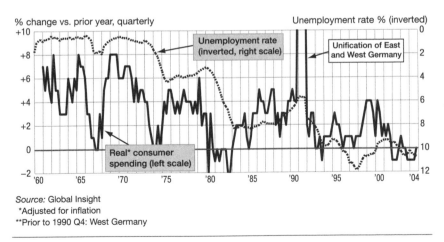

Source: Global Insight
*Adjusted for inflation
**Prior to 1990 Q4: West Germany

FIGURE B-14

Japan: Real* consumer spending and industrial production

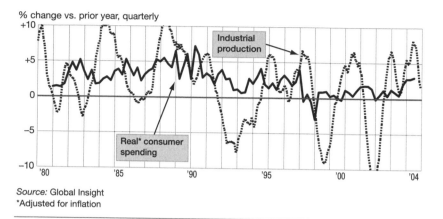

% change vs. prior year, quarterly

Source: Global Insight
*Adjusted for inflation

FIGURE B-15

Japan: Industrial production and real* capital spending

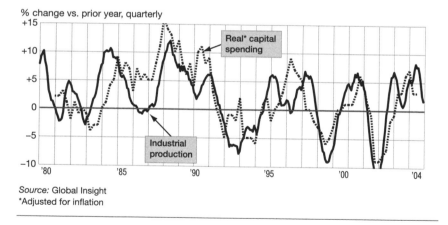

% change vs. prior year, quarterly

Source: Global Insight
*Adjusted for inflation

FIGURE B-16

Japan: Real* consumer spending and real* capital spending

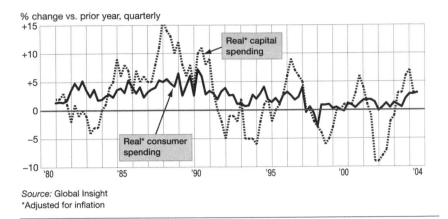

% change vs. prior year, quarterly

Source: Global Insight
*Adjusted for inflation

FIGURE B-17

Japan: Real* consumer spending and the unemployment rate

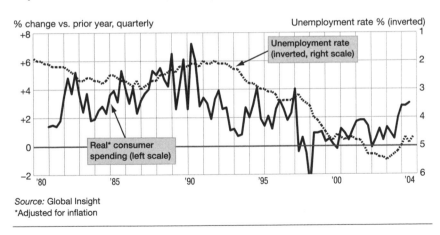

% change vs. prior year, quarterly   Unemployment rate % (inverted)

Source: Global Insight
*Adjusted for inflation

FIGURE B-18

United Kingdom: Real* consumer spending and industrial production

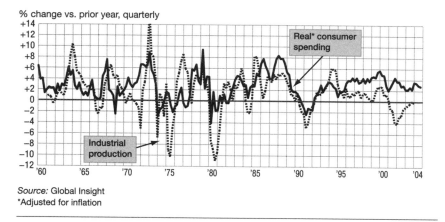

% change vs. prior year, quarterly

Source: Global Insight
*Adjusted for inflation

FIGURE B-19

United Kingdom: Industrial production and real* capital spending

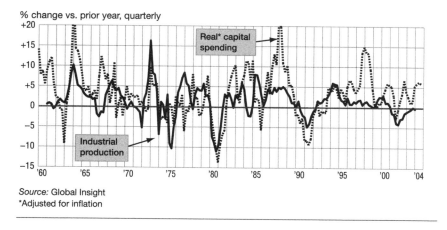

% change vs. prior year, quarterly

Source: Global Insight
*Adjusted for inflation

FIGURE B-20

United Kingdom: Real* consumer spending and real* capital spending

% change vs. prior year, quarterly

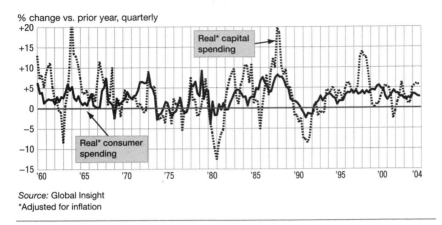

Source: Global Insight
*Adjusted for inflation

FIGURE B-21

United Kingdom: Real* consumer spending and the unemployment rate

% change vs. prior year, quarterly   Unemployment rate % (inverted)

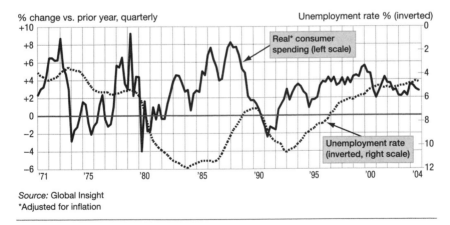

Source: Global Insight
*Adjusted for inflation

Major Industry Data Series

Personal Consumption Expenditures, by Type of Expenditure
(Source: Bureau of Economic Analysis)

Durable goods

Motor vehicles and parts
New automobiles
    New domestic automobiles
    New foreign automobiles
Net purchases of used automobiles
    Net transactions in used automobiles
    Used automobile margin
    Employee reimbursement
Other motor vehicles
    Trucks, new and net used
    Recreational vehicles
Tires, tubes, accessories, and other parts
    Tires and tubes
    Accessories and parts

Furniture and household equipment
Furniture, including mattresses and bedsprings
Kitchen and other household appliances
    Major household appliances
    Small electric appliances

China, glassware, tableware, and utensils
Video and audio goods, including musical instruments
  TVs, VCRs, videotapes
    Televisions
    Video equipment and media
  Audio equipment, media, instruments
    Audio equipment
    Records, tapes, and disks
  Musical instruments
Computers, peripherals, and software
  Computers and peripherals
  Software
Other durable house furnishings
  Floor coverings
  Durable house furnishings NEC
  Clocks, lamps, and furnishings
  Blinds, rods, and other
  Writing equipment
  Hand tools
  Tools, hardware, and supplies
  Outdoor equipment and supplies

Other
  Ophthalmic products and orthopedic appliances
  Wheel goods, sports and photographic equipment, boats
    Sport and photo equipment, cycles
    Guns
    Sporting equipment
    Photographic equipment
    Bicycles
    Motorcycles
  Pleasure boats and aircraft
    Pleasure boats
    Pleasure aircraft
  Jewelry and watches
  Books and maps

Nondurable goods

Food

Food purchased for off-premise consumption
    Food in off-premise food purchases
        Cereals
        Bakery products
        Beef and veal
        Pork
        Other meats
        Poultry
        Fish and seafood
        Eggs
        Fresh milk and cream
        Processed dairy products
        Fresh fruits
        Fresh vegetables
        Processed fruits and vegetables
        Juices and nonalcoholic drinks
        Coffee, tea, and beverage materials
        Fats and oils
        Sugar and sweets
        Other foods
        Pet food
    Alcoholic beverages purchased for off-premise consumumption
        Beer and ale, at home
        Wine and brandy, at home
        Distilled spirits, at home
    Purchased meals and beverages
        Food in purchased meals
        Elementary and secondary school lunch
        Higher education school lunch
    Other purchased meals
        Meals at limited service eating places
        Meals at other eating places
        Meals at drinking places

Alcohol in purchased meals
Food furnished to employees (including military)
   Food furnished to employees (including military)
      Food supplied to civilians
      Food supplied to military
   Food produced and consumed on farms

Clothing and shoes
Shoes
Women's and children's clothing and accessories except shoes
   Clothing and sewing for females
      Clothing for females
      Clothing for infants
      Sewing goods for females
   Luggage for females
Men's and boys' clothing and accessories except shoes
   Men's and boys'
      Clothing and sewing for males
         Clothing for males
         Sewing goods for males
      Luggage for males
   Standard clothing issued to military personnel

Gasoline, fuel oil, and other energy goods
Gasoline and oil
   Gasoline and other motor fuel
   Lubricants
Fuel oil and coal
   Fuel oil
   LPG and other fuel, and farm fuel
      LPG and other fuel
      Farm fuel

Other
Tobacco products
Toilet articles and preparations
   Soap

Cosmetics and perfumes
Other personal hygiene goods
Semidurable house furnishings
Cleaning and polishing preparations, and miscellaneous
Cleaning preparations
Lighting supplies
Paper products
Drug preparations and sundries
Prescription drugs
Nonprescription drugs
Medical supplies
Gynecological goods
Nondurable toys and sport supplies
Toys, dolls, and games
Sport supplies, including ammo
Film and photo supplies
Stationery and writing supplies
Stationery and school supplies
Greeting cards
Net foreign remittances
Expenditures abroad by U.S. residents
Governmental expenditures abroad
Other private services
Less: personal remittances in kind to nonresidents
Magazines, newspapers, and sheet music
Magazines and sheet music
Newspapers
Flowers, seeds, and potted plants

Services

Housing
Owner-occupied nonfarm dwellings—space rent
Owner-occupied mobile home
Owner-occupied station homes
Tenant-occupied nonfarm dwellings—rent
Tenant-occupied mobile homes

Tenant-occupied station homes
Tenant landlord durables
Rental value of farm dwellings
Other
    Hotels and motels
    Clubs and fraternity housing
    Higher education housing
    Elementary and secondary education housing
    Tenant group room and board
    Tenant group employee lodging

Household operation
Electricity and gas
    Electricity
    Gas
Other household operation
    Water and other sanitary services
        Water and sewerage maintenance
        Refuse collection
    Telephone and telegraph
    Local and cellular telephone
        Cellular telephone
        Local telephone
    Long-distance telephone
        Intrastate toll calls
        Interstate toll calls
    Domestic service
    Domestic service, cash
    Domestic service, in kind
Other
    Moving and storage
    Household insurance
        Household insurance premiums
        Less: household insurance benefits paid
    Rug and furniture cleaning
    Electrical repair
    Reupholstery and furniture repair

Postage
Household-operated services NEC

Transportation
User-operated transportation
   Repair, greasing, washing, parking, storage, rental,
   motor vehicle repair
   Motor vehicle repair
   Motor vehicle rental, leasing, and other
      Motor vehicle rental
      Motor vehicle leasing
         Auto leasing
         Truck leasing
      Other motor vehicle services
Other user-operated transportation
   Bridge, tunnel, ferry, and road tolls
   Insurance
Purchased local transportation
   Mass transit systems
   Taxicab
Purchased intercity transportation
   Railway
   Bus
   Airline
   Other

Medical care
Physicians
Dentists
Other professional services
   Home health care
   Medical laboratories
   Eye examinations
   All other professional medical services
Hospitals and nursing homes
   Hospitals
      Nonprofit

Proprietary
Government
Nursing homes
  Nonprofit nursing homes
  Proprietary and government nursing homes
Health insurance
  Medical care and hospitalization
  Income loss
  Workers' compensation

Recreation

Admissions to specified spectator amusements
  Motion picture theaters
  Legitimate theaters and opera
  Spectator sports

Other

Radio and television repair
Clubs and fraternal organizations
Commercial participant amusements
  Sightseeing
  Private flying
  Bowling and billiards
  Casino gambling
  Other commercial participant amusements
Pari-mutuel net receipts
Other
  Pets and pets services excluding veteranarians
  Veterinarians
  Cable TV
  Film developing
  Photo studios
  Sporting and recreational camps
  High school recreation
  Lotteries
  Videocassette rental
  Commercial amusements NEC

Internet service providers
Commercial amusements NEC

Other
Personal care
    Cleaning, storage, and repair of clothing and shoes
        Shoe repair
        Cleaning, laundering
        Drycleaning
        Laundry and garment repair
    Barbershops, beauty parlors, and health clubs
        Beauty shops, including combination
        Barbershops
    Other
        Watch, clock, and jewelry repair
        Miscellaneous personal services
Personal business
    Brokerage charges and investment counseling
        Equities commissions, including imputed
        Broker charges on mutual fund sales
        Trading profits on debt securities
        Trust services of commercial banks
        Investment advisory services of broker
        Commodities revenue
        Investment counseling services
    Bank service charges, trust services, and safe deposit
        Commercial bank service charges on deposit accounts
        Commercial bank fees on fiduciary accounts
        Commercial bank other fee income
        Charges and fees of other depository institutions
    Services furnished without payment by financial institutions
        Commercial banks
        Other financial institutions
    Expense of handling life insurance and pension plans
    Legal services
Funeral and burial expenses
    Other

Labor union expenses
Professional association expenses
Employ agency fees
Money orders
Classified ads
Tax return preparation services
Personal business services NEC
Education and research
Higher education
Private higher education
Public higher education
Nursery, elementary, and secondary schools
Elementary and secondary schools
Nursery schools
Other
Commercial and vocational schools
Foundations and nonprofit research
Religious and welfare activities
Political organizations
Museums and libraries
Foundations to religion and welfare
Social welfare
Childcare
Social welfare
Religion
Net foreign travel
Foreign travel by U.S. residents
Passenger fares, foreign travel
Travel outside the United States
U.S. student expenditures
Less: expenditures in the United States by nonresidents
Foreign travel in United States
Medical exports of foreigners
Exports of foreign students in United States

Private Fixed Investment by Type

(Source: Bureau of Economic Analysis)

Private Fixed Investment

Nonresidential

Structures

Nonresidential buildings, excluding farm
    Industrial
    Office buildings
    Other commercial buildings
    Religious
    Educational
    Hospital and institutional
    Other nonresidential buildings
Utilities
Telecommunications
Farm
Mining exploration, shafts, and wells
Other new nonresidential structures, excluding farm

Equipment and software

Information processing equipment and software
    Computer and peripheral equipment
    Software
    Communication equipment
    Instruments
    Photocopying and related equipment
    Office and accounting equipment
Industrial equipment
    Fabricated metal products
    Engines and turbines
    Steam engines
    Internal combustion engines
    Metalworking machinery
    Special industrial machinery NEC

General industrial, including materials handling equipment
Electric transmission and distribution equipment
Transportation equipment
Trucks, buses, and truck trailers
Autos
Aircraft
Ships and boats
Railroad equipment
Other equipment
Furniture and fixtures
Household furniture
Other furniture
Tractors
Farm tractors
Construction tractors
Agricultural machinery excluding tractors
Construction machinery excluding tractors
Mining and oil field machinery
Service industry machinery
Electrical equipment NEC
Household appliances
Miscellaneous electrical

Other
Less: sale of equipment scrap excluding automobiles

Residential

Structures
Single family
Multifamily
Other structures

Equipment

Residual

Appendix C

Industrial Production: Industry Groups

(Source : Federal Reserve Board)

Manufacturing

Primary processing

Advanced processing

Durable manufacturing

Lumber and products

Furniture and fixtures

Stone, clay, and glass products

Primary metals
  Iron and steel
  Nonferrous metals

Fabricated metal products

Industrial machinery and equipment
  Computer and office equipment

Electrical machinery
  Semiconductors and related electronic components

Transportation equipment
  Motor vehicles and parts
    Autos and light trucks
  Aerospace and miscellaneous transportation equipment

Instruments

Miscellaneous manufactures

Nondurable manufacturing
    Foods
    Tobacco products
    Textile mill products
    Apparel products
    Paper and products
    Printing and publishing
    Chemicals and products
    Petroleum products
    Rubber and plastics products
    Leather and products

Mining

Metal mining

Coal mining

Oil and gas extraction

Stone and earth minerals

Utilities

Electric utilities

Gas utilities

Industrial Production: Market Groups

Products, total

Final products
    Consumer goods
        Durable consumer goods
            Automotive products
                Automobiles and trucks, consumer
                Automobiles, consumer

Light trucks, consumer
Auto parts and allied goods
Other durable goods
Appliances and home computing, video, and
audio equipment
Household appliances
Computers, video and audio equipment
Carpeting and furniture
Miscellaneous durable goods
Nondurable consumer goods
Nondurable nonenergy consumer goods
Foods and tobacco
Clothing
Chemical products
Paper products
Consumer energy products
Fuels
Residential utilities
Equipment, total
Business equipment
Information processing and related equipment
Office and computing equipment, business
Industrial equipment
Transit equipment
Autos and trucks, business
Other equipment
Defense and space equipment
Oil and gas well drilling
Manufactured homes
Intermediate products
Construction supplies
Business supplies

Materials

Durable goods materials
Consumer parts

Equipment parts
   Semiconductors, printed circuit boards, and other electrical
   components
Other durable materials
   Basic metals

Nondurable goods materials
Textile materials
Paper materials
Chemical materials
Other nondurable materials

Energy materials
Primary energy
Converted fuel

Retail Sales and Food Services, by Type of Business
(Source: Department of Commerce)

Retail sales

GAF (general merchandise, apparel, and furniture and appliance) stores

Motor vehicle and parts dealers
Auto and other motor vehicle dealers
Automotive dealers
   New car dealers
   Used car dealers
Other motor vehicle dealers
   Boat dealers
Automotive parts, accessory, and tire stores

Furniture and home furnishings, electronics, and appliance stores
Furniture and home furnishings stores
   Furniture stores
   Home furnishings stores
      Floor covering stores

All other home furnishings stores
Electronics and appliance stores
   Appliance, TV, and other electronic stores
      Household appliance stores
      Radio, TV, and other electronic stores
   Computer and software stores
Building material and garden equipment and supply stores
   Building materials and supply stores
      Paint and wallpaper stores
      Hardware stores
Food and beverage stores
   Grocery stores
      Supermarkets and other grocery stores, excluding
         convenience stores
   Fruit and vegetable markets
   Beer, wine, and liquor stores
Health and personal care stores
   Pharmacies and drug stores
      Optical goods stores
Gasoline stations
Clothing and clothing accessories stores
   Clothing stores
      Men's clothing stores
      Women's clothing stores
      Children's and infants' clothing stores
      Family clothing stores
      Other clothing stores
   Shoe stores
   Jewelry stores
   Luggage and leather goods
Sporting goods, hobby, book, and music stores
   Sporting goods stores
   Hobby, toy, and game stores
   Sewing, needlework, and piece goods stores
   Bookstores
   Prerecorded tapes, CDs, and record stores
General merchandise stores

Department stores (excluding leased departments)
    Discount department stores
    Conventional and national chain department stores
Department stores (including leased departments)
    Discount department stores
    Conventional and national chaine department stores
Warehouse clubs and superstores
All other general merchandise stores
Miscellaneous store retailers
    Florists
    Office supply and stationery stores
    Gift, novelty, and souvenir stores
    Used merchandise stores
    Pet and pet supplies stores
    Manufactured (mobile) home dealers
    Tobacco stores
Nonstore retailers
    Electronic shopping and mail-order houses
    Vending machine operators
    Fuel dealers
      Heating oil dealers
      Liquified petroleum gas (bottled) dealers
    Other direct selling establishments
Food services and drinking places
    Full service restaurants
    Limited-service eating places
Drinking places

www.AheadoftheCurve-theBook.com

As noted in the preface, www.AheadoftheCurve-theBook.com will maintain monthly updated versions of the nineteen most important charts
in this book (see table D-1), so that readers may in the future easily
apply them to the current economic and stock market outlook. Readers may also wish to re-create the charts in this book and update them
on a regular basis. The www.AheadoftheCurve-the Book.com Web site
will also maintain links to the economic data series from governmental
and other data bureaus, to assist readers in replicating the charts.[1]

Appendix D

TABLE D-1

Figures with key economic data series available at
www.AheadoftheCurve-theBook.com

Figure 4-1: Recessions versus slowdowns in real GDP: A mismatch

Figure 7-3: Real consumer spending (PCE) and industrial production: The volatile effects of the inventory cycle

Figure 7-5: Swings in industrial production drive changes in real capital spending

Figure 7-7: Swings in real consumer spending (PCE) drive changes in real capital spending

Figure 8-4: Bear markets begin when growth in real consumer spending (PCE) peaks and begins to slow

Figure 9-3: Consumer Sentiment surveys: Coincident, not leading, indicators

Figure 10-4: How inflation affects growth in real average hourly earnings

Figure 10-7: Real hourly earnings: Best leading indicator of real consumer spending (PCE) downturns

Figure 10-9: Growth in employment and borrowing "leverages up" real hourly earnings

Figure 10:10: Real hourly earnings: A useful leading indicator of stock market declines

Figure 11-3: Employment's lagging relationship to consumer spending (PCE)

Figure 11-6: The unemployment rate's lagging relationship to real consumer spending (PCE)

Figure 11-11: Combined year-over-year increases in employment and real earnings growth approximate real consumer spending (PCE)

Figure 12-2: The discount or fed funds rate as a leading indicator of real consumer spending (PCE)

Figure 12-4: Inflation drives interest rates

Figure 13-2: Rising discount/fed funds rates: A harbinger of bear markets

Figure 13-3: Long-term interest-rate changes and the stock market

Figure 14-2: Increases in total domestic nonfinancial debt drive the prime rate

Figure 14-3: Increases in total domestic nonfinancial debt drive the 10-year Treasury yield

Notes

Preface

1. Appendix C contains a broad listing of industry classifications for which data are readily available as part of consumer spending (personal consumption expenditures), capital spending (gross domestic private investment), industrial production, and retail sales as reported by government bureaus.

2. Vertical gray bars are usually used in charts, primarily by economists, to denote recession.

Chapter 1

1. Another *New York Times* Business section article, on July 11, 2003, headlined "Data in Conflict: Why Economists Tend to Weep," amplified the ambiguity and confusion of economic data reports.

2. Paul A. Samuelson, *Collected Scientific Papers of Paul A. Samuelson* (Cambridge, MA: MIT Press, 1986).

Chapter 4

1. In defining *recession*, the National Bureau of Economic Research (NBER) states, "A recession is a significant decline in economic activity spread across the economy, lasting more than a few months, normally visible in real GDP, real income, employment, industrial production, and wholesale-retail sales. A recession begins just after the economy reaches a peak of activity and ends as the economy reaches its trough. Between trough and peak, the economy is in an expansion. Expansion is the normal state of the economy; most recessions are brief and they have been rare in recent decades." (Business Cycle Dating Committee, National Bureau of Economic Research, October 21, 2003 , http://www.nber .org/cycles/recessions.html) This definition, according the word "expansion" to even the most minor increases in total economic output at the end of a period of economic growth, is technically accurate. However, it is seriously at odds with

the significant difficulties faced by businesses and investors at this late and seriously deteriorated stage of the economic cycle.

The following is presented as a "frequently asked question" at the NBER Web site: "The financial press often states the definition of a recession as two consecutive quarters of decline in real GDP. How does that relate to the NBER's recession dating procedure?" The answer: "Most of the recessions identified by our procedures do consist of two or more quarters of declining real GDP, but not all of them . . . Our procedure differs from the two-quarter rule in a number of ways. First, we consider the depth as well as the duration of the decline in economic activity. Recall that our definition includes the phrase, 'a significant decline in economic activity.' Second, we use a broader array of indicators than just real GDP. One reason for this is that the GDP data are subject to considerable revision. Third, we use monthly indicators to arrive at a monthly chronology."

2. Chapter 10 shows how a downtrend in individuals' real average hourly earnings, our favored leading indicator of consumer spending, had for more than a year been foretelling the slowing of consumer spending that set this slowdown into motion.

Chapter 6

1. A second possibility exists: in some cases, trends in both series can be driven by a third series (series C). In such instances, a shorter lag time between series C and series A than between series C and series B would cause series A to move in advance of, and therefore appear to be a leading indicator of, series B.

2. It has been observed, correctly, that the National Football Conference team has won the Super Bowl more frequently than the American Football Conference team and that the stock market has advanced in more years than it declines, leading to a greater likelihood of these two events occurring together. Still, the relationship between these two occurences can only be viewed as spurious!

Chapter 7

1. The store must raise its purchases by 5% just to support the ongoing new, higher level of consumer demand, *plus* additional increases to bring inventory levels to the higher level necessary to support higher sales levels.

2. Many will note that the large portion of consumer purchases that is imported from abroad does not increase domestic industrial production. However, sales of imported goods are included in the Federal Reserve Board's calculation of industrial production; the net difference between imports and exports represents the balance of trade, data for which is reported monthly.

3. Year-over-year real consumer spending growth has typically reached a trough of between −2% and +2%.

4. In another example of the recession obsession, many commentators observed erroneously that consumer spending, because it had not declined in absolute terms, was "holding the economy up." Although true to some extent, this statement missed the more important point that it was the slowing growth of consumer spending in 2000 and 2001 that triggered the downturn in the first place.

5. Again, this is subject to the same issue of production and capacity being exported offshore, as discussed in chapter 2.

6. We might best think of the capital-spending boom of the late 1990s as having been a balloon that was inflated far beyond its normal capacity. However, the pin that burst it was, as always, a slowing of consumer spending. The bursting was simply louder because the balloon had been inflated beyond normal.

7. Robert L. Heilbroner and Lester C. Thurow, *Economics Explained* (New York: Touchstone, 1998) 96–97.

8. Ibid.

Chapter 8

1. A major anomaly to this pattern occurred from 1978 to 1980, but is easily explained. Despite slowing consumer demand during the late 1970s, unprecedented inflation in the extraction industries—energy, metals, and forest products—led stocks in those sectors to appreciate substantially as a result of the significant increase in asset values of companies in those sectors. This was accompanied by exceptional performance in high-tech stocks, which were seen as beneficiaries of the economy's need for higher productivity in a high-inflation environment. The stock market advance occurred despite a weakening overall corporate profit picture (see figure 8-4). The dramatic appreciation of stocks in "inflation-beneficiary" sectors resulted in a 1979–1980 advance for the stock market as a whole, even though a large number of stocks in consumer sectors and non–inflation-beneficiary manufacturing sectors experienced the equivalent of a bear market. Similarly, the ensuing 1981–1982 bear market resulted primarily from *deflation* and consequent stock declines in the inflation-beneficiary sectors, even as equities in consumer-spending and a number of other industrial sectors were advancing. Excluding the anomaly of inflation-beneficiary stocks, equity prices during this period generally behaved in a relatively classic fashion vis-à-vis the history of this chart.

2. This quotation originated in an article by Paul Samuelson in the September 19, 1966, issue of *Newsweek* and has been repeated or paraphrased frequently by market commentators, sometimes with attribution and sometimes not.

3. See the discussion of negative divergence in chapter 6.

Chapter 9

1. Chapter 10 will show that total consumer spending in the United States just about *equals* total personal disposable income—defined as all personal income after personal tax payments.

2. Think of consumer spending power as a big pond, with a stream—consumers' personal income—flowing in from above, and another stream of roughly equal size—consumer spending itself—flowing out from the bottom. Every now and then, the pond (personal wealth) gets higher or lower from rain (higher stock prices or home values) or drought (lower stock prices and home values). However, the flow from the lower end always results for the most part from the inflow from the stream above.

3. http://www.conference-board.org/economics/methodology.cfm.

4. University of Michigan Survey of Consumers, http://www.sca.isr.umich .edu/documents.php?c=i.

Chapter 10

1. Over the years, the savings rate has vacillated considerably. From the 1960s through the 1980s it ranged generally from 6% to 12% of disposable personal income, but over the past two decades it fell rather steadily to 1% to 4% at the end of the 1990s and since. Over the years, there has been no discernible predictive cyclical relationship between the savings rate and the direction of consumer-spending growth.

2. Usually, but not always: The extended period of strong growth in consumer spending during the mid-1990s did not produce higher inflation. Rising real average hourly earnings growth was sustained until 1998, when rising energy prices finally ended the period of declining inflation.

3. The duration and clarity of the advance warning provided by uptrends and downtrends in year-over-year hourly earnings at critical turning points in consumer spending have varied considerably from cycle to cycle over the past forty years. Year-over-year real earnings comparisons have experienced occasional short-lived upturns and downturns—particularly in the late 1980s and early 1990s—that never carried through for longer than six months; these comparisons might therefore have been considered as false indicators in signaling the direction of consumer spending. Forecasters who use this series to predict consumer spending need to take these short-lived false starts into account, but they shouldn't be considered as negating the general usefulness of this series.

4. Clearly, tax cuts represent a valuable fiscal tool for stimulating the economy through consumer spending in periods of severe economic stress. However, they must be used judiciously. Tax cuts can, and should, also be viewed as

government borrowing used simply to sustain higher-than-indicated rates of growth in consumer spending—in effect, papering over the normal economic cycle. Because this policy can result in massive increases in government debt, it can take a significant economic toll in another form. For example, federal debt more than tripled—from $995 billion at the end of 1981 to $3.2 trillion at the end of 1990—following the two Reagan administration tax cuts. Similarly, on a base of approximately $6 trillion, the federal debt has increased at an annual rate of more than $350 billion since the Bush administration tax cut of 2003.

5. Even now, many observers fail to see the real cause of the 2000–2002 economic downturn, feeling that the high-tech and Internet bubble simply burst. They miss the fact that, as in previous cycles, it was the slowing growth in consumer spending that set this process in motion (see chapter 7).

6. The differential between year-over-year increases in individuals' real average hourly wages and aggregate real consumer spending from 1982 to 1990 was significantly greater in degree and longer in duration than normal. As noted previously, because real average hourly wages is a pretax series, changes in taxation rates can materially increase (tax cuts) or decrease (tax increases) the differential.

7. The anomaly in 1978–1980 of a significant downtrend in real hourly earnings and consumer spending is explained earlier in footnote 1 of chapter 8.

Chapter 11

1. The end of the extended consumer boom of the late 1990s was a rare exception to this rule. The period of strong growth in consumer demand had continued so briskly and for so long that employment growth slowed from 1998 through 2000 as, quite literally, the nation ran out of workforce. Similarly, the sharp downtrend in consumer-spending growth in 1966 also did not produce a significant downturn in employment, a result of the absorption of much of the workforce into rapidly growing armed forces to support the growing Vietnam War effort.

2. The unemployment rate eventually increased to more than 6% in mid-2003.

Chapter 12

1. The discount rate in the late 1990s and early in the first decade of the 2000s was used less and less by member banks and, after December 2002, has no longer been a functioning mechanism in the monetary system. For most purposes, it has been replaced by the fed funds rate, the interest rate the Federal Reserve Board targets for banks to lend to each other on an overnight basis.

Therefore, although the discount rate was historically a better measure of the base interest rate set by the Fed, the fed funds rate now serves that role. Our charts therefore show the discount rate from 1960 to 2000, and only the fed funds rate since that time.

2. Year-over-year rates of change in the discount or fed funds rate (dotted line) in figure 12-2 are charted in *basis points* (100 basis points = 1.0% in interest-rate vernacular). For example, when the discount or fed funds rate is at 4.5% versus 3.0% a year earlier, the dotted line would be at +150 basis points; if the year-over-year change in the discount or fed funds rate increases to +250 basis points, it would move even lower in the chart (given the inverted scale on the right), matching up with a decline in consumer-spending growth in the solid line.

3. The Federal Reserve Board has two other significant tools: the management of the money supply and the setting of banks' reserve requirements. Both of these affect the flow of money in the economy and, in turn, bank lending to consumers as well as businesses.

4. The PCE deflator is the price deflator for the consumer spending portion of GDP and essentially is parallel to the Consumer Price Index.

Chapter 13

1. The S&P 500 index as of April 15, 2005, was 1143, representing a price-earnings ratio of 16X based on consensus estimated 2005 S&P 500 earnings per share of $71.00.

Chapter 14

1. A May 2003 paper, "New Evidence on the Interest Rate Effects of Budget Deficits and Debt," by Thomas Laubach of the Board of Governors of Federal Reserve System, concluded that "interest rates rise by about 25 basis points in response to a percentage point increase in the projected deficit-to-GDP ratio, and about 4 basis points in response to a percentage point increase in the projected debt-to-GDP ratio."

2. *Total domestic nonfinancial debt* is defined by the Federal Reserve Board as credit market debt owed by domestic nonfinancial sectors of the economy. It excludes debt owed by financial institutions, such as credit agencies, federally related mortgage pools, and private financial institutions. It also excludes trade debt, loans for the purpose of carrying securities, and funds from equity sources. However, it includes debt securities, mortgages, bank loans, commercial paper, consumer credit, and government loans owned by nonfinancial sectors.

3. Debt held by households also includes debt held by personal trusts and nonprofit organizations.

Chapter 15

1. The monthly tabulation is available on the Federal Reserve Board Web site at www.federalreserve.gov/releases.

2. This report is available on the National Association of Realtors Web site, www.realtor.org.

3. Food sales at Wal-Mart discount stores and its supercenters, where food represents roughly half of sales, are included; this somewhat distorts upward the GAF total, which is meant to measure primarily nonfood sales. Excluding estimated food sales of $54 billion at Wal-Mart in 2004, Wal-Mart's general-merchandise sales of approximately $138 billion would have accounted for 14% of total GAF store sales of $953 billion (ex food at Wal-Mart) in the United States.

Appendix A

1. Let's make two assumptions here: (1) that the new borrowing referred to is net of repayments and (2) that John will spend all of his net (after-tax) wages as well as any money he borrows (a valid assumption with regard to most lower- and middle-income consumers).

2. Note the arrow denoting secondary causality from employment to consumer borrowing in figure 2-1.

Appendix D

1. Those choosing to construct their own charts using the URLs on the www.AheadoftheCurve-theBook.com Web site may notice some discrepancies between charts constructed from data on these Web sites and the charts in this book. This results from the "rebasing" of the statistics by the government and other bureaus that issue them. As far back as the early 1980s, the elapsed time between peaks and troughs in the leading and lagging indicators was entirely clear in the years the data was reported and for five to ten years afterward. However, in following years these lead/lag times often shrank or disappeared altogether as the data was restated and rebased by the issuing bureaus. In other words, important timing sequences were "smoothed out" completely in this process.

I soon learned the importance of saving the original data every five to ten years, maintaining my cause-and-effect charts based on year-over-year changes in that original data, and then layering in new data as it was reported.

The Bureau of Economic Analysis has stated that the practice does not alter percentage changes in the series being rebased, but I have not found this to be the case—at least on the year-over-year basis used in virtually all of the charts in this book. While I am sure that rebasing makes perfect sense to professional statisticians, it has been detrimental to practical users of the data series it affects. It is illogical, I believe, that a clear pattern of lead/lag cause and effect consistently occurs between Series A and Series B when they are reported and for five or more years afterward, only to have it disappear through rebasing a decade or more later.

Economic data series in this book that were particularly affected were (1) real personal consumption expenditures and real capital spending, where in the rebased data a previously clear lead/lag relationship during the 1970s and 1980s virtually disappeared in data a decade later, and (2) the Department of Commerce's GAF-store sales data.

Bibliography

Achuthan, Lakshman, and Anirvan Banerji. *Beating the Business Cycle*. New York: Currency Books, 2004.

Carnes, W. Stansbury, and Stephen D. Slifer. *The Atlas of Economic Indicators*. New York: HarperCollins, 1991.

Cassidy, John. "The Decline of Economics," *New Yorker*, December 2, 1996.

Clements, Michael, and David Hendry. *Forecasting Economic Time Series*. Cambridge: Cambridge University Press, 1998.

De Rooy, Jacob. *Economic Literacy*. New York: Three Rivers Press, 1995.

Garnett, Robert F., Jr. *What Do Economists Know?* New York: Routledge, 1999.

Goldman, Sachs & Co. "Retail Economic Indicators," 1975–2003.

Granger, C. W. J., and Paul Newbold. *Forecasting in Business and Economics*. San Diego, CA: Academic Press, 1989.

Heilbroner, Robert L., and Lester C. Thurow. *Economics Explained*. New York: Touchstone (Simon & Schuster), 1998.

Hopkins, Peter J. B., and C. Hayes Miller. *Country, Sector, and Company Factors in Global Equity Portfolios*. Charlottesville, VA: Association for Investment Management and Research, 2001.

Keen, Steve, *Debunking Economics: The Naked Emperor of the Social Sciences*. New York: St. Martin's Press, 2002.

Keynes, John Maynard. *The General Theory of Employment, Interest, and Money*. New York: Harcourt, 1991.

Laubach, Thomas. "New Evidence on the Interest Rate Effects of Budget Deficits and Debt," Federal Reserve Board, Finance and Economics Discussion Series, May 2003.

Lipsey, Richard G., and Paul N. Courant, *Economics*. New York: HarperCollins College Publishers, 1996.

Malkiel, Burton G. *A Random Walk Down Wall Street*. New York: W.W. Norton, 1996.

Mankiw, N. Gregory. *Macroeconomics*. New York: Worth Publishers, 1992.

Mauldin, John. *Bull's Eye Investing*. Hoboken, NJ: John Wiley & Sons, 2004.

Ormerod, Paul. *The Death of Economics*. New York: St. Martin's Press, 1995.

Samuelson, Paul A. *Economics*. New York: McGraw-Hill, 1970.

Stein, Ben, and Phil DeMuth. *Yes, You Can Time the Market!* Hoboken, NJ: John Wiley & Sons, Inc., 2003.

Index

AheadoftheCurve-theBook.com,
  xvii–xviii, 255
  data available on, 256
annualized information, problems
  with, 51
apparel industry, 183
asymmetrical circular causality,
  66–67, 142
Australia, GDP and consumer data
  for, 218
Austria, GDP and consumer data for,
  218
automobile sales, interest rates and,
  156–157

balance of trade, 258
  international data on, 221
  U.S. deficit in, 20
bear markets
  beginning signs of, 102
  charted (1950–2004), 93
  consumer spending and, 96, 97–99
  defined, 36
  interest rates and, 164–166
  predicting beginning and end of,
    99–100
  real hourly earnings as leading
    indicator of, 129
  unemployment rate and, 146, 148

behavioral economics, 115–116
Belgium, GDP and consumer data for,
  218
borrowing. *See* debt
Brazil, GDP and consumer data for,
  218
bull markets
  beginning signs of, 102
  charted (1950–2004), 93
Bull's Eye Investing (Mauldin), 169
buy-and-hold strategy, 103–104

Canada
  economic charts for, 226–227
  exports of, 221
  GDP and consumer spending of,
    218
  imports of, 221
  trade balance of, 221
capital spending, 12
  boom in 1990s, 259, 261
  in Canada, 227
  composition of, 19, 20
  driven by consumer spending,
    79–83, 88–89
  effects of, 87
  in France, 229
  in Germany, 230, 231
  in Japan, 232, 233 [

capital spending (*continued*)
    influenced by production, 81–82
    influences on, 13
    influencing production, 80
    as lagging indicator, 102
    and manufacturing, 195, 197, 201
    overemphasis on, 87
    in the United Kingdom, 234, 235
cause and effect
    in charting, 59–60
    circularity in, 66–68
    distinguished from positive
        correlation, 68–69
change, seasonally adjusted rate of, 30
charting, 6
    application of, 203–204
    attitudes toward, 54
    benefits over econometric analysis,
        6–7
    case study of, 49–52
    ease of, 8–9
    housekeeping tips for, 59–60
    international application of,
        217–235
    principles of, 55–56
    and "seeing" the economy, 53–56,
        69–70
    short-term, ineffectiveness of, 30,
        49, 51–52, 73
    single versus multiline, 59
    value of, 189–190
    year-over-year, 51–52, 56–58, 73
China, GDP and consumer data for,
    218
coincident indicators, 102
consumer borrowing, 102
    coincident-to-lagging nature of, 214
    components of, 210–211
    and consumer spending, 215
    effect of, 213–215
    variability in, 214

consumer confidence indicators, 102
    as coincident indicators, 113, 114
    nature of, 111–112
    overreliance on, 112–115
Consumer Confidence Index, 59,
    111, 112, 113
consumer demand
    engines of, 104
    leading indicators of, 102
consumer psychology, and consumer
    spending, 110–111
consumer spending
    broken down by type, 237–246
    causal and secondary factors in,
        107–108
    charted from 1960–2004, 97
    composition of, 17
    consumer borrowing and, 209–211
    consumer psychology and, 110–111
    and corporate profits, 92, 94–96
    and demand chain, 73–89
    driven by personal income,
        118–128
    driving capital spending, 79–83
    driving economy, 11–12, 84–86
    driving employment, 138
    and economic cycle, 12–15
    forecasting of, 22–23, 107–116
    formula for, 149–152
    importance of forecasting, 21–22
    inflation and, 160, 161
    interest rates and, 154, 156–158,
        164
    international data for, 219
    as market indicator, 94–99
    percentage of GDP, 15, 21
    personal income and, 108, 121–122
    personal wealth and, 108–109
    power of, described, 260
    and production of goods and
        services, 12, 21, 76–77

real. *See* real consumer spending
on services, 19
and stock market, 13, 15, 21–22
tax cuts and, 126, 128
corporate profits. *See* profits
correlation, versus causality, 68–69
credit
effect on economy, 213–215
nonrevolving, 211
revolving, 210–211
second-derivative change in,
211–213
as swing factor, 209
credit card use, 157–158

debt
and consumer spending, 209–210
and interest rates, 172
leveraging real wages, 130–132
second-derivative change in,
211–213
total domestic nonfinancial, 172,
173–175, 177
deficit
and interest rates, 171
party political views on, 171
demand chain, 92
consumer spending and, 73–89
illustrated, 74
demand-pull inflation, 132
discount rate, 154. *See also* federal
funds rate
historical value of, 261–262
replaced by federal funds rate, 261
discretionary purchases, interest rates
and, 157
disposable personal income, 119
dis-saving, 209
downturn of 1969–1970, 39
economic data for, 40–42

downturn of 2000–2002, 43
causes of, 261
economic data for, 44–46
relation of unemployment to
spending during, 147, 149

earnings yield, of stocks, 166
econometric analysis, 6
shortcomings of, 6–7
economic cycle
capital spending and, 12, 13
chronology of, 14, 205
consumer spending and, 12–13
inevitability of, 78, 84
stock market and, 101
production and, 12, 13
economic growth
defined, 12
effects of slowing of, 28–29
and Federal Reserve, 160
ROCET-based perspective on,
206–207
traditional perspective on, 206
economic slowdowns
correlated to recessions, 37, 99
economic indicators in, 39
effects of, 36, 38
patterns of, 25–26
stages of, 26–29
Economics Explained (Heilbroner and
Thurow), 86
emotions, overcoming, 102–103
employment
driven by consumer spending, 22,
109, 138
driving consumer spending, 22,
142, 150
influences on, 21
as lagging indicator, 15, 102, 109,
117, 138–141, 151

employment (*continued*)
  leveraging real wages, 130–132
  rate of, 118
engine, turbine, and power-transmission industry, consumer spending and, 197, 200
Excel (Microsoft program), 204
exports and imports, and economic growth, 20

federal funds rate, 154
  and bear markets, 165
  charting of, 262
  leading consumer spending trends, 158–160
Federal Reserve
  factors affecting, 160
  tools of, 262
final sales, 17
forecasting
  amenability of individual industries to, 183–184
  anecdotal approach to, 4–6
  attitudes toward, 3–4
  banishing emotion from, 108–110
  case studies of, 185–189
  cause and effect in, 59–60
  consumer confidence indices and, 111–115
  corporate apathy toward, 184–185
  importance of, 4
  Lowe's–Home Depot case study, 195, 196
  at micro level, 181–182
  Wal-Mart case study, 194–195
France
  economic charts for, 228–229
  economic conditions in, 222–223
  economic vulnerability of, 220
  exports of, 221

GDP and consumer spending of, 218
  imports of, 221
  trade balance of, 221

GAF (general merchandise, apparel, and furniture) stores, 191
  forecasting of, 191–193
Germany
  economic charts for, 230–231
  economic conditions in, 223–224
  economic vulnerability of, 220
  exports of, 221
  GDP and consumer spending of, 218
  imports of, 221
  trade balance of, 221
Goldman Sachs GAF Sales Forecast Index, 191–192
  components of, 192
  effectiveness of, 192–193
Goldman Sachs Retail Composite Comparable-Store Sales Index, 193
government spending, 20
  components of, 20–21
Grantham, Jeremy, 170
Greenspan, Alan, 153, 155
gross domestic product (GDP)
  composition of, 16
  consumer spending and, 15
  rate of change, 1950–2004, 36
gross private domestic investment. *See* capital spending
growth recession, 34

health care industry, noncyclical nature of, 183
Heilbroner, Robert, 86, 87, 88

Home Depot's sales, forecasting of, 195, 196
home improvement industry
  case study of, 186, 188
  housing turnover and, 197, 198
  value of forecasting in, 189
housing market, interest rates and, 156

Index of Consumer Sentiment, 111, 112–113
India, GDP and consumer data for, 218
industrial production, 17. *See also* production
  in Canada, 226
  and capital spending, 13
  elements included in, 258
  in France, 228
  in Germany, 230
  in Japan, 232
  types of enterprises, 249–250
  in the United Kingdom 234
industries, individual
  amenability to cyclical analysis, 183–184
  forecasting of, 181–182
  relative performance of, 182
inflation
  demand-pull, 132
  effect on growth in earnings, 122, 124
  and interest rates, 160–162
installment credit. *See* consumer borrowing
interest rates
  and automobile sales, 156–157
  and bear markets, 164–166
  bellwether, 169–170
  and consumer spending, 154, 156–158, 164
  and discretionary purchases, 157
  federal deficit and, 171

and Federal Reserve decisions, 160
  future of, 169–170, 175–178
  and housing market, 156
  inflation rates and, 160–162
  long-term changes in, 168
  and profits, 163
  ROCET tracking of, 158, 159
  and stock market, 163–170
  total debt and, 172, 173, 177–178
inventory effect on industrial production cycle, 74–76
investment, characteristics of, 86–87
Italy, GDP and consumer data for, 218

Japan
  economic charts for, 232–233
  economic conditions in, 224–225
  consumer spending in, 217
  exports of, 221
  GDP of, 217, 218
  imports of, 221
  trade balance of, 221

Kahneman, Daniel, 116
Keynes, John Maynard, 132
Korea, GDP and consumer data for, 218

lagging indicators, 62, 63
  false solace offered by, 101
  identifying, 102
  relationships with leading indicators, 64–65
leading indicators, 61
  cycles of, 62–64
  identifying, 102
  nature of, 63

leading indicators (*continued*)
  relationships with lagging
    indicators, 64–65
Lowe's, forecasting of, 195, 196

market. *See* stock market
Mauldin, John, 169–170
metalworking industry, trends in
    production in, 197, 199
Mexico, GDP and consumer data for,
    218
mortgages, minimal effects of, 210

negative concurrence of economic
    indicators, described, 63
negative divergence of economic
    indicators, described, 62
net exports and imports, 20
Netherlands, GDP and consumer data
    for, 218
nonrevolving credit, 211

personal consumption expenditures
    (PCE). *See* consumer spending
personal consumption expenses
    (PCE) deflator, 16, 121, 262
personal income
  and consumer spending, 13, 108
  defined, 118–119
  disposable, 119
  driving consumer spending,
    119–128
personal wealth, and consumer
    spending, 108–109
pharmaceutical industry, noncyclical
    nature of, 183
plastics industry
  case study of, 186

industrial production and
    consumer spending in, 187
  value of forecasting in, 189
positive concurrence of economic
    indicators, described, 62
positive divergence of economic
    indicators, 64
  described, 62
price-earnings ratio, 163, 166
prime rate, 154
  total domestic nonfinancial debt
    and, 174
private fixed investment
  broken down by type, 247–248
production, 12
  and capital spending, 13, 80–82
  consumer spending and, 12, 21,
    76–77
  inventory effect and, 74–79
  types of industry groups,
    249–250
  types of market groups, 250–252
profits
  and employment trends, 21
  consumer spending and, 92,
    94–96
  interest rates and, 163
  and market, 94
prospect theory, 116

quarter-to-quarter charting
  ineffectiveness of, 30, 39
  obfuscatory aspects of, 52–53
  as obstacle to analysis, 55–56

Reagan, Ronald, 126
real average hourly earnings, 118,
    258, 261
  criteria for, 152

and employment growth, 150
inflation and, 122
as leading indicator of consumer
   spending, 117–118, 121–122,
   123–124, 125, 127, 128–130,
   133, 151
reliability of indications by, 260
underemphasis on, 133–135
real capital spending. *See* capital
   spending
real consumer spending, 15
and bear markets, 97, 98
calculation of, 15–16
in Canada, 226–227
charts of, 57, 58, 140–141
consumer credit and, 215
discount rate and, 158–160
forecasting of downturns in, 125
forecasting of upturns in, 127
in France, 228–229
in Germany, 230–231
in Japan, 232–233
and industrial production, 199
influence of growth in employment
   and earnings on, 151
influencing real capital spending,
   88–89
relation to unemployment rate, 145
in the United Kingdom, 234, 235
recession(s), 25
advent of, 27, 28–29
correlated to economic downturns,
   37, 99
definitions of, 257–258
examples of (1950–2004), 35
growth, 34
as lagging event, 42
obsession with, 36, 38, 73, 259
traditional attitudes toward, 29–30
traditional definition of, 34
utility of concept, 46

recession of 1969–1970, 33–34
retail sales
   broken down by type, 252–254
   components of, 191
   data on, 18
   of GAF stores, 191–193
   rates of growth, 190
revolving credit, 210–211
ROCET (rate of change in economic
   tracking) method, 8
   case studies of, 185–189
   total nonfinancial debt and, 173–175
   mandate for, 46–47
   and tracking interest rates, 158, 159
Russian Federation, GDP and
   consumer data for, 218

Samuelson, Paul, 7, 99
savings rate, 119
   changes in, 260
seasonal adjustments, 30, 50–51, 55
Spain, GDP and consumer data for, 218
stock market
   consumer spending and, 13, 15,
   21–22
   company profits and, 94
   as discounting mechanism, 4
   drivers of, 91
   intellectual versus emotional
   approaches to, 102–103
   interest rates and, 163–170
   long-term interest rates and, 168
   paradoxical attitudes toward,
   100–103
   secondary market influencing, 100
   timing, 103–104
stock valuations
   earnings yield, 166
   factors in, 167
   price-earnings ratio, 163, 166

supply-side debate, 86–89
Sweden, GDP and consumer data for, 218
Switzerland, GDP and consumer data for, 218

tax cuts
  and consumer spending, 126, 128
  effects of, 260–261
  and interest rates, 171, 175
Thurow, Lester, 86, 87, 88
total domestic nonfinancial debt, 172, 173
  defined, 262
  and interest rates, 173–175
  paradoxical effects of, 209
  recent increases in, 177–178
trade associations, as source of information, 189
Treasury yield, 175, 176
Tversky, J., 116

unemployment, 118, 138
  as lagging indicator, 102
unemployment rate, 118, 138, 143
  as lagging indicator, 102
  in bear markets, 146, 148
  in Canada, 227
  consumer spending and, 143–144
  in France, 229
  in Germany, 231
  in Japan, 233
  misleading aspect of, 146–147

and real consumer spending, 145
  in the United Kingdom, 235
unit purchasing power of consumers, 117
United Kingdom
  economic charts for, 234–235
  economic conditions in, 225–226
  exports of, 221
  GDP and consumer spending of, 218
  imports of, 221
  trade balance of, 221
United States
  consumer spending in, 217
  currency of, 221
  exports of, 221
  GDP of, 217, 218
  imports of, 221
  trade balance of, 221

wage growth, and consumer spending, 109–110, 150
wage rates, and consumer spending, 22
Wal-Mart sales
  food sales at, 263
  forecasting of, 194–195
wealth effect, 128
World Trade Center tragedy, 129

year-over-year charting, 51–52
  benefits of, 56–58, 73
  and ROCET technique, 56

About the Author

Joseph H. Ellis is an Advisory Director at Goldman, Sachs & Co. in New York City. Born in Watertown, New York in 1942, Mr. Ellis received a Bachelor of Arts degree from Columbia University in 1964 and also attended Columbia University Graduate School of Business. He headed the Retail Research Group in the Investment Research Department at Goldman, Sachs & Co. from 1970 to 1994, was named a General Partner of Goldman Sachs in 1986, and became a Limited Partner in 1994. During his tenure as Goldman Sachs' senior retail-industry analyst, Mr. Ellis was cited by *Institutional Investor Magazine* as the first-ranked retail investment analyst on Wall Street for eighteen consecutive years. Since 1994, Mr. Ellis has served as the firm's principal liaison and consultant with retailers around the world.

Before joining Goldman Sachs in 1970, Mr. Ellis was Vice President and Investment Analyst with The Bank of New York. From 1984 to 1991, he was a Trustee of Prep for Prep, a nonprofit organization dedicated to the furthering of minority education, and served as Treasurer from 1987 to 1991. He was also a Trustee of The Brearley School from 1987 to 1990, was Vice Chair of the Board of Trustees of The New York State Nature Conservancy from 1995 to 2003, and served on the Board of Directors of the National Retail Federation from 1998 to 2001. Mr. Ellis is currently on the Board of Trustess of RARE (a nonprofit organization specializing in environmental conservation and sustainable economic development in developing countries), serves on the Steering Committee of the Center for Environmental Research and Conservation (CERC) of Columbia University, and is a Northeast Trustee of CARE.

Mr. Ellis currently sits on the Board of Directors of Coach, Inc. and Waterworks, Inc. He is also founder and principal owner of Blue Tulip, which operates five stores selling better paper products, gifts, and other items marking personal occasions, and has stores located in Princeton, New Jersey; Paoli, Pennsylvania; Marlton, New Jersey; Fairfield, Connecticut; and Bronxville, New York. Additional stores are soon to open in Middletown, New Jersey and Canton, Connecticut.